THIRTEENTH CENTURY ENGLAND XIII

PROCEEDINGS OF
THE PARIS CONFERENCE
2009

THIRTEENTH CENTURY ENGLAND XIII

PROCEEDINGS
OF THE PARIS CONFERENCE
2009

Edited by

Janet Burton
Frédérique Lachaud
Phillipp Schofield
Karen Stöber
Björn Weiler

THE BOYDELL PRESS

First published 2011
The Boydell Press, Woodbridge

ISBN 978 1 84383 618 6

ISSN 0269–6967

The Boydell Press is an imprint of Boydell & Brewer Ltd
PO Box 9, Woodbridge, Suffolk IP12 3DF, UK
and of Boydell & Brewer Inc.
668 Mt Hope Avenue, Rochester, NY 14620, USA
website: www.boydellandbrewer.com

A CIP catalogue record for this book is available
from the British Library

The publisher has no responsibility for the continued existence or
accuracy of URLs for external or third-party internet websites referred to
in this book, and does not guarantee that any content
on such websites is, or will remain, accurate or appropriate

Papers used by Boydell & Brewer Ltd are natural, recyclable products
made from wood grown in sustainable forests

Printed in Great Britain by
CPI Antony Rowe Ltd, Chippenham and Eastbourne

CONTENTS

ILLUSTRATIONS

John of Crakehall

Credit Finance

PREFACE

By convening in Paris, the 2009 meeting broke with precedent: this was the first Thirteenth-Century England conference to be held outside the British Isles. We very much hope that this will set a precedent, and that in future other meetings, too, will reflect by their venue the degree to which England formed part of a larger cultural, political, religious, economic and social whole. In 2009, the specific occasion for crossing the Channel was the 750th anniversary of the Treaty of Paris, the agreement in which Henry III surrendered his claim to Normandy, Anjou and Poitou, and which inaugurated a period of relative and, though temporary, nonetheless largely unparalleled calm in dealings between the rulers of England and France. This context is reflected in the papers published here, many of which focus on dealings between the kingdoms of England and France and their inhabitants, with a separate group of papers specifically on the Treaty of Paris and its aftermath. Yet, in keeping with the traditions of the conference, the venue did not determine the range of topics discussed.

The papers on the Treaty of Paris, which sat at the heart of the conference and are published here as a self-contained group, reflect the variety of ways in which the Treaty and its associated history, especially its later history, can be addressed. Daniel Power considers the ways in which an Anglo-Norman aristocracy struggled to elide their dynastic ambitions with the machinations of high politics in this period. The movement of familial land and access to it was constrained by the claims of the separated English and French states; while the Treaty of Paris did not occasion a final rupture and in fact served to ease some cross-Channel management of family lands, the futures of English and French dynasties were frequently quite discrete by the later thirteenth century. This Anglo-Norman tension over rights and property is also evident in William Chester Jordan's paper, in which he discusses the significance of the dispute concerning the status of the small Gloucestershire priory of Deerhurst following its purchase by Earl Richard of Cornwall in 1250 from the French abbey of St Denis, of which Deerhurst had been a dependency since the days of Edward the Confessor. The purchase was followed by the dispersal and then the reassembly of the monks but, as Jordan argues, the ramifications lasted longer, and are intertwined with the political controversies and diplomatic manoeuvrings of the 1250s and early 1260s. Florent Lenègre discusses the later treaties of Paris of 1295, between France and Norway and between France and Scotland. The context of these treaties, both short and long term, was discussed over fifty years ago by R. Nicholson, but Lenègre raises broader questions Nicholson did not consider. Why did Edward I react so violently to the ratification of the two treaties? What was France's interest in renewing the treaties at that particular time? Was it a symbolic gesture, the importance of which has been overestimated? Lenègre offers a different perspective, that of an economic and political entity centred on the North Sea over which the English king had sought to affirm his authority throughout the thirteenth century.

The nature of politics and political society, always an important theme in the *TCE* volumes published to date, is considered in both the general and particular in a number of studies included in this latest volume. Caroline Burt's paper is concerned with the development of political discourse in the Europe of the twelfth and thirteenth centuries, especially as it related to the nature of kingship and the public authority of kings. She discusses the influence of both Roman and canon law, as well as the Bible and Aristotelian ideas – the latter fully integrated into western thought during the period – on the developing political dialogue of the period. Julie Kanter explores evidence for royal itineraries in the reigns of John and Henry III. Using the published itineraries and setting out a range of data on distances travelled, duration and frequency of stay, she examines some fundamental differences of government operating between, as well as within, the two reigns, above all noting a distinction between a 'sedentary' Henry III whose itinerary, especially during the years of the minority, stood in real contrast to the 'frantic' movements of the royal household under John.

In her discussion of Peter of Aigueblanche, bishop of Hereford 1240–68, Julia Barrow demonstrates that there is more to his career than the participation in the Sicilian scheme, on which historians have previously tended to base their assessment and on which his historical reputation has rested. In particular she considers his support network – his patrons, his family and especially his household – which facilitated his remarkable achievements. Much of Barrow's reappraisal is based on her edition of the acta of the bishop, published in the English Episcopal Acta series. Adrian Jobson also explores the career of a significant political figure of the mid-thirteenth century. His examination of John of Crakehall, treasurer of England 1258–60, reveals an energetic and conscientious administrator, charged with the reform of the king's finances. Jobson illustrates the ways in which Crakehall's earlier career, including his stewardship of the estates of the bishopric of Lincolnshire, must have informed his subsequent career as well as facilitating his appointment. His study also reveals the significance of competent individuals within the royal administration, a competence at least as evident in the reversals suffered by the exchequer after Crakehall's death.

Continuing the discussion of finance but moving from exchequer to wardrobe, Adrian Bell, Chris Brooks and Tony Moore explore the changing relationship of Edward I's government and its Italian bankers. They pay particular attention to the ways in which Edward managed, or attempted to manage, these external finances and they illustrate the process which led to a collapse in the financial relationship with the Ricciardi in the 1290s. Presenting this case as a 'precocious, if doomed, experiment in government credit finance', they also argue that, in its failure, it encouraged different kinds of revenue creation, especially direct taxation. The political tension occasioned by ordinary and extraordinary means of generating revenue is also evident in Benjamin Wild's chapter, in which he considers challenges to royal authority in thirteenth-century England, looking specifically at the case of Henry III's captivity at the hands of Simon de Montfort between May 1264 and August 1265. Examining the chancery rolls from Henry III's reign, Wild discusses the ways in which de Montfort made use of the royal wardrobe to achieve his own goals in this intriguing power struggle.

Dialogue, an incidental theme that runs through many of the papers in the collection and especially those dealing with the treaties, is also at the core of David Trotter's discussion. He focuses on the issue of communication between people in thirteenth-century England and France, considering questions such as 'How did people make themselves understood across the Channel?' 'To what extent were their languages mutually intelligible?' and 'How significant are the differences in orthography between these languages?' An examination of a range of documents from thirteenth-century England and France leads him to conclude that the spoken language either side of the Channel was essentially the same. A dialogue of sorts, between God and the Devil but also between law and theology, is discussed by William Marx who, in a subtle reading of the text *Conflictus inter Deum et Diabolum*, offers an exploration of the relationship between this later medieval study of redemption and a worldly familiarity with pleading at law, and more particularly Roman civil law, which clearly informs the narrative and its structure. But whether this is a text written by lawyers to reflect their grasp and use of theology, or the reverse, remains, as the author notes, quite unclear. The use of language in law also features prominently in Caroline Dunn's study of definitions of *raptus* in legislation and in cases in medieval England. She notes that, while *raptus* was consistently applied in cases of sexual violence, its incidence in relation to abduction and elopement increased only in the later thirteenth century, as legislators and litigants sought to secure the property associated with ravishment; as such they were prepared to admit more than sexual violence within the legal definition of the term.

The 2009 meeting in Paris came about at the invitation of Frédérique Lachaud and Xavier Hélary at the Université de Paris IV (Sorbonne), and was generously supported by the ANR Derniers Capétiens. We would like to thank our hosts, and our sponsors, for their indefatigable good cheer, superb organisation and generous hospitality (including a wonderful concert at the Musée de Cluny). They have set a high standard to match when the next conference will convene, on more familiar but no less exotic ground, at Aberystwyth and Lampeter in 2011.

Janet Burton, Lampeter
Frédérique Lachaud, Université de Paris IV (Sorbonne)
Phillipp Schofield, Aberystwyth
Karen Stöber, Aberystwyth
Björn Weiler, Aberystwyth

CONTRIBUTORS

Julia Barrow, University of Nottingham
Adrian R. Bell, ICMA Centre, University of Reading
Chris Brooks, ICMA Centre, University of Reading
Caroline Burt, Pembroke College, University of Cambridge
Caroline Dunn, Clemson University
Adrian Jobson, The National Archives
William Chester Jordan, Princeton University
Julie E. Kanter, King's College London, University of London
Florent Lenègre, Archives départementales de la Seine-Maritime, Rouen
William Marx, University of Wales Trinity Saint David
Tony K. Moore, ICMA Centre, University of Reading
Daniel Power, Swansea University
David Trotter, Aberystwyth University
Benjamin L. Wild, Sherborne School

ABBREVIATIONS

In the following list all works are published in London unless otherwise specified.

Actes de Philippe Auguste	*Recueil des actes de Philippe Auguste, roi de France,* ed. H. Delaborde and others, 6 vols (Paris, 1916–2005)
AD	Archives départementales [de]
AN	Archives Nationales (Paris)
Ann. Mon.	*Annales Monastici*, ed. H.R. Luard, 5 vols (RS 36, 1864–9)
ANS	*Anglo-Norman Studies*
BBCS	*Bulletin of the Board of Celtic Studies*
Becket Materials	*Materials for the History of Thomas Becket*, ed. J.C. Robertson, 7 vols (RS 67, 1875–85)
BIHR	*Bulletin of the Institute of Historical Research*
BL	British Library, London
BNF	Bibliothèque Nationale de France, Paris
Bodleian	Bodleian Library, Oxford
Burton	'Annals of Burton', in *Ann. Mon.*, i. 183–500
CAC Wales	*Calendar of Ancient Correspondence concerning Wales*, ed. J.G. Edwards (Cardiff, 1935)
CAD	*A Descriptive Catalogue of Ancient Deeds in the PRO* (1890–1915)
CARD	*Calendar of Ancient Records of Dublin*, ed. J.T. Gilbert, 19 vols (Dublin, 1889–1944)
CChR	*Calendar of Charter Rolls*, 6 vols (PRO Texts and Calendars, 1903–27)
CCR	*Calendar of Close Rolls* (PRO Texts and Calendars, 1892 onwards)
CDI	*Calendar of Documents Relating to Ireland*, ed. H.S. Sweetman, 5 vols (1875–86)
CDS	*Calendar of Documents relating to Scotland*, ed. J. Bain, 4 vols (Edinburgh, 1881–8)
CFR	*Calendar of Fine Rolls*, 22 vols (PRO Texts and Calendars, 1911–1962)
CFR Henry III	*Calendar of the Fine Rolls of the Reign of Henry III Preserved in the National Archives*, ed. P. Dryburgh and B. Hartland, 3 vols (Woodbridge, 2007–9)
Champollion-Figeac	Champollion-Figeac, *Lettres de rois, reines et autres person-nages des cours de France et d'Angleterre*, 2 vols (Collection de documents inédits sur l'histoire de France, Paris, 1839 and 1847)

CIMisc	*Calendar of Inquisitions Miscellaneous*, 7 vols (PRO Texts and Calendars, 1916–68)
CIPM	*Calendar of Inquisitions Post Mortem*, 20 vols (PRO Texts and Calendars, 1904–95)
CLR	*Calendar of Liberate Rolls*, 6 vols (PRO Texts and Calendars, 1916–64)
CM	Matthew Paris, *Chronica Majora*, ed. H.R. Luard, 7 vols (RS 57, 1872–83)
CN	*Cartulaire Normand de Philippe Auguste, Louis VIII, Saint Louis et Philippe-le-Hardi*, ed. L. Delisle (Caen, 1852)
Complete Peerage	G.E. Cokayne, *The Complete Peerage of England, Scotland, Ireland, Great Britain and the United Kingdom*, ed. V. Gibbs and others, 14 vols in 15 (1910–98)
CPL	*Calendar of Papal Letters*, ed. W.H. Bliss and others, 13 vols in 14 (1893–1955)
CPR	*Calendar of Patent Rolls* (PRO Texts and Calendars, 1891 onwards)
CR	*Close Rolls of the Reign of Henry III*, 14 vols (PRO Texts and Calendars, 1902–38)
CRR	*Curia Regis Rolls of the Reigns of Richard I, John and Henry III preserved in the Public Record Office*, 17 vols (PRO Texts and Calendars, 1922–91)
CS	Camden Society, Camden Series
CSMLT	Cambridge Studies in Medieval Life and Thought
CStM	*Chartularies of St Mary's Abbey, Dublin*, ed. J.T. Gilbert, 2 vols (RS 80, 1884–6)
DBM	*Documents of the Baronial Movement of Reform and Rebellion 1258–1267*, selected R.F. Treharne, ed. I.J. Sanders (Oxford, 1973)
DD	*Diplomatic Documents 1101–1272*, ed. P. Chaplais (1964)
DNB	*Dictionary of National Biography*
Dunstable	'Annals of Dunstable', *Ann. Mon.*, iii. 3–408
EcHR	*Economic History Review*
EEA	*English Episcopal Acta* (1980–)
EETS	Early English Text Society
EHD	*English Historical Documents*, ed. D.C. Douglas, 12 vols in 13 (1953–77)
EHR	*English Historical Review*
English Medieval Diplomatic Practice	Pierre Chaplais, *English Medieval Diplomatic Practice, Part I: Documents and Interpretation*, 2 vols (London, 1982)
English Royal Documents	*English Royal Documents: King John – Henry VI (1199–1461)* (Oxford, 1971)
Exc. e Rot. Fin.	*Excerpta e Rotulis Finium in Turri Londiniensi asservatis*, ed. C. Roberts, 2 vols (Record Commission, London, 1835–6)
EYC	*Early Yorkshire Charters*, i–iii, ed. W. Farrer (Edinburgh, 1914–16), and iv–xii, ed. C.T. Clay (Yorks. Archaeological Soc., Record Soc., extra series, I–X, 1935–65)

FDMPV	Fuentes documentales medievales del País Vasco
Fees	*Liber Feudorum: The Books of Fees Commonly Called Testa de Nevill, 1198–1293* (1920–31)
Feudal Aids	*Inquisitions and Assessments relating to Feudal Aids, with Other Analogous Documents preserved in the PRO, 1284–1431* (1899–1920)
Flores	*Flores Historiarum*, ed. H.R. Luard, 3 vols (RS 95, 1890)
FMST	*Frühmittelalterliche Studien*
Foedera	*Foedera, Conventiones, Litterae, et ... Acta Publica*, ed. T. Rymer, amended edition by A. Clarke and F. Holbrooke, 4 vols in 7 (Rec. Comm., 1816–69)
Gerald, *EH*	*Expugnatio Hibernica. The Conquest of Ireland, by Giraldus Cambrensis*, ed. A.B. Scott and F.X. Martin (Dublin, 1978)
Guisborough	*The Chronicle of Walter of Guisborough*, ed. H. Rothwell (Royal Historical Society, Camden Third Series 89, London, 1957)
HKF	W. Farrer, *Honors and Knights Fees*, 3 vols (1923–5)
HMC	Historical Manuscripts Commission
HMDI	*Historic and Municipal Documents of Ireland A.D. 1172–1320*, ed. J.T. Gilbert (RS 53, 1870)
HMSO	Her/His Majesty's Stationery Office
Howden, *Chronica*	*Chronica Magistri Rogeri de Houedene*, ed. W. Stubbs, 4 vols (RS 51, 1868–71)
Howden, *Gesta*	*Gesta Regis Henrici Secundi Benedicti Abbatis*, ed. W. Stubbs, 2 vols (RS 49, 1867)
HR	*Historical Research*
HRH	*Heads of Religious Houses in England and Wales, II: 1216–1377*, ed. D.M. Smith and V.C.M. London (Cambridge, 2001)
IHS	*Irish Historical Studies*
J.	*Journal [of the]*
Joinville	*Joinville Vie de Saint Louis*, ed. Jacques Monfrin (Paris, 1995)
Jugements	*Recueil des Jugements de l'Échiquier de Normandie au XIIIe siècle*, ed. L. Delisle (Paris, 1864)
King's Works	*The History of the King's Works: The Middle Ages*, ed. R.A. Brown, H.M. Colvin and A.J. Taylor, 2 vols (HMSO, 1963)
Langtoft	*The Chronicle of Pierre de Langtoft, Rerum Britannicarum medii aevi scriptores*, ed. T. Wright (London, 1869)
Layettes	*Layettes du Trésor des Chartes*, ed. A. Teulet and others, 5 vols (Paris, 1863–1909)
Margam	'Annals of Margam', in *Ann. Mon.*, i. 3–40
Med. Dublin	*Medieval Dublin I* [etc.]: *Proceedings of the Friends of Medieval Dublin Symposium*, ed. S. Duffy (Dublin, 2000–)
MGH	Monumenta Germaniae Historica
Na Buirgéisi	G. Mac Niocaill, *Na Buirgéisi XII–XV Aois*, 2 vols (Dublin, 1964)
NAI	National Archives of Ireland, Dublin

ODNB	*Oxford Dictionary of National Biography*, ed. H.C. Matthew and B. Harrison, 60 vols (Oxford, 2004)
Osney	'The Chronicle of Osney', in *Ann. Mon.*, iv. 3–352
PatR	*Patent Rolls of the Reign of Henry III [1216–32]*, 2 vols (PRO Texts and Calendars, 1901–3)
PL	*Patrologia Latina Cursus Completus*, series latina, ed. J. P. Migne, 221 vols (Paris, 1844–64)
PR	*Pipe Rolls*, published by the Pipe Roll Society
PRO	The National Archives: Public Record Office
Proc.	*Proceedings of [the]*
PRS	Pipe Roll Society
PW	*Parliamentary Writs and Writs of Military Summons*, ed. F.T. Palgrave, 2 vols (Rec. Comm., 1827–34)
QN	'Querimoniæ Normannorum, 1247', in *RHF*, xxiv, I (Paris, 1904), pp. 1–73
RBE	*Red Book of the Exchequer*, ed. H. Hall, 3 vols (RS 99, London, 1896)
RC	*Rotuli Chartarum in Turri Londinensi Asservatis*, ed. T.D. Hardy (Rec. Comm., 1837)
RDBR	*The Royal Domain in the Bailliage of Rouen*, ed. J. Strayer, 2nd edn (London, 1976)
Rec. Comm.	Record Commission
Reg.	*Register [of]*
Registres	*Les Registres de Philippe Auguste*, ed. J.W. Baldwin, i, *Texte* (Paris, 1992)
RF	*Excerpta e Rotulis Finium in Turri Londinensi Asservatis, 1216–72*, ed. C. Roberts (Rec. Comm., 1835–6)
R. Gasc.	*Rôles Gascons*, ed. F. Michel and C. Bémont, 3 vols (Paris, 1885–1904); ed. Yves Renouard (London, HMSO, 1962)
RH	*Rotuli Hundredorum temp. Hen. III et Edw. I* (Rec. Comm., 1812–18)
RHF	*Recueil des Historiens des Gaules et de la France*, 24 vols (Paris, 1793–1904)
RIA	Royal Irish Academy
RLC	*Rotuli Litterarum Clausarum in Turri Londinensi Asservati, 1204–27*, 2 vols, ed. T.D. Hardy (Rec. Comm., 1833–44)
RLP	*Rotuli Litterarum Patentium in Turri Londinensi Asservati, 1201–16*, ed. T.D. Hardy (Rec. Comm., 1835)
Rot. Fin.	*Rotuli de Oblatis et Finibus in Turri Londinensi Asservati*, ed. T.D. Hardy (Rec. Comm., 1835)
Rot. Parl.	*Rotuli Parliamentorum*, 6 vols (Rec. Comm., 1783)
Royal Letters	*Royal and Other Historical Letters Illustrative of the Reign of Henry III*, 2 vols, ed. W.W. Shirley (RS 27, 1862–6)
RS	Rolls Series (*Rerum Britannicarum Medii Aevi Scriptores*, 1858–96)
Rymer	Thomas Rymer, *Foedera, conventiones, literae et cujuscunque generis acta publica*, 2 vols (London, 1704, 1705)
Saint-Pathus	*Vie de Saint Louis par Guillaume de Saint-Pathus*, ed. H.-F. Delaborde (Paris, 1899)

ser.	series
Soc.	Society [of]
Soc. Antiqs.	Society of Antiquaries of London
SR	*The Statutes of the Realm*, ed. A. Luders and others, 11 vols (Rec. Comm., 1810–28)
TCE, i–xiii	*Thirteenth Century England*, 13 vols so far, i–iv, ed. P.R. Coss and S.D. Lloyd; vi–x, ed. M.C. Prestwich, R.H. Britnell and R.F. Frame; xi–xii, xiii, ed. J. Burton, P. Schofield, K. Stöber, B. Weiler (Woodbridge, 1986–)
Tewkesbury	'Annals of Tewkesbury', in *Ann. Mon.*, i. 43–182
TNA	The National Archives, *see* PRO
Torigni	Robert of Torigni, in *Chronicles of the Reigns of Stephen, Henry II and Richard I*, ed. R. Howlett, 4 vols (RS 82, 1884–9), iv
Treaty Rolls	P. Chaplais, *Treaty Rolls preserved in the Public Record Office*, vol. 1, *1234–1325* (London, 1955)
TRHS	*Transactions of the Royal Historical Society*
VCH	*The Victoria History of the Counties of England*, ed. H.A. Doubleday and others (1900– , in progress)
Waverley	'Annals of Waverley', in *Ann. Mon.*, ii. 129–412
Wendover	*Rogeri de Wendover, Chronica sive Flores Historiarum*, ed. H.O. Coxe, 5 vols (English Historical Soc., 1841–4)
WHR	*The Welsh History Review*
Winchester	'Annals of Winchester', in *Ann. Mon.*, ii. 3–128
WL	*The Royal Charter Witness Lists: Henry III*, ed. M. Morris (List and Index Soc. 291–2, 2002); *Edward I*, ed. R. Huscroft (List and Index Soc. 279, 2000)
Worcester	'Annals of Worcester', in *Ann. Mon.*, iv. 355–562
Wykes	'Thomas Wykes' Chronicle', in *Ann. Mon.*, iv. 6–354

Political Ideas and Dialogue in England in the Twelfth and Thirteenth Centuries

Caroline Burt

In the years between the start of the twelfth century and the end of the thirteenth, ideas about kingship developed significantly across Europe and new forms of political dialogue emerged. To this, England was no exception.[1] While what follows is a reminder of England's historical integration with Europe, most importantly it discusses the way in which widely shared ideas merged with local, in some ways very distinctive, traditions and circumstances to produce a particular political dialogue within England. At the beginning of the twelfth century, many ideas about kingship were well established. First, it was accepted that the king had both private, or personal, and public authority.[2] The former was conveyed by the fact that he was the greatest lord in the land – the head of the feudal hierarchy; as such, he held territory (the royal demesne) and property, and had tenants and vassals from whom he was entitled to expect military service, an arrangement which was replicated further down the feudal chain. The king's public authority, on the other hand, was derived from the fact that he was the accepted ruler of a realm. This meant that certain regnal rights, such as entitlement to taxation, were conferred on him, but it also brought with it responsibilities. Order within the kingdom was, in theory, his to maintain – hence the contemporary phrase 'the king's peace'. In practice this usually meant ultimate jurisdiction over crimes and could, under the most active rulers, lead to the promulgation of law codes. The king had at the same time a duty to defend his subjects from external foes. In short, the rights the king could claim were directly related to his responsibility for the overall maintenance of the common welfare, the 'communis utilitas', of his subjects.

Such was the situation in c. 1100 and although these fundamental tenets of royal authority never really changed, the public authority of the king was subjected to a process of increasing definition during the course of the following two centuries. The further spread of literacy, and, with it, techniques of accounting and administration, the emergence of the universities, and particularly the study of the 'learned' canon and Roman laws, as well as the work of theologians (especially the scholastics) all contributed to these developments.[3] In essence, practical changes equipped rulers with greater latitude in what they could actually do within their realms, and an enhanced ability to disseminate governmental decisions, thus bolstering their claims to authority, both personal and public. At the same time, developments in political language provided them with the linguistic, or rhetorical, tools to express aspects of

[1] I should like to thank Dr Magnus Ryan, Dr John Watts, Mr Richard Partington and Professor Rosamond McKitterick for their help with this article. Many of its points draw on and will be developed more fully in my forthcoming monograph on the reign of Edward I.
[2] For further discussion of this and what follows, see J.L. Watts, *The Making of Polities: Europe, 1300–1500* (Cambridge, 2009), 68–71.
[3] See again Watts, *The Making of Polities*, 73–4.

their authority in newly exalted terms. It is with the specific effects of new political language and ideas generated by the study of canon and Roman law, the Bible, and of Aristotle by the scholastics, that this paper will be concerned.

I

Canon law studies had, under papal auspices, been growing in sophistication since at least the eighth century.[4] From the eleventh century, however, under the influence of the reform movement and its desire to invest ever more centralised authority in the pope, canon lawyers became increasingly concerned with stressing the plenitude of papal power. Thus, canonists, either under the pope's direct influence (as was the case most of the time), or simply under the influence of reforming ideas, sought texts which could be used to justify papal centralisation. Yet at this stage canon law existed as a series of compilations of material. Jurisprudence did not exist, and that is where the Roman lawyers, or civilians, had an impact.[5] The study of Roman law had itself only been reinvigorated in the late eleventh century by the re-discovery of Justinian's *Digest* in Italy, after which lawyers based in Bologna and elsewhere began to study it intensively.[6] In the twelfth century, both sets of lawyers came to influence each other on a number of different levels. Indeed, so interwoven did the ideas of Roman and canon lawyers become thereafter that it is difficult at times to distinguish between civilian and canonist contributions to political dialogue, especially in view of the integral importance of Roman law jurisprudence in the education of every canonist.[7]

The influence of the canon and Roman lawyers on ideas about princely authority was profound, because the detail and specificity of their sources encouraged a much more precise and nuanced analysis of the nature of governmental authority than had hitherto been made.[8] Initially the emphasis was on further defining and justifying the public, jurisdictional authority of the prince. He, like the Roman emperor, was said to have been given supreme executive authority in his realm by God, what was known as 'plenitudo potestatis'. Indeed, he came frequently to be referred to as 'emperor in his kingdom', his collection of powers known as his 'imperium'. This was in a sense simply a bolstering of arguments about the king's unrivalled jurisdiction within his realm. However, it made an important difference at a time when princes were, with increasingly sophisticated practical mechanisms at their disposal, making particular attempts to assert their authority at the expense of, for example, the nobility or the church. By reference to this logic, what had previously

---

[4] For this and what follows, see G. Post, *Studies in Medieval Legal Thought* (Princeton, 1964), 61–8; K. Pennington, 'A Short History of Canon Law from Apostolic Times to 1917', http://faculty.cua.edu/Pennington/Canon%20Law/ShortHistoryCanonLaw.htm (consulted 30 September 2009); J. Canning, 'Introduction: Politics, Institutions and Ideas', in *The Cambridge History of Medieval Political Thought c.350–c.1450*, ed. J.H. Burns, 5th edn (Cambridge, 2005), 347–9; and L.S. Robinson, 'Church and Papacy', in ibid., 266–77.

[5] Pennington, 'Short History of Canon Law from Apostolic Times to 1917'.

[6] On Roman law, see P. Stein, *Roman Law in European History* (Cambridge, 1999); J. Canning, 'Ideas of the State in Thirteenth and Fourteenth Century Commentators on the Roman Law', *TRHS* 5th ser. 33 (1983), 1–27; E. Kantorowicz, *The King's Two Bodies: A Study in Medieval Political Theology* (Princeton, 1957, repr. 1997), 126–43.

[7] Overview: K. Pennington, 'Law, Legislative Authority and Theories of Government, 1150–1300', in *Cambridge History of Medieval Political Thought*, ed. Burns, 425–42; J.A. Brundage, *The Medieval Origins of the Legal Profession: Canonists, Civilians and Courts* (Chicago, 2008), 126–218.

[8] For discussion of this elsewhere, see Watts, *The Making of Polities*, 74–8.

been regarded as the king's personal inheritance and property was now increasingly presented and viewed 'as public goods, which ... were required for the rule of the realm'.[9] This inheritance and property (the royal demesne), alongside the rights and powers required for the governance of the realm, pertained to what became known as the 'crown', which was coincidental first with the king himself as head of the body politic, and secondly, by extension, with the body – the realm as a whole. Importantly, though, property held and jurisdiction exercised by others were *also* often represented as inalienable rights of the crown. In short, a firm notion emerged in the twelfth century that all authority emanated from the king and was rightly exercised by him; others exercised authority in a realm only by royal concession. Once established, this idea of the king's supreme public jurisdiction was followed in the thirteenth century by discussion of exactly how it should be utilised, and the focus came to fall principally on the role of the prince to legislate, to provide common rules by which all his subjects must abide.

However, despite the tendency of lawyers to stress the authority of the prince in these ways, his was not always seen as untrammelled power.[10] Arguments about the authority of the prince were in fact often coupled with the long standing notion that his duty in exercising power was to uphold the 'communis utilitas', or common profit. In other words, the king's public authority was conferred to enable him to fulfil his role as guardian of the realm; rights and responsibilities were, as in earlier notions of kingship, inextricably linked. As will be seen, this led unsurprisingly to claims by princes that the authority they claimed to act in a variety of matters was sanctioned by the fact that it was for the common profit (even if, at times, their assertions in this regard were tenuous). Yet, despite this, the prince's 'imperium' was not necessarily considered to be revocable: some, like Azo, felt that it was, but others argued that it was the prerogative of the prince to decide whether he acted in the interests of the common profit: the king, they argued, quoting Justinian's *Digest*, 'is not bound by the law', and, furthermore, 'what pleases the prince has the force of law'. The prince's will was sufficient reason for law ('voluntas pro ratione in principe').[11] Subjects were thus in theory reliant on the king being minded to act for the common good; most practitioners of the learned laws agreed that he could not be forced to do so.

Among lay rulers, the Holy Roman emperors were early protagonists in the deployment of ideas and arguments emerging from the study of Roman and canon law, as they sought to emphasise their authority in the empire and in relation to the Church and the pope. Within the empire, the emphasis was initially on using exalted language about the emperor's public authority to emphasise, clarify or expand his existing feudal jurisdiction and rights. Such rights were often spoken of in public terms to claim that they were not solely the personal possession of the emperor, but the inalienable appurtenances of the imperial crown. In the mid twelfth century, Frederick Barbarossa (1152–90) was speaking, for example, of 'this our dignity of the imperial crown and governance'.[12] Such direct and indirect usage of Roman and canon law continued in the thirteenth century, but increasingly the emphasis now fell on the legislative authority of the emperor: in 1231, for example, when Emperor

---

[9] Watts, *The Making of Polities*, 75.

[10] On what follows, see Pennington, 'Law, Legislative Authority and Theories of Government, 1150–1300', 425–42.

[11] For a discussion of these ideas see M.J. Ryan, 'Bartolus of Sassoferrato and Free Cities', *TRHS* 6th ser. 10 (2000), 65–89.

[12] www.exclassics.com/foxe/foxe40.htm (accessed 4 May 2010).

Frederick II was making law in Sicily, he was again to turn to texts produced by canonists and civilians to emphasise his authority to do so; the origin and protection of the law, he said, concur in one hand, that of the king. To the senators and people of Rome he was also to write that 'our imperial majesty is free from all laws'.[13] There is, then, no doubt that Roman and canon law furnished the Holy Roman emperors with a powerful language with which to express their claims to authority. It was not, however, the only language to be used in this way; Philippe Buc has shown how, in the twelfth century, Frederick Barbarossa also manipulated in his own favour the work of biblical exegetes, who were ironically broadly arguing *against* lordship.[14] In a speech made by Obert, archbishop of Milan, at the Diet of Roncaglia (1158) for example, which made use of the language of the exegetes of Genesis 1, Barbarossa was portrayed as a second Adam, a saviour for Italy, unlike previous kings. In sum, 'the Roncaglia speech', writes Buc, 'shows how exegetical models could be adjusted to praise the prince'.[15]

With the rise of territorial states in the same period, kings, anxious to emphasise their own authority vis-à-vis other rulers, particularly the Holy Roman emperor and the pope, and their own subjects, soon followed the example set by the pope and the emperor. Both Louis VII (1137–80) and Philip Augustus (1180–1223) of France, for example, worked hard to assert their feudal jurisdiction, placing evergreater emphasis on their public authority in so doing.[16] They did so when claiming wider powers too. By 1202, Innocent III, possibly quoting the words used by Philip Augustus in a petition to him in 1201, wrote that the French king 'does not recognise a superior in temporal matters'.[17] And in around 1300, the French king Philip IV spoke of himself as 'emperor in his own kingdom'.[18] In addition, the Capetians were linked with a fundamental shift in favour of the French king in the tenor of arguments by biblical exegetes based in Paris. Those who followed Amaury of Bene, for example, who were secretly patronised by Philip Augustus's son, the future Louis IX, argued that all orders would be excised at the end of the world, except those of the king of France and his son, who would receive 'potestas'. Thereafter, arguments in favour of lordship, particularly of the French king, came increasingly to prevail.[19] In other words, unlike Barbarossa, the French kings did not simply manipulate the work of exegetes in their own favour, but sought to change the direction of exegetical thoughts. Elsewhere, Alfonso X of Castile (1252–84) similarly argued that the king had no superior in temporal matters and that he was equivalent to the emperor in his own kingdom.[20]

In order to ensure, so far as possible, the acceptance and implementation of their laws and mandates, princes furthermore began to adapt to their own ends the developing idea in private law that the wishes of corporations could be represented by proctors given full powers ('plena potestas') to act on the corporation's behalf.

13 Kantorowicz, *The King's Two Bodies*, 105–6, 155.
14 P. Buc, *L'Ambiguité du livre: prince, pouvoir, et peuple dans les commentaires de la Bible au moyen âge* (Paris, 1994); P. Buc, '*Principes Gentium Dominantur Eorum*: Princely Power between Legitimacy and Illegitimacy in Twelfth Century Exegesis', in *Cultures of Power: Lordship, Status and Process in Twelfth Century Europe*, ed. T.N. Bisson (Philadelphia, 1995), 310–28.
15 Ibid., 316.
16 Watts, *The Making of Polities*, 73.
17 R. Fawtier, *The Capetian Kings of France: Monarchy and Nation 987–1328* (London, 1960), 85–6.
18 Ibid., 88.
19 Buc, 'Princely Power', 317–18. See also an interesting further piece by Buc: 'David's Adultery with Bathsheba and the Healing Power of the Capetian Kings', *Viator* 24 (1993), 101–20.
20 Post, *Studies in Medieval Legal Thought*, 483.

Representatives of communities (ecclesiastical and lay), they ordered, should come before them with full power to give consent to executive action.[21] In the mid-thirteenth century, Emperor Frederick II soon summoned proctors in these terms, and his actions were in turn replicated by rulers elsewhere, in Spain and France.[22] The consent obtained in this way by rulers was, as they intended, important in increasing the force of princely action, but it should be noted that it was a predominantly procedural consent: in other words, although it allowed representation and the expression of the Roman law maxim that 'what touches all should be approved by all', representatives were in fact obliged to give consent to executive action where it could be shown to be necessary for upholding the 'utilitas publica'.

In making relatively grand assertions about their authority, princes were of course sometimes speaking of a practical reality which did not exist. In 1183, when Frederick Barbarossa issued the Treaty of Constance, the preamble emphasised his authority, while in the body of the treaty the emperor actually made what Holt has called 'massive alienations of real power'.[23] Indeed, Barbarossa was one in a long line of princes forced by their subjects to make concessions in this period despite the wide-ranging authority they claimed. Subjects had, like their rulers (in fact often because of their rulers), imbibed notions of rights and authority which pervaded the atmosphere of twelfth- and thirteenth-century Europe, and, in the face of princely claims which threatened their own liberties, they often fought successfully for those liberties. It was in the context of war, and failure in war, that most concessions were wrested. The Treaty of Constance was issued by Barbarossa after his defeat by the Lombard League at Legnano, granting the towns of the League a number of liberties, and providing them, in practice, with far-reaching powers of self-governance.[24] And over a hundred years later, Alfonso X of Castile was being forced to make a number of concessions to his greatest subjects.[25] Thus, although princes had used the language of the political thought of the period to express their supreme public authority, in so doing they often found themselves in conflict with those who felt their own authority was being challenged, in practice mainly nobles, the Italian cities and the Church. The twelfth and thirteenth centuries represented, in sum, a period in which, aided by the development of the learned law, the parameters of princely authority within Europe underwent greater definition; it was a process which was often violent and frequently bloody.

In the second half of the thirteenth century, a new influence came to bear on political theory, the work of Aristotle, which was fully re-absorbed in the West during this period.[26] Where earlier theologians had often seen politics as a necessary evil, now, inspired by Aristotle, they increasingly came to see politics in a more positive light, akin to the Roman tradition, but of course with God at the heart of their interpretations. They argued that politics provided a way of achieving the life of virtue necessary for man to attain salvation. In this, kingship was deemed to have a special function: in the 1260s, Thomas Aquinas, one of the most famous and influential of the scholastic theologians, argued in a work written for Hugh de Lusignan, king of

---

[21] For this and what follows, see Post, *Studies in Medieval Legal Thought*, 86–7.

[22] Post, *Studies in Medieval Legal Thought*, 89.

[23] J.C. Holt, *Magna Carta*, 2nd edn (Cambridge, 1992), 87.

[24] I am grateful to Dr Magnus Ryan for pointing this out to me.

[25] Watts, *The Making of Politics*, 172–3.

[26] For a discussion of the reception of Aristotelian ideas, see M. Kempshall, *The Common Good in Late Medieval Political Thought* (Oxford, 1999); J. Dunbabin, 'Aristotle in the Schools', in *Trends in Medieval Political Thought*, ed. B. Smalley (Oxford, 1965), 65–86; R.W. Dyson, 'Introduction' to T. Aquinas, *Political Writings* (Cambridge, 2002).

Cyprus, that 'the king's duty is to secure the good life for the community in such a way as to ensure that it is led to the blessedness of heaven'.[27] Aquinas was soon followed by others, including Giles of Rome (Egidius Romanus) in the late 1270s, who produced another 'Mirror' commissioned in 1277 by Philip III of France for his son, Philip, which enjoyed wide circulation in Europe from around 1280.[28] In some ways, the arguments produced by the scholastic theologians were not so very different from those that had gone before: they continued to emphasise the supreme authority of the prince, and in a sense the duty to preserve the common good did not diverge much in practice from any of the earlier notions of the common utility. Yet the scholastics celebrated kingship in a way that few in the Christian tradition, if any, had before. The king could, by acting for the common good, play a crucial role in securing the salvation of his subjects, and eternal life, 'the blessedness of heaven', for himself, and politics could be an intrinsically noble business. It is unsurprising that kings should have made use of such ideas in their own favour.

II

The language of politics thus underwent a transformation in the twelfth and thirteenth centuries, influenced by not one, or two, but arguably three major sets of thinkers: the canonists, the civilians, and the theologians. As we have seen, this had a profound influence on politics across the continent, but how far and in what particular ways did these ideas affect England? It is self-evident that centralised royal authority was not brought to England by Roman or canon law. First, by the time Roman and canon law ideas came to influence political thought in western Europe, England was already highly centralised. Furthermore, as George Garnett has shown, a notion of the crown, and of rights and land pertaining to it, had emerged in the decades following the Conquest. Henry I had, for example, spoken of the 'liberties, dignities and penalties belonging to the king's crown' at the turn of the twelfth century.[29] Later, the Angevins were just as likely to refer for support to traditional notions of kingship as they were to the language of the two laws. So, remarks Jim Holt, when John needed to invoke a defence against Innocent III, he did not turn to Justinian, but instead to St Wulfstan, and when talking about the relationship between the prince and the law, he stated that new assizes could not, he had heard, be introduced anywhere without princely assent – a statement, Holt emphasises, which was a long way from Justinian.[30] Similarly, in seeking to subject their king to the law in 1215, John's subjects were appealing to long-standing ideas about the subordination of the ruler to the law.[31]

That said, ideas from the Roman and canon law did enter England rapidly and became important in the language deployed by kings in support of the extension of their public authority. Henry II was the first king to use Roman law language, in connection with the rights of the crown, arguing that the 'iura' pertaining to it had

---

[27] For this and what follows, see T. Aquinas, *Political Writings*, 1(b), '*De Regimine Principum* or *De Regno*', 5–45.
[28] Kempshall, *The Common Good in Late Medieval Political Thought*, 130–56.
[29] G. Garnett, 'The Origins of the Crown', in *The History of English Law: Centenary Essays on Pollock and Maitland*, ed. J. Hudson (Proceedings of the British Academy 89, 1996), 171–214 (p. 199). Despite attempts to do so, it has proved impossible to trace the origins of Henry's references.
[30] Holt, *Magna Carta*, 88.
[31] Ibid., 89.

to be maintained 'illibata' or 'illaesa' (inviolate). The exact point at which Henry first used these Roman law terms in England is debated, but it may have been as early as 1154, through the addition of a clause to the coronation charter.[32] As with many other monarchs, what particularly prompted this stress on crown rights was, Harriss has argued, Henry's policy of 'recovering and exploiting the rights of the crown', particularly through the resumption of royal lands soon after his accession, the latter fact reinforcing the idea that he did indeed add a new clause to the coronation charter in 1154.[33] It was, in other words, part of a practical need to justify royal policy. However, there is no convincing evidence that he made any more grandiose claims to authority based on Roman or canon law principles.

Following Henry II's death, foreign policy imperatives and ambitions meant in practice that developing Roman and canon law ideas about princely authority came most commonly to be used within a quite specific frame of reference: war finance. King John, for example, linked the 'magna et ardua' of the conflict with Philip Augustus with the 'utilitas communis' of England.[34] In other words, John sought to define the war in national rather than feudal terms, claiming authority to wage war and call on his subjects' resources for the good of the realm, or common profit. Henry III too sought more than once to define conflict abroad in national terms. In 1237, his request for taxation was couched in references to the 'status noster et regni nostri', while that of 1242 spoke of Henry's rights in France *and* those parts which pertained 'ad regnum suum Angliae'.[35]

At the same time, John and Henry further developed the ideas first utilised by Henry II about the inalienability of crown lands and rights mainly in order again to increase the revenue they could raise to fulfil their military commitments. First, the royal demesne began to emerge, Harriss has shown, 'as a separate administrative entity in which the king's unlimited rights over the land could facilitate extensive fiscal exploitation'. Tallage, a tax on all the lands pertaining to the ancient demesne, also developed, which, argues Harriss, 'further assisted this'.[36] Henry III also broadened the focus from lands to liberties and franchises, making it clear in the early 1250s that only those who could present charters or show long usage could legitimately exercise liberties and franchises. In 1255, he went further, ordering an enquiry into encroachments on royal rights.[37] The treatise by the author known as Bracton reinforced the idea which was developing here when it described franchises concerned with justice and peace-keeping as pertaining to the crown 'because they make the crown what it is'; as a consequence, it argued, they were inalienable.[38] Potentially this meant that all previous grants were invalid, though Henry never pursued a policy of resumption. The language of inalienability was also used by Henry when he began, with the acquisition of the earldom of Chester, to develop a royal patrimony, land which belonged to the king as private rather than public property, and was intended to provide for members of the royal family. Initially he argued that this land must not be separated from the crown, though its distinctive-

---

[32] Post, *Studies in Medieval Legal Thought*, 415–31; H.G. Richardson, 'The Coronation Oath in Medieval England: The Evolution of the Office and the Oath', *Traditio* 16 (1960), 111–202 (at 151–69, 174–80).

[33] G.L. Harriss, *King, Parliament and Public Finance in Medieval England to 1369* (Oxford, 1975), 131–2.

[34] Post, *Studies in Medieval Legal Thought*, 384.

[35] Ibid., 384–5.

[36] Harriss, *King, Parliament and Public Finance*, 134.

[37] M.C. Clanchy, 'Did Henry III have a Policy?' *History* 53 (1968), 203–16 (at 209–10).

[38] Post, *Studies in Medieval Legal Thought*, 373.

ness from the ancient demesne of the crown soon became clear, rendering such arguments less useful to him. Thereafter the royal patrimony became an accepted part of the king's (or rather the dynasty's) private belongings.[39]

It can be shown, then, that Roman and canon law ideas were utilised by English kings in the thirteenth century, particularly as they could be made relevant to arguments about national taxation and crown lands and rights. Indeed, it should be noted that Henry III in particular was connected with other monarchs using ideas from the two laws: in the 1230s, the famous canonist Hostiensis was on Henry's staff, while, in the same decade, Frederick II's chief justice and legal draughtsman, Peter de Vinea, was in receipt of an annual salary from the exchequer.[40] But what has not yet been seen are any more grandiose statements about royal authority from English monarchs. In fact, Henry III is the only ruler who (unsurprisingly) may have come close to such utterances. In 1248, according to Matthew Paris, he argued that

> no more should vassals judge their prince or confine him to their conditions, than servants would their lords. For, whosoever are deemed inferiors have rather to be directed at the will ('arbitrium') of the lord and the pleasure ('voluntas') of the ordinary.[41]

This was all very close to the Roman law notion that 'the will of the prince has the force of law'. Henry may also have made claims to the pope which drew on the idea that he was 'emperor in his kingdom': Innocent IV complained in 1244 that he had said that his power in temporal affairs was the equivalent of the pope's in spiritual matters.[42]

Henry was, however, the only English king to date to make such grandiose statements; more usually arguments made about royal authority were designed, as we have seen, to help the Angevins justify requests for taxation, or claims to rights and lands in order to raise money by an alternative means. It is true that the requests for taxation made by John and Henry III often involved the invocation of the notion of the common profit to couch military ventures in national rather than feudal terms, but neither king engaged in action which suggested that they had really absorbed ideas about upholding the common profit. At times it is even clear that such notions were being forced on them by others. The Statute of Merton of 1236, for example, whose preamble states that discussion had taken place at the king's coronation about 'the common good of the realm' which had led to 'the underwritten articles', was the work of a baronage on whose support Henry III was reliant to be able to pursue the foreign ambitions he harboured. It was a trade-off rather than a statement of Henrician policy.[43] Indeed, ideas from the two laws were readily seized upon by the English king's subjects to express his responsibilities to maintain the common profit over his executive authority at other times too. Mention has already been made of the most famous instance of this, Magna Carta, but ten years earlier, in 1205, for example, John's barons forced him, through the threat of rebellion and invasion, to swear that he would preserve the 'iura' of the realm by their advice. As Holt notes, 'The right, interest, or utility of the realm was a weapon which both sides in the argument could use.'[44] Major crisis came in 1215 because the failure of

---

[39] Harriss, *King, Parliament and Public Finance*, 142–4.
[40] Clanchy, 'Did Henry III have a Policy?' 210.
[41] Paris is quoted in Clanchy, 'Did Henry III have a Policy?' 207–8.
[42] Ibid., 213.
[43] *SR*, I, 1.
[44] Holt, *Magna Carta*, 119.

John's allies to defeat the French at Bouvines in 1214 made it possible to challenge a king who, through arbitrary impositions on his barons, which had been designed to increase his security (as he saw it) by indebting those whose loyalty he deemed suspect, and to raise money for war, had not fulfilled his duties to his subjects. The principle that the king ruled for the good of the realm was re-stated in 1216 when Magna Carta was reissued in the first year of Henry III's minority: Henry and his Council, it was said, would take care of 'those things which suggested themselves for correction, all those things which pertained to the 'communis omnium utilitas' and the 'pax et status noster et regni nostri'. These were, of course, the words of the nobility (and the papal legate, who seems to have injected quite a lot of up to date canon law into English governance), not the child-king.[45] Later, in 1242, the magnates were to justify their refusal of an aid on the basis that the money raised in 1237, which should have been spent for the '*utilitas* of the king and the realm as was necessary', had not been disposed of in this way. Two years later they lamented that aids raised had yielded no profit to the king or the realm.[46] It was thus perhaps inevitable that, by the time of the major crisis of Henry's reign in 1258, they should be styling themselves the defenders of the common profit: in the Provisions of Oxford of that year they spoke of the common needs of the realm and the king, and at the same time turned the king's doctrine of inalienability back on him: it seems that some resumption of royal lands may have been considered at the Oxford meeting, and members of the royal council later swore not to receive any such lands themselves or to allow Henry to give away any of the demesne of the crown.[47] Influences on the reformers in 1258 came from elsewhere too. Montfort himself was connected directly with Bishop Grosseteste (who was interested in Aristotelian ideas) and Louis IX of France, who had, following his return from crusade in 1254, published his *Grand Ordonnance*, which aimed at rooting out abuses by royal servants. Both Grosseteste's *Rules*, written for the countess of Lincoln, and his *Statuta*, created to regulate the conduct of his own household, were utilised in England in 1258, as was the *Grand Ordonnance*.[48] What had prompted the crisis of the late 1250s does not require lengthy explanation: Henry's continental policy was not one in which the interests of the English realm could really be invoked no matter what the king claimed: unlike in the 1290s, the French never, for example, raided the English south coast, to pose a direct threat to the king's subjects. A number of crises resulted from Henry's relentless pursuit of his continental ambitions, the major one of 1258–67 being caused by the denial of justice to some of his greatest subjects combined with his decision to fund his expeditions by placing arbitrary burdens on his subjects, particularly the knightly class.[49]

In the two centuries before 1272, political ideas and dialogue in England had, alongside the growing practical remit of the king's authority, developed significantly. New, or newly resurrected, ideas about public authority had an effect on the way English kings perceived themselves and their rights, as well as on their subjects' perceptions of princely responsibility to maintain the common profit. Yet the local perspective should not be forgotten: these ideas had become interwoven in England with traditional notions of kingship and kingly obligations, such as the principle

---

[45] Post, *Studies in Medieval Legal Thought*, 385.
[46] Harriss, *King, Parliament and Public Finance*, 37–8.
[47] Ibid., 137–8; R.F. Treharne, *Documents of the Baronial Movement of Reform and Rebellion 1258–1267* (Oxford Medieval Texts, 1973), 96–8.
[48] J.R. Maddicott, *Simon de Montfort* (Cambridge, 1994), 167–9.
[49] D. Carpenter, 'What happened in 1258', in his *The Reign of Henry III* (London, 1996), 183–97.

that the king should be below the law; the contingent development of the common law, rather than the absorption of civil law which took place in most of Europe, also added to the development of an identity which to some extent set it apart from its continental neighbours. That said, the similarities between the crises John and Henry III faced as they sought to expand their authority and define policy, and those faced by other European monarchs in the same period, cannot be ignored. This was an era of definition: rulers now had the linguistic facility to stake greater claims to authority to act for the common profit than ever before, but the practical extension of royal authority and the conjoining of the 'communis utilitas' and greater executive power created, at the same time, expectations which subjects demanded their rulers should fulfil. By 1272 these principles were as well established in England as in many other European realms. Under Edward I, however, such ideas were deployed afresh. In some ways, this was a matter of rehearsal; but in others it represented a departure – and one whose consequences for English – and, indeed, British – politics – were profound.[50]

---

[50] This will be explored in my forthcoming monograph on Edward I.

Peripatetic and Sedentary Kingship:
The Itineraries of John and Henry III

Julie Elizabeth Kanter

The itineraries of the thirteenth-century English kings have not yet been given the attention they merit. Little in the way of thorough research has been produced beyond the compiling of the actual itineraries themselves. These compiled itineraries are of particular importance as it is only in the thirteenth century that the royal itineraries become complete enough to enable a detailed study to be undertaken. King John is the first English monarch whose travels can be followed on a near daily basis. This paper sets out to examine the itineraries of King John from 1199 to 1216 and of Henry III during both the minority government from 1216 to 1226 and the first phase of his personal rule from 1234 to 1241. The royal itinerary is not only of interest to modern historians – it was of great importance to contemporaries as well. For instance, *The History of William Marshal* has a plethora of references detailing where John went and when he went there.[1]

There are various types of questions which can be addressed. There are those relating to the nature of the itinerary itself – how fast and how far did the royal household travel, as well as where the king travelled to and how long he remained stationary at each location. There are also those questions concerned with the purpose of the itinerary – why the king travelled. One of the most fundamental questions relating to the itinerary is to what extent there was a capital-based government at Westminster. One of the clearest declarations of the view that there was not – and perhaps the most well known – was made by Jolliffe who wrote 'it was a government *in itinere* – not one which went out intermittently and for limited commissions, but one in perpetual movement, a government of the roads and roadsides ... England had no capital but the king's highway'.[2] John Le Patourel agreed and expressed just how ingrained this lifestyle was, stating 'Before 1066 the Norman dukes had not attempted to rule their duchy from a fixed seat of government ... After 1066 it is equally clear that the Norman kings continued this life of movement.'[3] Although Robert Bartlett has gone so far as to state that 'A sedentary court was not inconceivable ... Itineration was not forced on kings and lords, it was chosen by them.'[4] As Nicholas Vincent has stated, 'the Plantagenet kings were of their essence itinerant'.[5]

As for the purposes of the kings' itinerations, historians have tended to focus on five main categories: Economics, Politics, Ceremony, Religion and Pleasure. However, any analysis of the itineraries of John and Henry III should begin with

---

[1]   A.J. Holden, ed., S. Gregory, trans., *History of William Marshal*, 3 vols (London, 2006).
[2]   J.E.A. Jolliffe, *Angevin Kingship*, 2nd edn (London, 1963), 140.
[3]   J. Le Patourel, *The Norman Empire* (Oxford, 1976), 123.
[4]   R. Bartlett, *England under the Norman and Angevin Kings 1075–1225* (Oxford, 2000), 141–3.
[5]   N. Vincent, 'The Pilgrimages of the Angevin Kings of England, 1154–1272', in *Pilgrimage: The English Experience from Becket to Bunyan*, ed. C. Morris and P. Roberts (Cambridge, 2002), 12–45 (at 14–15).

an acknowledgement of those great endeavours which enable such an examination, namely the compilations of the itineraries. The itinerary of King John was compiled by Sir Thomas Duffus Hardy, first as an article in *Archaeologia* published in 1827[6] and additionally, in a more comprehensive form, as part of the introduction to the Patent Rolls of John's reign, which he also edited and which were published in 1835.[7] The 1835 itinerary is derived mainly from the attestations of the king – the date and the location of which are found on the enrolments in the Charter, Close and Patent Rolls that exist for all but three years of John's reign. These sources were supplemented by information derived from the Household rolls, seven of which are still in existence for John's reign[8] (and five of which were also edited by Hardy), by a list of fines levied by the Court of the King's Bench in John's presence which was compiled by the Rev. Joseph Hunter,[9] and by unspecified original charters which Hardy claimed to have found both in the Public Record Office and in private collections.[10]

The itinerary of Henry III was originally compiled by T. Craib in 1923.[11] Craib, like Hardy, derived his itinerary through the use of attestations on the enrolments of the chancery rolls. There also exists a revised edition of Henry III's itinerary for the years 1234–42 which is printed in volumes XV and XVI of the *Curia Regis Rolls*.[12] Additionally, Steven Brindle and Stephen Priestly have edited and annotated a version of Henry III's itinerary (excluding his time in France) which is based on the *Curia Regis Rolls* version of 1234–42 and primarily on Craib's for the rest of the time.[13]

As will be seen, when the itineraries are engaged with rigorously, a wealth of information is there to be discovered. I will begin then with the itinerary of King John 1199–1216. As has already been mentioned, John is the first English king whose itinerary is complete enough to enable a detailed examination, but to what extent exactly is his itinerary known? John's location is recorded for 69% of the days in his reign. This figure includes the three years – his eleventh, twelfth and thirteenth regnal years (7 May 1209 – 3 May 1212) – for which there are no Charter, Close or Patent Rolls extant. However, it should be remembered that there are Household rolls surviving from his eleventh and twelfth regnal years, meaning that it is only 13 John (12 May 1211 – 3 May 1212) for which there is a real dearth of information. If this regnal year is omitted from the calculations then the percentage of days with a known location for the king is 73% (see Table 1).

As John's itinerary is indeed complete enough to enable conclusions based upon it to be made, just what can be said regarding the nature of John's itinerary? The first thing that leaps into focus is how far John travelled: see Table 2. John is recorded as having travelled approximately 79,612 miles (128,123km) during his reign. This works out to be a daily average of 12.5 miles (20km) per day.

---

6   T.D. Hardy, '*Itinerarium Johannis Regis Angliae*', *Archaeologia* 22 (1827), 124–60.
7   *RLC*. This version of the itinerary was also published with a slightly different layout in *Description of the Patent Rolls in the Tower of London; to which is added an Itinerary of King John, with Prefatory Observations* (London, 1835) [hereafter, *Description*].
8   *Rotuli Liberate ac Misis et Praestitis regnante Johanne*, ed. T.D. Hardy (London, 1844); H. Cole, ed., *Documents Illustrative of English History in the Thirteenth and Fourteenth Century* (London, 1844).
9   *Description*, 152–6 n. 1.
10   *Description*, 156.
11   T. Craib, 'The Itinerary of Henry III' (1923), in typescript in the Map Room of The National Archives at Kew.
12   *CRR*, xv. pp. lviii–lxi; xvi. pp. xliv–xlviii.
13   S. Brindle and S. Priestly, eds, *The Itinerary of King Henry III, 1216–1272* (English Heritage, n.d.).

Table 1. John 1199–1216: Days when his location is recorded

Year	No. of recorded days	No. of days in his regnal year	Recorded days (%)
1199	101	209	48
1200	237	366	65
1201	183	365	50
1202	264	365	72
1203	313	365	86
1204	300	366	82
1205	333	365	91
1206	226	365	62
1207	304	365	83
1208	217	366	59
1209	210	365	58
1210	199	365	55
1211	71	365	19
1212	225	366	61
1213	318	365	87
1214	272	365	74
1215	337	365	92
1216	281	293	96
Overall	4391	6346	69
Years with adequate sources	4095	5615	73

Source: 'Itinerary of King John', in *RLP*; analysis is my own.

It is simply remarkable just how consistently, how relentlessly, John was travelling. Even more astonishing is that it was not just in the summer – with its many hours of daylight and potentially good weather – that John and his household were covering great distances. John travelled consistently throughout the year. Indeed, most of his trips to the north of England occurred during the winter months.

It has been remarked that John was a restless king, frequently remaining in the same place only one night before moving on again.[14] This is certainly supported by the record of his itinerary: the average length of time that John spent at a location per visit was just 2.1 days (Table 3).

Another way to look at this is by examining the percentage of his reign that King John spent on visits of various lengths. The greatest amount, 43% of his time on the throne, was spent on visits of two or three days' duration and the least, just 12% of his time as king, on visits of a week or more. The longest period of time John spent at one location is the 55-day stay at Rochester between 13 October and 6 December 1215. This was when he was engaged in besieging Rochester Castle.[15] Indeed, his time at Rochester was twenty days longer than any other continuous period of time at any location during his reign. The next longest stay is between 16 June and

14   J.C. Holt, *King John* (London, 1963), 13.
15   *Flores*, ii. 145–6.

Table 2. John 1199–1216: Distances travelled

Year	Distance (in miles)	Average distance per day
1199	3141	15
1200	4589	12.5
1201	4409	12
1202	5168	14.2
1203	4956	13.6
1204	4899	13.4
1205	4929	13.9
1206	4638	12.7
1207	4524	12.4
1208	4449	12.2
1209	4667	12.8
1210	4184	11.5
1211	2008	5.5
1212	4372	11.9
1213	4831	13.2
1214	6300	17.3
1215	4012	11
1216	3418	11.7
Overall	79494	12.5
Years with adequate sources	73258	13

Source: Locations taken from 'Itinerary of King John', in *RLP*; distances calculated using the shortest route by road between locations as determined by Google Maps; all other analysis is my own.

Table 3. John 1199–1216: Average number of consecutive days spent in one location

Year	Average no. of consecutive days
1199	1.9
1200	1.9
1201	1.8
1202	2.4
1203	2.7
1204	2.3
1205	2.3
1206	2.2
1207	2.1
1208	2
1209	1.5
1210	1.6
1211	1.6
1212	1.8
1213	2.1

Year	Average no. of consecutive days
1214	2
1215	2.9
1216	2.5
Overall	2.1

Source: 'Itinerary of King John', in *RLP*; analysis is my own.

18 July 1203 when John remained at Rouen in order to protect the Norman capital from Philip Augustus.

A slightly different way of thinking about the peripatetic nature of John's itinerary is by looking at how many times a month he changed location (Table 4).[16] In total, there is a recorded change in John's location 2,702 times during his reign, which gives an average of thirteen changes per month.

Having examined the rate at which John was coming and going between locations, it seems only right to take a closer look at the locations themselves. There are 630 at which John is recorded at least once during his reign. Of these, 415 are in England, 177 are in France, 26 are in Ireland and the remaining 12 are in Wales. Obviously though, John was not dividing his time equally between all 630 places. The ten locations where John spent the most time[17] (if all locations in central London are grouped together[18]) are shown in Table 5.

What is striking is just how little time John actually spent at even these, his 'top' locations, with 7% of his time spent at Westminster and within central London, and 3% at each of Winchester, Rouen, Marlborough and Clarendon, with the remaining 81% in other locations.

John's itinerary is characterized by its fast pace, frequent changes and by the wide variety of locations visited. This leads one to wonder just what was driving this whirlwind of activity. It can often be difficult to establish what was the main motivation behind any particular section of John's itinerary. The king was able to multi-task and often he was travelling through a region for many purposes. While it may be impossible to completely disentangle the strands of the royal motivations, it is possible to highlight the more prominent ones by examining the impact they made.

Primarily, John was travelling in order to conduct routine governmental business: the collection of revenue, the dispensation of justice and maintaining of the peace of the realm. John's need to maintain the peace – including monitoring and exercising political control – was one reason for his itineration. The first example of this is John's tour of his realm (with the exception of Ireland) in 1200–01. In part this

---

[16] This is indeed slightly different in that there are a few times in John's reign when his household seems to be based at one location, for instance, Lambeth Palace, while John was travelling back and forth each day to an alternative location, say the Tower of London. In effect, John was spending consecutive days at both locations at the same time.

[17] For the purposes of this paper the king is assumed to have been at a location when he is recorded there, or on a day or days for which no location is recorded if (1) he is recorded at the same location on both the day before and the day following the day(s) with no recorded location and (2) the gap in day(s) with a recorded location is three or less.

[18] The locations included under the term 'central London' and the respective number of times John was at each are as follows: Lambeth (101 days recorded/104 estimated); Westminster (101); the Tower (73); Temple (43); London – non-specific (34); St Bride's (11); Southwark (9); Clerkenwell (1); St Paul's (1).

Table 4. John 1199–1216: Changes of location

Year	No. of recorded changes	Average per Month
1199	69	8.6
1200	129	13.3
1201	113	9.4
1202	155	13
1203	160	13.3
1204	143	11.9
1205	228	19
1206	132	11
1207	185	15.4
1208	142	11.8
1209	169	14.1
1210	139	11.8
1211	51	4.3
1212	178	14.8
1213	212	18
1214	166	13.8
1215	175	14.6
1216	156	15.6
Overall	2702	13
Years with adequate sources	2473	13.4

Source: 'Itinerary of King John', in *RLP*; analysis is my own.

Table 5. John 1199–1216: Most frequently visited locations

Most frequently visited locations	No. of days
Central London	378
Winchester	176
Rouen	159
Marlborough	136
Clarendon	136
Woodstock	117
Nottingham	102
Rochester	97
Freemantle	81
Reading	64

Source: 'Itinerary of King John', in *RLP*; analysis is my own.

tour was probably concerned with impressing his new subjects through his personal presence.

Another primary reason that John travelled was the collection of revenue. Although John travelled for this purpose throughout his reign, one of the clearest ways of looking at it is through his trips to the north of England. It can be particularly difficult to determine the primary motivation for these trips; John might meet with the king of Scotland at York, but also travel around in the north a good deal in order to monitor the area and to drum up revenue. However, the very fact that John did visit many locations on what Sir James Ramsay termed his 'rambling' trips to the north when meeting with the king of Scotland, rather than going directly to and from York as Henry III did, perhaps indicates that John was motivated by more than diplomacy.[19] It is unfortunate that the Fine Roll entries from John's reign bear only locations and not dates. However, the great number of fines concerning the north of England – more than the average – during the trips John made to there, suggests a correlation between the presence of the king and the amount of money raised.[20] Through travelling around the realm John was able both to encourage offers of money to be made willingly and to coerce more from the unwilling. Indeed, Beth Hartland and Paul Dryburgh have calculated that the total value of the fines from four surviving fine rolls of John's reign is £103,875 plus a great number of renders in kind.[21] While not all of the offers would actually have been paid, the revenue John did collect must have made it more than worth John's while to travel for the purpose of increasing his wealth.

Ceremonial aspects of kingship, such as his two coronations at Westminster (first in 1199 and in 1200 with Isabella), crown wearing at Easter and the holding of the Christmas court, held often but not always, in the old Wessex region, also played their part in determining John's itinerary.[22] As for dispensation of justice influencing the king's itinerary, much has been made of this by Lady Stenton. But while there is evidence to support the notion that John concerned himself with the judicial aspects of kingship, there is less evidence suggesting that this was actually governing his itinerary. It must be remembered that there is a great difference between the judicial courts determining the royal itinerary and the judicial courts that simply accompany the royal household on an itinerary which was governed by other factors.[23]

If aspects of routine government determined John's itinerary, so too did extraordinary aspects such as political crises, diplomacy and warfare. John's 1210 trip to Ireland in pursuit of the de Broase family is but one example. Likewise, John's meetings with King William of Scotland in 1200, 1206, 1207, 1209 and 1212 are prime examples of when the itinerary was influenced by diplomacy. The times when

[19] J.H. Ramsay, *The Angevin Empire or the Three Reigns of Henry II, Richard I and John* (New York, 1903), 433.

[20] *Rot. Fin.*, 42–143.

[21] Renders in kind amount to: 411 palfreys, 400 hens, 360 capons, 300 cows, 100 iron arrowheads, 100 cheeses, 100 bacons, 55 hawks, 47 horses, 30 lampreys, 30 oz. of gold, 20 *destroiers*, 20 gold coins, 9½ quarters of wheat, 9 hounds, 7 tuns of wine, 6 otter skins, 2 scarlet robes and 1 gold ring with rubies. All figures come from *Calendar of the Fine Rolls of the Reign of Henry III. Volume II: 1224–1234*, ed. P. Dryburgh and B. Hartland (Woodbridge, 2008) (hereafter, *CFR II*), vii–viii. For more on the values of the fines from John's reign see, B. Hartland and P. Dryburgh, 'The Development of the Fine Rolls', *TCE*, xii. 193–205.

[22] Howden, *Chronica*, iv. 90.

[23] For more information on John's preoccupation with the courts, see D.M. Stenton, 'King John and the Courts of Justice', in *English Justice between the Norman Conquest and the Great Charter 1066–1215*, ed. D.M. Stenton (Philadelphia, 1964), 89–114.

active warfare governed the itinerary are of course readily apparent: the hostilities with King Philip II over John's inheritance prior to the treaty of Le Goulet, the struggle against Arthur in 1202, the fight to keep control of Normandy whilst John was present in the duchy in 1203, the expedition to Poitou in 1206, and again in 1214, the two campaigns against the Welsh in 1211 and in the civil war of 1215–16. But outside these times of active hostilities, the build up to warfare also controlled the king's ambulations – such as the preparations for the aborted expeditions of 1205 and 1213. The itinerary in the winter and spring of 1215 when the king travelled to many of his castles including Knepp, Winchester, Corfe, Marlborough, Northampton, Nottingham, Sauvey, Melbourn and Oxford, presumably to ensure they were well prepared for the coming civil war, can also be viewed in the same light.

Pleasure too, at times, may have governed the royal itinerary. There is reason to suppose that John spent much of 1207 hunting and that it was this that was determining where he went and when.[24] It was the only year in which this was the case. However, during other years the king spent certain periods of time at his favourite hunting grounds and indeed for at least nine months of the year the hunt accompanied John on his travels.[25]

As for the notion that religion or piety was governing the itinerary of King John, there is not a great deal of evidence to support it. But there is some. There are, for instance, the eight days when John is recorded at Bury St Edmunds.[26] Although John's itinerary only tangentially touched on the East Anglian holy sites, more piety may be detected in John's time at Reading Abbey. John spent sixty-four days of his reign there – making it one of the locations that he spent the most time at. It is known that John was rather attached to a relic, the hand of St James, housed there; indeed, he had even given money to construct a new shrine for it.[27]

Beyond that there is not much to indicate other occasions when religion or piety was governing John's itinerary. Certainly John never visited Worcester, where he is buried, on either 19 January or 7 June, the feast days of St Wulfstan or on 28 February, the feast of St Oswald of Worcester. With respect to St Edward the Confessor, just twice was John at Westminster for one of his two feast days: 13 October in 1204 and 1213. A similar situation applies to Canterbury, where only once was John present for one of Becket's feast days: 2 December 1205.

Finally, was there an aspect of tradition governing John's itinerary? To a certain extent, John may have been itinerant because this was a normal aspect of Norman and Angevin kingship. However, it is difficult to evaluate this hypothesis further. John was incessantly itinerant and he was travelling for the purpose of routine government. But all this was brought to a halt when John died. Under the minority government of Henry III England had a capital-based government.

The itinerary of the minority government is well documented. There is a recorded location(s) on 75% of the days of the minority (Table 6).

---

[24] Out of the 100 locations that John is recorded at in 1207, 48 are royal residences. Of these, 42 are located within or adjacent to royal hunting grounds. Additionally, the majority of the 52 locations which are not royal residences are also located in close proximity to these same royal forests.

[25] S.D. Church, 'Some Aspects of the Royal Itinerary in the Twelfth Century', *TCE*, xi. 31–45 (at 37).

[26] 19 March 1201, 18–19 December 1203, 18–20 May 1205, 4 November 1214 and 9 March 1216.

[27] *The Great Roll of the Pipe for the Second Year of the Reign of King John*, ed. D.M. Stenton, PRS n.s. 12 (London, 1934), p. xviii; W.L. Warren, *King John*, new edn (New Haven, CT, and London, 1997), 172.

Table 6. Henry III 1216–26: Days when his location is recorded

Year	No. of recorded days	No. of days in his regnal year	Recorded days (%)
1216	41	73	56
1217	277	365	76
1218	235	365	64
1219	213	365	58
1220	267	366	73
1221	253	365	69
1222	255	365	70
1223	306	365	84
1224	318	366	87
1225	325	365	89
1226	310	365	85
Total	2800	3725	75

Source: S. Brindle and S. Priestley, eds, *The Itinerary of King Henry III, 1216–1272* (English Heritage, n.d.); analysis is my own.

Table 7. Henry III 1216–26: Distances travelled

Year	Distance (in miles)	Average distance per day
1216	451	6.2
1217	2601	7.1
1218	2870	7.9
1219	1546	4.2
1220	2077	5.7
1221	2543	7
1222	1767	4.8
1223	2371	6.5
1224	2418	6.6
1225	1891	5.2
1226	1918	5.3
Total	22453	6

Source: Locations taken from S. Brindle and S. Priestley, eds, *The Itinerary of King Henry III, 1216–1272* (English Heritage, n.d.); distances calculated using the shortest route by road between locations as determined by Google Maps; all other analysis is my own.

As such we can be confident that it is not because of any lack of sources that the itinerary appears relatively static. In total the minority government is recorded as travelling just 22,453 miles (36,135km) between 28 October 1216 and 31 December 1226. This works out to an average distance per day of just 6 miles (9.6km) per day (Table 7) – as compared to the 12.5 miles per day during John's reign.

But it is not simply that the minority government was travelling shorter distances; the regent, justiciar and king were often spending more days at each location per visit (Table 8). The average for John was 2.1 days, while under the minority it was 3.3 days.

Table 8. Henry III 1216–26: Average number of consecutive days spent in one location

Year	Average no. of consecutive days
1216	3.9
1217	3.4
1218	2.3
1219	3.8
1220	4.4
1221	2.9
1222	4.2
1223	2.4
1224	3.7
1225	3.8
1226	4
Overall	3.3

Source: S. Brindle and S. Priestley, eds, *The Itinerary of King Henry III, 1216–1272* (English Heritage, n.d.).

Table 9. Henry III 1216–26: Changes of location

Year	No. of recorded changes	Average per month
1216	13	4.3
1217	121	10.1
1218	121	10.1
1219	49	4.1
1220	62	5.2
1221	102	8.5
1222	62	5.2
1223	114	9.5
1224	98	8.2
1225	108	9
1226	108	9
Total	958	7.8

Source: S. Brindle and S. Priestley, eds, *The Itinerary of King Henry III, 1216–1272* (English Heritage, n.d.).

This becomes clearer when one compares the percentage of time that the minority government spent on visits of different durations: visits of 7 days or more accounted for 53 % of all visits, 4 to 6 days 13%, 2 to 3 days 17%, and visits of one day also accounted for 17% of all visits.

This difference between John's reign and the minority is seen also in the number of times the minority government changed its location (Table 9), which it did an average of 7.8 times per month (as compared to John's average of 13 changes per month).

There is also a very recognizable shift in the locations that the minority government visited. Between 1216 and 1226 there are 239 locations recorded as part of the itinerary, 235 in England and 4 in Wales. The overwhelming majority of the minority government's time was spent at Westminster and the most frequently visited locations are set out in Table 10:[28]

Table 10. Henry III 1216–26 : Most frequently visited locations

Most frequently visited locations	No. of days
Central London	1598
Winchester	126
Gloucester	124
Oxford	104
Bedford	64
Marlborough	57
Reading	52
Canterbury	40
Woodstock	37
Windsor	38

Source: S. Brindle and S. Priestley, eds, *The Itinerary of King Henry III, 1216–1272* (English Heritage, n.d.).

The amount of time spent in central London, particularly Westminster, by the minority government, dwarfs the time that was spent anywhere else. Again, this can be looked at in terms of percentages of time spent at various locations, with 50% of the monarch's time spent in central London, 4% in Winchester, 4% in Gloucester, 3% in Oxford, and 39% in various other locations. That half of the period from 1216 to 1226 was spent by the minority government in central London is remarkable when compared to John who spent just 7% of his time there.

If the nature of the itinerary of Henry III during the minority is so markedly different from that of King John, so too are the influences which governed it. It was only in exceptional circumstances that the minority government left the capital. Even without examining these factors in the same detail, it is possible to see how they contrast to those governing John's itinerary. War and other political crises necessitated leaving the capital, namely the siege of Rockingham in 1220, Bytham and Blyth in 1221 and Bedford in 1224.[29] Finally, diplomacy also acted as an influence on the itinerary outside central London, as is shown by the trip to York for the marriage of Henry III's sister Margaret to King Alexander II of Scotland in 1221.[30]

By the dawn of the thirteenth century the financial and judicial aspects of royal government had come to be based at Westminster. However, the extent to which John avoided capital-based government is demonstrated by the suspension of the Bench at Westminster between 1209 and 1214, when the Court of Common Pleas

---

[28] The locations included under the term 'central London' and the respective number of times the minority government was at each are as follows: Westminster (1332); the Tower (144); London, non-specific (38); Temple (37); Lambeth (37); Southwark (4); Clerkenwell (3); St Paul's (3).

[29] *CM*, iii. 59, 61, 64, 88.

[30] *CM*, iii. 66–7.

once again followed the king, and by John's establishment of provincial treasuries at Bristol, Devizes, Marlborough, Corfe, Exeter, Nottingham, Salisbury and Rochester – changes which combined with his peripatetic itinerary. In contrast with this, the functioning capital-based government established under Henry III's minority looks all the more dramatic.

Having examined the way the itinerary and royal government functioned under John, and how this relationship altered during the minority, it is logical to investigate how it operated under the personal rule of Henry III, particularly from 1234 to 1241. One of the wonderful things about looking at this particular group of years is that the king's itinerary is recorded on 93% of the days during this time (Table 11).

Table 11. Henry III 1234–41: Days when his location is recorded

Year	No. of recorded days	No. of days in his regnal year	Recorded days (%)
1234	340	365	93
1235	336	365	92
1236	331	366	90
1237	348	365	95
1238	333	365	91
1239	341	365	93
1240	345	366	94
1241	354	365	97
Total	2728	2922	93

Source: S. Brindle and S. Priestley, eds, *The Itinerary of King Henry III, 1216–1272* (English Heritage, n.d.).

Table 12. Henry III 1234–41: Distances travelled

Year	Distance (in miles)	Average distance per day
1234	2609	7.1
1235	2868	7.9
1236	2351	6.4
1237	1861	5.1
1238	1957	5.4
1239	1366	3.7
1240	1292	3.5
1241	1696	4.6
Total	16000	5.5

Source: Locations taken from S. Brindle and S. Priestley, eds, *The Itinerary of King Henry III, 1216–1272* (English Heritage, n.d.); distances calculated using the shortest route by road between locations as determined by Google Maps; all other analysis is my own.

From 1234 to 1241, Henry III is recorded as having travelled approximately 16,442 miles (26,461km), which equates to just 5.6 miles (9km) per day (Table 12). This is slightly less than during the minority and dramatically less than during John's reign.

If anything, Henry III travelled less and less as time progressed. Likewise, the king also remained longer at each location per visit than either under the minority or John's reign. From 1234 to 1241 Henry averaged 3.7 days at a location per visit (Table 13).

Table 13. Henry III 1234–41: Average number of consecutive days spent in one location

Year	Average no. of consecutive days
1234	3.3
1235	2.4
1236	3.2
1237	4.2
1238	3.5
1239	4.6
1240	6.8
1241	5.1
Overall	3.7

Source: S. Brindle and S. Priestley, eds, *The Itinerary of King Henry III, 1216–1272* (English Heritage, n.d.).

During this period Henry III also spent a greater percentage of his time on visits which lasted for a week or more at one location (54%) (and also more time on visits of two or three days (19%) and four to six days (16%)) than had occurred under the minority government or King John.[31] While Henry III spent over 50% of his time on visits of seven days or more, he also averaged 9.2 changes of location per month (Table 14).

The locations that Henry III visited are mainly the same as those visited during the minority from 1223 onwards; however, the proportion of time spent is very different. Henry was not based at Westminster to the same extent, although it was there that he visited the most from 1234 to 1241. Overall Henry III is recorded as having been to just 182 locations during this period, 181 in England and one, Rhuddlan, in Wales. The most frequently visited locations (with the two locations in central London, Westminster and the Tower, grouped together[32]) are set out in Table 15.

Henry III's later itinerary was not capital-based as under the minority, but it was still greatly dominated by the capital in a way that neither John's nor any previous Norman or Angevin king's ever had been. This difference between Henry's 1234–41

---

[31] 11% of Henry's recorded visits during this period lasted only a day.
[32] The locations included under the term 'central London' and the respective number of times that Henry III was at each are as follows: Westminster (854); the Tower (8).

Table 14. Henry III 1234–41: Changes of location

Year	No. of recorded changes	Average per month
1234	142	11.8
1235	160	13.3
1236	128	10.7
1237	98	8.2
1238	109	9.1
1239	87	7.3
1240	60	5
1241	95	7.9
Total	879	9.2

Source: S. Brindle and S. Priestley, eds, *The Itinerary of King Henry III, 1216–1272* (English Heritage, n.d.).

Table 15. Henry III 1234–41: Most frequently visited locations

Most frequently visited locations	No. of days
Central London	862
Windsor	299
Woodstock	271
Reading	128
Kempton	125
Marlborough	114
Clarendon	101
Winchester	74
Gloucester	64
Marwell	52

Source: S. Brindle and S. Priestley, eds, *The Itinerary of King Henry III, 1216–1272* (English Heritage, n.d.).

itinerary and the itineraries during either the Minority or the reign of King John can also be noted when examining the percentage of time Henry III spent at the various locations he frequented, with 29% of his time in this period spent at Westminster and in central London, 10% at Windsor, 9% at Woodstock, 4% at each of Reading, Kempton and Marlborough, and the remaining 40% at various other locations.

Henry III's itinerary was sedentary where his father's had been nearly frantic, but it was not as sedentary as it had been under the minority. What, then, was governing this royal itinerary? Henry III had to itinerate to some extent in reaction to specific events such as political crises, diplomacy and warfare – such as when in 1241 Henry travelled to Rhuddlan with the aim of invading Wales,[33] or his rush to London following the trouble of the de Montfort marriage in 1238.[34] Travel for another

[33] *CM*, iv. 149–50.
[34] *CM*, iii. 475–9.

extraordinary reason, to please his wife, can be seen in 1236, when Henry appears to have embarked on to show to his new queen Eleanor of Provence, including a visit to Glastonbury.

Henry also regularly travelled for reasons of religion and piety. Nicholas Vincent has shown that he was at Westminster on 13 October for the feast of the translation of St Edward the Confessor in all but fifteen years of his reign and on 5 January in twenty-six years – about half his reign.[35] However, it is in precisely this period, the first part of his personal rule, that Henry's devotion to the Confessor – and hence his presence at Westminster – emerges.[36] 1238 was the first year that he was present at Westminster on 5 January. From that point on he was only absent on that date seven times (including four years when he was abroad) during the rest of his reign.[37] Likewise, it is in the mid 1230s that Henry's itinerary begins to reflect his desire to be in Westminster for 13 October as well. His growing devotion to the Confessor may go some way towards explaining his abandonment of the various other central London residences, particularly the Tower, that occurred during his years of personal rule. Henry only visited the Tower once between 1234 and 1241 – and this visit was made at a time of crisis following the de Montfort marriage in 1238. Henry's primary motivation for visiting the capital was piety. As such, Westminster was the place for him to be. Even on those occasions when he travelled to the capital for other reasons, Westminster's familiarity – as well as the improvements carried out on the palace during Henry's reign – may have contributed to his ceasing to base himself at the other royal and ecclesiastical residences in the capital.[38]

Although the greatest impact of piety on the itinerary of Henry III is the time he spent at Westminster due to his devotion to the Cult of St Edward the Confessor, it is not the only example of piety's influence. In nine years of his reign Henry III was at Canterbury for at least one of the feast days of Thomas Becket.[39] Additionally, in half of the eight years from 1234 to 1241, Henry made pilgrimages to the various holy sites of East Anglia including Bury St Edmunds, Bromholm and Walsingham.[40] Apart from pilgrimages, Henry also travelled to meet with leaders of the Church in England. The Patent Roll entries for June and July 1235 show Henry arranging a tour to try and speak with the heads of various religious houses, such as Westminster, Bolton, Bath and Hereford.[41]

For the most part, though, it is pleasure that seems to have governed the king's itinerary – Henry's pleasure in his various royal residences. He left his favourite residences only a handful of times each year and all of these departures can be explained by extraordinary events. Between 1234 and 1241 Henry abandoned the capital-based government pioneered during his minority, though he did not abandon the capital, because of his devotion to the Confessor. However, there was no return to the ultra-peripatetic form of itineration that occurred while his father was on the throne. Perhaps John travelled at a rather more punishing rate than was strictly necessary, but to a large degree he needed to move so quickly and so frequently because he was travelling for the purposes of routine government. John had also

---

[35] Vincent, 'Pilgrimages of the Angevin Kings', 26 n. 63.

[36] D.A. Carpenter, 'King Henry III and Saint Edward the Confessor: The Origins of the Cult', *EHR* 122 (2007), 865–91 (at 868).

[37] Henry III was abroad in 1243, 1254, 1260 and 1264 and also missed 1252, 1266 and 1272 when he was in England: Carpenter, 'King Henry III and Saint Edward the Confessor', 868 n. 21.

[38] *King's Works*, i. 494–504, 547–8.

[39] Vincent, 'Pilgrimages of the Angevin Kings', 26 n. 64.

[40] Those years are: 1234, 1235, 1236 and 1238.

[41] *CR*, iii. 109–21

inherited a royal itinerary formed under his Norman and Angevin predecessors whose vast empire demanded burdensome itinerations – though after the loss of most of the Continental component of the empire the pace of John's itinerary was as relentless as ever, but mainly confined to England. Under the minority of Henry III this came to a sudden and distinct halt and in its place a fully functioning capital-based form of government was instituted. When Henry III began his personal rule he was, therefore, free to leave the machinations of government in Westminster while he himself was able to pursue an itinerary based on piety and pleasure. Additionally, Henry would not have profited from following his father's style of itineration in the way previous kings had. Magna Carta had ended the king's ability to extract excessive amounts of money, or promises of such, as he travelled about his realm. The average value of offers in the Fine Rolls from the first eighteen years of Henry III's reign, £4,257, is more than £22,000 less than the average for the four years of John's reign for which the amounts have been calculated.[42] This downward trend in the profitability of a peripatetic itinerary was to continue and by 1304–5 Edward was able to obtain offers of just £1,121 and thirty-eight 'reasonable reliefs'.[43] This shift in the pattern of the king's itinerary may therefore be seen as a reflection of the change in the nature of English kingship that had begun with Magna Carta – and as such it merits greater and more detailed attention than it has previously attracted.

[42] Hartland and Dryburgh, 'Development of the Fine Rolls', 195.
[43] D.A. Carpenter, 'The English Royal Chancery in the Thirteenth Century', in *English Government in the Thirteenth Century*, ed. A. Jobson (London, 2004), 49–69 (at 54).

Peter of Aigueblanche's Support Network

Julia Barrow

Peter of Aigueblanche, bishop of Hereford between 1240 and 1268, was one of Henry III's leading diplomats and one of his hardest-working and longest-serving supporters.[1] It is true that his reputation has never recovered from his work towards the Sicilian scheme, for the funding of which he dreamed up the idea of getting the richer English abbeys to provide void schedules (in other words, sealed blank pieces of parchment, the medieval equivalent of blank cheques), and which of course proved to be a disastrous failure and a bottomless hole for mid-thirteenth-century English finances.[2] Matthew Paris hardly ever mentioned Peter without criticism.[3] However, in view of the length of time he worked for Henry and the scale of his achievements (treaties with Savoy and Castile,[4] lengthy negotiations with Popes Innocent IV and Alexander IV,[5] a final legal adjudication of the question of whether Henry had ever been legally married to Joanna of Ponthieu,[6] assistance for the absentee Boniface of Savoy in running the diocese of Canterbury,[7] and reporting to Henry on events in the Welsh Marches[8]) some acknowledgement of his abilities is overdue. There is absolutely no question that he was useful to Henry, and also to Eleanor of Provence, in whose train he made his original entry into England.[9] Peter's Savoyard origins

---

[1] François Mugnier, *Les savoyards en Angleterre au XIIIe siècle et Pierre d'Aigueblanche évêque d'Héreford* (Chambéry, 1890); T.F. Tout, 'Peter of Aigueblanche', *DNB*, xv. 946–51; R.G. Griffiths with W.W. Capes, eds, *Reg. Thomas de Cantilupe* (Canterbury and York Society II, 1906–7), pp. xxiii–xxv; W.W. Capes, ed., *Reg. Richard de Swinfield, Bishop of Hereford (AD 1283–1317)* (Canterbury and York Society VI, 1909), pp. vii–viii; A.T. Bannister, *The Cathedral Church of Hereford: Its History and Constitution* (London, 1924), 47–56; J.-P. Chapuisat, 'Le chapitre savoyard de Hereford au XIIIe siècle', *Sociétés savantes de Savoie, Congrès de Moûtiers 5 et 6 septembre 1964* (Moûtiers, 1966), 43–51; W.N. Yates, 'Bishop Peter de Aquablanca (1240–1268): A Reconsideration', *Journal of Ecclesiastical History* 22 (1971), 303–17; Nicholas Vincent, 'Aigueblanche, Peter d'<|>', *ODNB*, i. 475–8; Julia Barrow, ed., *English Episcopal Acta*, xxxv. *Hereford, 1234–1275* (Oxford, 2009; hereafter *EEA*, xxxv.), xxxvii–lxvi, 177–89, 197–9 and nos 33–125.
[2] In general on the Sicilian affair, see Björn Weiler, 'Henry III and the Sicilian Business: A Reinterpretation', *HR* 74 (2001), 127–50; on the void schedules, see *CPR 1247–58*, 389, dated 28 October 1254, at Bordeaux, and also J.E. Sayers, ed., *Original Papal Documents in England and Wales from the Accession of Pope Innocent III to the Death of Pope Benedict XI (1198–1304)* (Oxford, 1999), nos 484, 501, 510, and *CM*, v. 510–13, for Matthew Paris's view of these proceedings.
[3] *CM*, iv. 48, 61, 75, 171, 190, 286, 294–5, 298, 318, 320, 323, 349, 351, 403, 508, 550; v. 98, 229, 324, 351, 373, 375, 422, 442, 510–12, 520–1, 523, 525–7, 533, 558, 581, 587, 591, 622, 647, 679.
[4] *EEA*, xxxv. nos 58 (Savoy), 41–2 (Castile); cf. *CM*, vi. 284 (Castile).
[5] *EEA*, xxxv. pp. xliv–xlv, xlvi–xlvii, xlviii, l, lii, lvi–lviii.
[6] David d'Avray, 'Authentication of Marital Status: A Thirteenth-Century English Royal Annulment Process and Late Medieval Cases from the Papal Penitentiary', *EHR* 120 (2005), 986–1013; *EEA*, xxxv. nos 61–2.
[7] *EEA*, xxxv. p. xliii, and cf. pp. xliv, lviii.
[8] Ibid., nos 74, 83.
[9] David Carpenter, *The Reign of Henry III* (London, 1996), 271; Hugh Ridgeway, 'King Henry III and the "Aliens", 1236–1272', *TCE*, ii. 81–92 (at 85, 87, 91); R.F. Treharne, *The Baronial Plan of Reform,*

gave him a handle on southern French and Italian events and personalities, but also a politically independent stance (Savoyards were subjects of the emperor, but in practice, even though loyal down to 1250, might go their own way).[10] Moreover, his mother tongue would presumably have been Franco-Provençal, which would have enabled him to cope with southern forms of French, including the form of Occitanian spoken in Gascony, unlike French-speaking English people, who would be used to northern French in the form of Anglo-Norman. In addition, Franco-Provençal would have been closer than northern French to the Italian and Castilian he would have encountered on some of his embassies. We might note, for example, that Peter would have been better equipped linguistically than his partner on the 1254 Castilian mission, John Mansel.[11] Above all, his tireless enthusiasm for work and travel must have endeared him to his employer. After a very brief biography and a comment on sources, this paper will then look at the various features of Peter's support network: the people in his employment, his property portfolio and his communication system.

Biography and sources

The Aigueblanches were a cadet branch of the Briançon family in Savoy.[12] Peter was presumably born early in the thirteenth century and his early patrons included Archbishop Herluin of Tarentaise and members of the comital family of Savoy.[13] William, bishop-elect of Valence and brother of Count Amadeus IV of Savoy, took Peter into his following as his paymaster ('procurator expensarum') before he escorted his sister Beatrice's daughter Eleanor of Provence to England to marry Henry III in 1236.[14] Peter had switched over to Henry's service by the spring of 1238[15] and in December 1240 he was consecrated bishop of Hereford.[16] During the course of his pontificate, which lasted nearly three decades, Peter made nine trips abroad, the longest lasting three years; the first eight of these largely consisted of diplomatic missions for Henry III, combined with periods of royal service in

1258–1263 (Manchester, 1971), 102–3, 194, 272, 278–9, 293, 301, 302; F.M. Powicke, *King Henry III and the Lord Edward*, 2 vols (Oxford, 1947), i. 265, 232–3, 309n, 361, 371–3, ii. 461n, 495; Margaret Howell, *Eleanor of Provence: Queenship in Thirteenth-Century England* (Oxford, 1998), 33–4, 37, 43, 47, 49–50, 58–9, 107, 111, 122, 193, 202–3, 214.

[10] For context, see Björn Weiler, *Henry III of England and the Staufen Empire, 1216–1272* (Woodbridge, 2006), 126–8.

[11] J.O. Baylen, 'John Maunsell and the Castilian Treaty of 1254: A Study of the Clerical Diplomat', *Traditio* 17 (1961), 482–91; Robert C. Stacey, 'John Mansel', *ODNB*, xxxvi. 530–3 (at 532), thinks Mansel was the dominant figure in the 1254 mission, but it is more likely that he and Aigueblanche worked together as a team.

[12] *EEA*, xxxv. pp. xxxviii–xxxix; Léon Vercoutere, *Les seigneurs de Briançon et d'Aigueblanche en Tarentaise du Xe au XIVe siècle* (Paris, 1933), 46; see also Joseph Garin, *Histoire féodale des Seigneurs de Briançon* (Albertville, 1942), 80, 107–8, though his account of Peter's parentage needs to be treated with caution.

[13] *EEA*, xxxv. pp. xxxix–xl; cf. Archives départementales de Savoie, S A 162 of 1236, and also Peter's respectful comments about Herluin (whom he calls 'Hercules') in his will: *EEA*, xxxv. nos 123–4.

[14] *CM*, iv. 48; see also *EEA*, xxxv. p. xl.

[15] Henry gave Peter a benefice in Lancashire on 6 March 1238: *CPR 1232–47*, 211; *EEA*, xxxv. p. xl.

[16] *CM*, iv. 74–5 for date (Sunday 23 December 1240) and place (St Paul's Cathedral) and for the presence of the archbishop of York and the legate; according to the Annals of Osney and the Chronicle of Thomas Wykes the date was 22 December, and according to the former the consecration was carried out by the bishop of Worcester (*Ann. Mon.*, iv. 88); the Annals of Worcester also say that Peter was consecrated by the bishop of Worcester (*Ann. Mon.*, iv. 432); for discussion, *EEA*, xxxv. p. xli.

Gascony.[17] In addition to the diplomatic dealings already mentioned, Peter undertook several negotiations with the French to establish Gascon truces in the 1250s and later to ensure Louis IX's full support for Henry during the Montfortian crisis of 1263–65.[18] Peter's last continental journey, to Savoy in 1266–68, was probably largely to sort out his personal affairs.[19] He returned to England by early in the autumn of 1268 and died at Sugwas near Hereford on 27 November 1268.[20] His working life also involved fairly lengthy periods of residence in his diocese and long stays at court, mostly at Westminster or otherwise in south-eastern England. He could not have achieved what he did without a support network – a very large number of people, mobile and stationary, and also a significant number of dwelling-places and stopping-off points; in addition, he needed a means of moving information and money from place to place. Luckily, enough sources survive to allow us to form some impression about how Peter's communications nexus worked. Peter's own surviving letters and charters, reasonably numerous, shed light on many of these issues; in particular his will (surviving in two versions, together with a codicil) is informative about the members of his entourage at the end of his life.[21] Equally, a great deal of information emerges from the Close and Patent Rolls, since at the start of each of Peter's foreign trips Henry III would arrange for letters of safe conduct (Peter's passport and ambassadorial credentials), money to supply immediate needs and also shipping from Dover or occasionally Bristol,[22] and in general throughout Peter's career Henry organised fairly frequent payments and gifts to him and his servants,[23] save in the rather gloomy period between the late 1250s and the early 1260s, when the Montfortians forced the king to withdraw his favour from his supporter. Much of this documentation has been in print for a long time, but I have been able to obtain a more rounded picture of Peter's activities and personnel through editing his acta and compiling his itinerary as part of volume XXXV in the *English Episcopal Acta* series.

In what follows the people in Peter's network will form the first object of discussion and then his means of communication.

---

[17] For full details, see *EEA*, xxxv. pp. xlii–xliii (1242–43; dealings with rulers of several different polities, including Champagne, Flanders, Savoy and Provence), pp. xliv–xlvii (late 1244–46; Innocent IV at Lyons and Savoy), p. xlviii (1247–48; Innocent IV), pp. xlviii–liii (late 1249 – late 1252; Louis IX, Savoy on personal business, Innocent IV at Lyons, judicial process at Sens to annul Henry III's betrothal to Joanna of Ponthieu, Innocent IV at Perugia), pp. lv–lviii (October 1253 – October 1255; Gascony, Vendôme to meet papal envoys, Toledo to meet Alfonso X of Castile, Assisi to meet Innocent IV, Gascony, Naples to meet Alexander IV, Savoy on personal business), pp. lix–lx (September 1256 – late 1257; Gascony, with negotiations with Alfonso X, though it is uncertain whether or not he went to Castile), p. lx (February–autumn 1258; negotiations with Louis IX and personal business in Lyons), pp. lxiii–lxiv (October 1263 – November 1265; negotiations with Louis IX in Paris and also at Amiens and St-Omer) and p. lxv (February 1267 – September 1268; personal business in Savoy). Henry III had also intended to send Peter overseas early in 1256, but he was too ill to go then (ibid., p. lviii).

[18] *EEA*, xxxv. pp. xlix, lx, lxiii–lxiv; it should also be noted that Peter had dealings with Welsh rulers, cf. ibid., pp. xli, xliv, lxi.

[19] *EEA*, xxxv. pp. lxiv–lxv.

[20] Ibid., pp. lxv–lxvi.

[21] Now edited together in *EEA*, xxxv. nos 33–125; the wills and codicil are edited as nos 123–5.

[22] *EEA*, xxxv. p. xlii n. 73, pp. xlviii, xlix, liv–lv, lix, lx, lxiii, lxiv–lxv.

[23] Ibid., pp. xl, xli, xliii, xliv, xlviii, lvi, lix, lxii and cf. also p. liv.

People

This section considers Peter's own patrons, his family, his household and his use of patronage. Peter originally made his career with the help of Archbishop Herluin of Tarentaise, Aimeric IV of Briançon, who was a kinsman,[24] and the family of the counts of Savoy. Herluin probably helped with his education and Aimeric with early contacts, but it was thanks to the family of Amadeus IV, count of Savoy from 1233 to 1253, notably William of Valence and Eleanor of Provence, that he made real progress. Thanks to William he reached England; thanks to Eleanor he entered Henry III's service. Eleanor of Provence, Henry III, Boniface of Savoy and Amadeus IV were to remain Peter's patrons for life and he was loyal to all of them, even when relations with Henry III chilled in the late 1250s. In his will he left silver basins to Eleanor with the request that she pray for him;[25] his feelings about Henry are perhaps represented on his counterseal, which bore the legend 'Virgo Petrum rege, propiciante rege' ('Virgin, rule Peter, with the king propitiating'), leaving the identity of the king, God or Henry III, ambiguous;[26] he held land in fee from Amadeus and Boniface,[27] as well as from Henry III; he worked hard for both Henry and Boniface. Peter's services to Henry have been summarised already; for Boniface, he acted as proctor,[28] took seisin of the archiepiscopal estates after Boniface's election had been confirmed by the pope in 1243,[29] looked after the estates in 1247,[30] helped to do up Lambeth Palace[31] and collected money.[32]

Medieval bishops might often employ members of their own family in their households; perhaps Peter also had thoughts of doing this when Henry made him bishop of Hereford in 1240. In fact, however, Peter was far more valuable to his family than they were to him. There were a number of reasons for this. Firstly, Peter's appointment as bishop of Hereford raised him to a financial status far above anything that his Savoyard relatives could dream of. It is true that Hereford was merely a middle-ranking see in English terms, but it was much wealthier than, for example, the Savoyard dioceses of Tarentaise and Maurienne. Peter's kin were noble but probably struggled to maintain this status on limited resources. Savoy's main economic resource was the collection of tolls from travellers across the Alps, which was essentially a perquisite of the counts. Peter had four brothers, Hugh, Aymo, Gonthier and Master Aimeric, and one sister, Agnes.[33] Peter obtained promise of a benefice for his brother Aimeric from Henry III in 1243,[34] and probably made him precentor of Hereford, though he seems to have resigned this dignity after 1264 in favour of one of his (and Peter's) nephews. He was still alive at Peter's death.[35]

---

[24] Garin, *Histoire féodale*, 107–8 says Peter's cousin; Vercoutere, *Les seigneurs*, p. 46, says his grand-father.

[25] *EEA*, xxxv. no. 124.

[26] Ibid., p. xcix and no. 107.

[27] Ibid., no. 39 and pp. 197–9.

[28] Ibid., p. xliii.

[29] TNA, C60/41, m. 10 (Fine Roll, 28 Henry III, item 25 of 26 November 1243 or just after: see Fine Rolls Project at http://www.finerollshenry3.org.uk/cocoon/frh3/content/calendar/roll_041.html).

[30] *EEA*, xxxv. p. xlvii, citing Canterbury Cathedral Archives, DCc/ChAnt/B/393/2.

[31] *EEA*, xxxv. p. xliii, citing *CCR 1242–7*, 140 of 9 December 1243.

[32] *EEA*, xxxv. p. xlvii, citing *CPL*, i. 233 of 13 June 1247.

[33] *EEA*, xxxv. pp. xxxviii–xxxix, 197–9 and no. 124.

[34] Ibid., p. xliii, citing *CPR 1232–47*, 395.

[35] In fact he should probably be identified with the Master Aimeric of Aigueblanche who became precentor of Hereford in 1249; in John Le Neve, *Fasti Ecclesiae Anglicanae 1066–1300*, viii. *Hereford*, ed. J.S. Barrow (London, 2002; hereafter *Fasti*, viii.), 15–16, I assumed that the Aimeric of Aigueblanche

In the next generation, Peter had four clerical nephews. One of these was James, perhaps Hugh's son, whom he made archdeacon of Shropshire in 1253; in 1254–55 he also occurs as keeper of the wardrobe to Eleanor of Provence, but he did not spend long in this position and it did not lead to further promotion.[36] The three other clerical nephews were all sons of Aymo, and Peter made them all dignitaries of Hereford Cathedral, John dean at some point after 1262,[37] Aimeric chancellor by 1268, and Aymo precentor by 1268.[38] The young Aigueblanche who made most impact was John, who, against some difficulties, remained dean until his death in 1320; his services to his uncle included acting as executor and ordering a very fine tomb for him.[39] Peter's will shows that he was strongly attached to his family – he made bequests to his siblings, his sisters-in-law and his nieces and nephews – but he was more helpful to them than they were to him.[40]

For active support Peter relied on his household. Thanks to the final version of his will, his codicil, some of his other charters and to documents issued by his officials we know the names of twenty-six clerical members of his *familia* and of twenty-seven secular members of his household, and in addition of four servants on two of his episcopal manors, Prestbury and Sugwas.[41] These totals include everyone over the course of the pontificate, but the final version of the will and codicil (both issued at Sugwas on 26 November 1268, a day before Peter's death) gives us a clearer idea of the size of his staff at any one point. At his death, Peter had about thirty people in his household, at least seven of whom were clerics, and at least ten of whom were laymen; there were also two laywomen, a laundress, whose name is not given, and Ysota, the daughter of one of the chaplains.[42] Besides the laundress Peter's immediate domestic staff included two cooks, a baker, a kitchen servant and several grooms. About eighteen of the household seem from their names to have

who held the dignity of precentor between 1249 and a point between 1264 and 1270 was Peter of Aigue-blanche's nephew, but it is more likely that Peter's brother Master Aimeric was precentor by 1249 and then to after 12 June 1264, perhaps then resigning his dignity so that his and Peter's nephew Aymo might succeed (by 1268 when he occurs, as Peter's nephew, in *EEA*, xxxv. no. 124), while Aymo's brother Aimeric became chancellor (*Fasti*, viii. 16, 22; Aimeric occurs as chancellor and as Peter's nephew in *EEA*, xxxv. no. 124). However, only one Aimeric of Aigueblanche occurs in Hereford Cathedral's obit book (*Fasti*, viii. 103).

[36] *Fasti*, viii. 28; *EEA*, xxxv. p. xxxix, citing T.F. Tout, *Chapters in the Administrative History of Medi-aeval England*, 6 vols (Manchester, 1920–33), i. 255 and *List of Foreign Accounts Enrolled on the Great Rolls of the Exchequer* (PRO Lists and Indexes XI, 1900), 104.

[37] *EEA*, xxxv. 192; see also ibid., no. 124, both refining the dating provided in *Fasti*, viii. 12–13.

[38] See n. 32 above and *EEA*, xxxv. no. 124; the entries in *Fasti*, viii. 15–16 and 22 which say Aymo had become precentor by 1270 and Aimeric chancellor by 1270 need to be revised. Peter presumably encour-aged Worcester Cathedral to present Aimeric to the rectory of Lindridge (cf. *EEA*, xxxv. nos 69–70, 73, 76).

[39] John, Aimeric and Aymo are named as Peter's executors in the bishop's codicil (*EEA*, xxxv. no. 125).

[40] Ibid., no. 124.

[41] Ibid., lxxviii–lxxix. The four named manorial servants were Adam, based at Prestbury in 1249 (*CRR*, xix. no. 2402), and three others mentioned in Peter's will and codicil (*EEA*, xxxv. nos 124–5), Philip of Prestbury, Guienocus of Prestbury and Roger formerly parker of Sugwas.

[42] *EEA*, xxxv. nos 124–5: the seven people who can definitely be identified as clerics were Bartholomew and James, clerks, James of Aosta or of Aoste, notary, Peter (of Ugine?) and Peter Eymer, both canons, William the chaplain and Jordan of London, the chaplain; the others were Jordan of London's daughter Ysota, Theobald, William de Busell', Bernard, Geoffrey the cook, Thomas Seccus, William Parvus, Gingoneccus and Guilloccus the two bakers, Willekin, Gunnieccus of the kitchen, Merineccus, Gayta (probably identifiable with Gaye the serjeant who occurs ibid., no. 50), Iufflecus, Gussinus, John de Bercye, Aquinus le Mougne, Hugh of Montmayeur (who married Peter's niece Beatrice), an unnamed laundress, Aymentatus Parvus and Alan the messenger; James of Maurienne, formerly Peter's messenger, was also a legatee.

been Savoyards or Burgundians, occurring at all social levels from senior clerks down to the kitchen staff; one of them was the husband of Peter's niece Beatrice. The really senior lay members of Peter's entourage, for example his stewards, who occur in other sources, were English and probably mostly episcopal tenants; they were not listed in the will, presumably because they did not live with the bishop but would have had houses and households of their own.[43]

The clerical members of Peter's household, roughly evenly divided between Englishmen and Savoyards (and with the occasional Welshman), had no formal hierarchy.[44] Nonetheless an informal one certainly existed, reinforced by the selection of particular individuals for certain tasks and also by the chronological order in which Peter bestowed preferment. Of prime importance was the official. A sequence of eight men held this position during the episcopate. Peter inherited Master John Bacon from his predecessors (he occurs working for Peter in 1245); Robert, prior of Wormsley, was termed official when he represented Peter in court in Berkshire at Michaelmas 1249.[45] By 1251 Bernard, prior of Champagne, was official; when Bernard was murdered in 1252 he was succeeded by Master Nicholas of Preston and then by William of Ross in the latter months of 1252 on a temporary basis,[46] and then more lastingly by the Savoyard Master Peter of Sollières, who held the position from 1253 until at least the late 1250s.[47] He was succeeded by Master Stephen de Gurunville by January 1262 and finally by Master Simon of Radnor, who was official from 1265 to 1268.[48] The official had to deal with routine diocesan business in Peter's absence overseas; much of the documentation has not survived, but large numbers of significations of excommunication (the official letters to the king requesting the help of the secular arm in distraining people who contumaciously remained excommunicate beyond the 40-day limit) survive in the names of Master Peter of Sollières and Master Simon of Radnor.[49]

Peter probably chose most of his officials himself, but one of them was pressed on him by Eleanor. This was Bernard, prior of Champagne, who during Peter's absence in 1251–52 proceeded to annoy the dean and chapter of Hereford, a major Marcher lord and also Henry III by refusing candidates presented to him for institution.[50] Bernard may possibly also have been implicated in an arson attack carried out in the summer of 1251 by some of Peter's estate servants on the barns of the then dean of Hereford, Master Giles of Avenbury.[51] In the summer of 1252 Bernard was murdered by a large group of clerics and laymen while attending mass in the epis-

---

[43] The senior laymen in Peter's entourage, probably with their own independent households, were Philip of Willington who occurs as steward in 1250, Richard of Thingland, William de Lecche of Hereford, Walter who occurs as marshal in 1253 and Stephen le Arblester who occurs as marshal in 1264. By the early 1260s Peter's steward was a cleric, Master Roger of Gloucester (*EEA*, xxxv. no. 113).

[44] For Peter's household clergy see *EEA*, xxxv. pp. lxxiv–lxxviii.

[45] Ibid., p. lxxiv.

[46] Ibid., pp. lxxiv–lxxv.

[47] Ibid., p. lxxv and *Fasti*, viii. 80–1; he also occurs as *auditor causarum* in the court of the count of Savoy in 1265 (ibid.).

[48] *EEA*, xxxv. pp. lxxv–lxxvi.

[49] TNA, C85/85, nos 6–8, 11, 24–7, 29–31, 43; no. 28 omits the official's name, but was probably the work of Simon, while no. 35, undated, was issued by Master John Bacon.

[50] John fitzAlan, lord of Clun, wanted to present Giles of Avenbury, dean of Hereford, to the church of Clun: *Original Papal Documents*, ed. Sayers, no. 681; Henry III wanted to present John, chaplain of Coventry, to the church of Munslow in Shropshire: *CCR 1251–53*, 206 of 20 March 1252; see also *EEA*, xxxv. p. li.

[51] Ibid., p. li.

copal chapel in Hereford.[52] Matthew Paris states that Bernard claimed to be a cousin of Eleanor; certainly her reaction to his death suggests that he was a close connection.[53] Assuming that Bernard was related to Eleanor on her mother's side and was thus also a kinsman of Boniface of Savoy, this would suggest that the Champagne of which he was prior was Champagne in Bugey, a non-conventual priory attached to the cathedral of Belley;[54] Boniface had been bishop-elect of Belley from 1232 until his election as archbishop of Canterbury in 1241.[55] Bernard's murder caused a major shock both within Hereford and at court, where Henry III and Eleanor were vehement in their demands for retribution.[56] The archdeacon of Hereford (a Norman called Master Henry Boistard) and another cathedral canon, Gervase of London, were among the suspects and lost their positions;[57] the chief suspect, a clerk called John of Frome, eventually escaped from custody in Newgate Gaol late in 1254 and fled abroad, leading Henry III to slap a 3000 mark fine on the citizens of London.[58] Peter of Aigueblanche's reactions to the murder may have been privately mixed; losing Bernard was perhaps a blessing in disguise, since he could now appoint a more docile cleric as official and also exploit the departure of Henry Boistard and Gervase as an opportunity for exercising patronage. Against this, however, he had to appease a very angry Eleanor. He therefore established an elaborate anniversary arrangement for Bernard and for himself, to be celebrated eventually on the day of his own death.[59]

Low down in the clerical pecking order came the scribes. Although (if we exclude the three notaries) only one of Peter's eight identifiable scribes can be named (Roger of Bosbury), we can tell from the script and spelling of his acta that he employed a mixture of English and French scribes.[60] From the places of issue of the original acta we see that he was equally likely to have an English or a French scribe with him whether he was in England or France (thus, for example Scribe I, who was English, wrote a charter dated at Lyons and one which, to judge from its date, must have been issued at or near Ledbury, while Scribe IV, who was French, wrote charters dated at London and at Bazas).[61] The dates of the items written by each identifiable scribe show that normally scribes only wrote for Peter for a period of about two years at

---

[52] Ibid., pp. lii–liii. He is also almost certainly John Leland's 'Bernard Quarre, a provost or ruler of St Peter's in Herford afore the erectynge of S. Guthlak's Priory, slayne at the altar, and aftar in continuaunce translatyd to the chapiter of S. Guthlake' (Lucy Toulmin Smith, ed., *Leland's Itinerary in England*, 5 vols (London, 1906–10), ii. 68): the term 'ruler' suggests that Bernard had probably been rector of St Peter's church in Hereford, whose advowson Peter of Aigueblanche claimed for himself, before recognising Gloucester Abbey's rights in the church in 1247 (*EEA*, xxxv. no. 53), while the term 'provost' will refer to him being prior of Champagne. Leland has clearly assumed that Bernard's position at St Peter's referred to the period when it was a collegiate church, before the merger of the communities of St Peter and St Guthlac in 1143 to form the priory of St Guthlac's, on a new site, after which St Peter's church continued in use as a parish church only.

[53] *CM*, v. 486–7; *EEA*, xxxv. p. li and ibid., p. liii for Henry III's reaction.

[54] J.-M. Besse, *Abbayes et Prieurés de l'Ancienne France: Recueil Historique des Archevêchés, Evêchés, Abbayes et Prieurés de France*, 14 vols, in progress (Ligugé and Paris, 1905–), ix. 244.

[55] Clive H. Knowles, 'Savoy, Boniface of', *ODNB*, xlix. 133–6 (at 133).

[56] Cf. T. Stapleton, ed., *De antiquis legibus liber: cronica maiorum et vicecomitum Londoniarum* (Camden original series XXXIV, 1846), 21–2; *CM*, v. 486–7.

[57] *EEA*, xxxv. pp. liii and 193–4.

[58] Ibid., p. liv.

[59] *Fasti*, viii. 153; *EEA*, xxxv. no. 89.

[60] Ibid., pp. xcvi–xcvii.

[61] Ibid., nos 107, 53, 38, 90, respectively.

the most,[62] which probably means that they were junior clerks undergoing training and that they then moved on to more senior roles, for example being responsible for the wording of documents. In Savoy Peter employed a notary (Master William of Bonvilaret), but only did so in England for the final version of his will (Master James of Aosta) and for his codicil (Lambert).[63]

Medieval bishops thought hard about how to reward service and Peter was usually good at doing this. Master John Bacon was probably already a canon of Hereford and William of Ross already a rector when they began to work for him.[64] All Peter's officials save Nicholas and Bernard became canons, though Master Simon of Radnor probably did so only after Peter's death.[65] Master Peter of Ugine, one of Peter's longest-serving and most trusted clerks, was rewarded with a benefice in 1247 – his employer leant on Abbey Dore to present him to the rectory of Bacton.[66] Later Peter of Aigueblanche collated him to a prebend.[67] He also gave prebends to two other household clerics of Savoyard origins, Master Alexander de Acu (also known as Alexander of Savoy) and Peter Eymer,[68] and since his physician Master John Canturinus occurs after Peter's death as rector of Eastnor it was probably Peter who collated him.[69] Rewards for lay servants are less well recorded (save for all the bequests of money in Peter's will) but Gaye, servant of Peter and of his clerk William of St Agatha, received a small estate on the bottom reach of the River Wye.[70]

More generally on Peter of Aigueblanche's patronage we might note that between his consecration in 1240 and Prior Bernard's murder in the summer of 1252 five Savoyards, five or six Englishmen, two Italians, a Welshman and a Frenchman obtained Hereford prebends (which were all in Peter's gift).[71] The Italians and two of the English clerks were provided by the pope;[72] Master Alexander Secular was a clerk in the Exchequer and Henry III would have urged Peter to collate him;[73] Master William de Montfort might have been pressed on Peter by Simon de Montfort or perhaps by Bishop Walter de Cantilupe of Worcester.[74] This fairly even pattern of collation changed overnight after Bernard's murder. Between the summer of 1252 and 27 November 1268 no fewer than twelve Savoyards and two men from the Bugey were collated as opposed to four English canons, an Italian and a Welshman.[75] Not only this but in the course of the year 1253 Peter was able to persuade Master Giles of Avenbury to accept demotion from the deanery to the treasurership,

---

[62] Ibid., pp. xcvi–xcvii; however, Scribe II, who was English, wrote for Peter between August 1249 and May 1257.

[63] *EEA*, xxxv. nos 39, 124–5.

[64] *Fasti*, viii. 73–4 (Bacon), and 19–20, 46–7, 96–7 (Ross, here as le Rus).

[65] For Simon, see *Fasti*, viii. 89 and John Le Neve, *Fasti Ecclesiae Anglicanae, 1066–1300*, ix. *The Welsh Cathedrals*, compiled by M.J. Pearson (London, 2003), 19, 30, 70.

[66] *EEA*, xxxv. p. lxxvi.

[67] *Fasti*, viii. 81.

[68] *Fasti*, viii. 48, 63; *EEA*, xxxv. pp. lxxv, lxxvi n. 424, p. lxxvii.

[69] Ibid., p. lxxvii.

[70] Ibid., no. 50 (which survives in an eighteenth-century English translation).

[71] See Appendix.

[72] Almost certainly Huguicio son of Peter Leo and Master Stephen of Anagni were provided by the pope; Thomas Foliot II was a kinsman of Robert of Somercotes, cardinal deacon of Sant'Eustachio, and was provided to a prebend; Master Peter of Radnor was provided to the prebend of Huntington: *Fasti*, viii. 36, 44–5, 73, 80, 91.

[73] TNA C60/44, m. 13 (Fine Rolls, 13 November 1246, cited from http://www.finerollshenry3.org.uk/cocoon/frh3/content/calendar/roll_044.html

[74] *Fasti*, viii. 96, and see also ibid., 16, 47 for his later career.

[75] See Appendix.

thus freeing the deanery for a Savoyard, Master Anselm of Clermont.[76] In other words, Peter turned Prior Bernard's murder to his advantage by packing the cathedral chapter with Savoyards.

Means of communication

Peter's extensive travels meant that he had to take great care over organisation. He needed accommodation in places that he visited frequently; he had to ensure that the episcopal estates were managed effectively to supply his income, and he had to have a secure means of transferring money and information from place to place. Here, property, travel, messengers and money will be looked at in turn.

In moving around Europe, Peter liked having a number of homes of his own in strategic places. He built up an impressive range of properties. First there were all the manors that went with the bishopric of Hereford – admittedly, only a middlingly wealthy see by English standards, but providing him with a reasonable income. According to the Red Book of Hereford, a description of the episcopal estates compiled about twenty years after Peter's death but including some material from his lifetime, the temporalities were worth £672 19s 6d in the late thirteenth century.[77] By the late thirteenth century there were just over twenty demesne manors, predominantly in Herefordshire, but also including a large estate on the western edge of Shropshire (Lydbury North, 53 hides) and a big estate near Cheltenham in Gloucestershire (Prestbury, 30 hides); five of these manors had boroughs, set up in the twelfth century (Ledbury, Ross, Bromyard, Bishop's Castle and Prestbury).[78] Peter can be found staying at six of his episcopal manors (Prestbury, Ledbury, Bosbury, Ross on Wye, Whitbourne, Sugwas), and also at the episcopal palace at Hereford, where he was insulted by the Montfortians.[79] Sugwas, two miles west of Hereford, may have been his favourite, and it was where he died, but Ledbury and Prestbury (an alternative route was Ross and Prestbury) were equally important as they were the first stepping stones on his journeys east to London. Within London, he could make use of the inn near Old Fishstreet Hill granted to the see by his predecessor Ralph of Maidstone,[80] but in fact in 1240 and 1243 we actually find him using Lambeth Palace; in 1240 it was vacant, and in 1243 Peter was being allowed to use it provided that he did it up for Boniface of Savoy.[81] Subsequently (by 12 November 1255) Boniface gave him Wimbledon, part of the great 80-hide archiepiscopal manor of Mortlake.[82] In Savoy Peter was granted his family's castles of Aigueblanche and Feissons-sur-Isère by Amadeus IV in 1250;[83] in 1255 Boniface and Peter made an agreement over the castle of Sainte-Hélène-sur-Isère, which Peter had been holding

---

[76] Peter had originally made Anselm dean in 1247, but since Giles started to be dean later in that year Anselm presumably was removed from office at that point, perhaps because he was too young: see discussion in *EEA*, xxxv. pp. xlvii–xlviii, lv.

[77] Calculated from A.T. Bannister, ed., *A Transcript of 'The Red Book' of the Bishopric of Hereford (c. 1290)*, Camden Miscellany XV (Camden 3rd series XLI, 1929), passim.

[78] W.W. Capes, ed., *Charters and Records of Hereford Cathedral* (Cantilupe Society III, 1908), 8, 19–20; see also *EEA*, xxxv. no. 95.

[79] *EEA*, xxxv. pp. lxii, 180–2, 186–9. On the episcopal palace at Hereford, see John Blair, 'The 12th-century Bishop's Palace at Hereford', *Medieval Archaeology* 31 (1987), 59–72; for comment on surviving fabric at Bosbury, see Anthony Emery, *Greater Houses of England and Wales 1300–1500*, ii. *East Anglia, Central England, and Wales* (Cambridge, 2000), 512–15.

[80] *Fasti*, viii. 104 and n.

[81] *CCR 1237–42*, 253; *CCR 1242–47*, 41, 140.

[82] *CPR 1247–58*, 449; see also *CIPM*, i. 301, no. 884; *VCH Surrey*, iv. 122.

[83] *EEA*, xxxv. 197–9. Peter may have been inheriting them on the death of his eldest brother.

from Boniface's family since at least 1252.[84] In Lyons, Peter had a house near the Hôtel-Dieu by the time of his death,[85] but it is likely that he acquired it in the 1240s when he spent a lot of time in Lyons.[86] By the time he died he also owned a house in the Rue des Prêcheurs in Paris, and land near Charenton-sur-Marne, a property now represented by the Parisian suburb of Maisons-Alfort (the name Alfort is a corruption of Hereford).[87] Maisons-Alfort possibly came Peter's way between 1263 and 1265 when he was negotiating on Henry III's behalf with Louis IX; here he would have been a tenant of the abbey of Saint-Maur-des-Fossés.

Peter evidently mapped out parts of his itineraries according to his own property network, but even he, with his very large number of houses, had to make use of other places to stay on his long journeys; overnight stops would presumably have been every fifteen or twenty miles on journeys he undertook with a large household group, moving slowly, and at much longer intervals apart on fast journeys, notably the very fast journey he undertook from Meilhan in Gascony to Toledo to negotiate with Alfonso X in 1254, where he apparently covered 650 kilometres in nine and a half days (22 to 31 March), about 70 kilometres a day – very heavy going, but possible if relays of horses were supplied by Henry III and Alfonso X, as presumably was the case here. Peter probably treated his own horses rather more leniently; they figure quite prominently in his will, including his most valuable palfreys, the 'Wigmore' palfrey, which he kept in England, and the 'Belley' palfrey, which he kept in Savoy (the adjectives perhaps refer to the stud farms where they had been bred).[88] Most of Peter's stopping places we have no information about; however, on one of the long trips that he made quite often, Lyons to London, his stopping-points would have included the Carthusian monastery of Montmerle, about 45 kilometres north of Lyons and 25 kilometres south of Mâcon, and the Cistercian monastery of Pontigny near Auxerre, as well as his own property in Paris. Peter's name is entered in Montmerle's list of benefactors, and he issued an indulgence for Pontigny in 1246 at about the time of the canonisation of St Edmund of Abingdon, who had been buried at Pontigny.[89]

To transmit information elsewhere Peter always had a messenger permanently in employment; this was a position of some responsibility, since much of Peter's correspondence was politically sensitive, and he also sometimes sent money. In 1253, Geoffrey of Bosbury, one of his messengers, stole money from Peter and sought sanctuary in a church in London, still hanging on to money and sealed documents.[90] By 1256 Peter was employing a clerk (also termed a varlet) called Guy de Castello to travel from Gascony to Henry III in England, who rewarded Guy with warm clothing for his journeys – a cloak lined with hindskin, a furred surcoat and a tunic.[91] Guy then disappears from sight; subsequent messengers were James of Maurienne and finally Alan.[92] Messages within the diocese of Hereford did not require a high-

---

[84]   Ibid., no. 39 and note thereto.

[85]   Ibid., nos 123–4; the house lay between the 'hospital near the bridge over the Rhône' (the Hôtel-Dieu) and the house of the Dominicans.

[86]   *EEA*, xxxv. pp. xliv–xlvii, xlviii, l.

[87]   Ibid., nos 123–4.

[88]   Ibid., no. 124.

[89]   Georges Guigue and Jacques Laurent, eds, *Obituaires de la province de Lyon*, i. (Recueil des Historiens de la France: Obituaires V, Paris, 1951), 467; for Peter's indulgence for Pontigny, see *EEA*, xxxv. no. 107.

[90]   *CCR 1251–53*, 505.

[91]   *CCR 1256–59*, 17; *CLR 1251–60*, 354.

[92]   *EEA*, xxxv. no. 125.

level messenger, and according to the *Red Book of Hereford* this duty was performed by a customary tenant on the manor of Ledbury.[93]

For large cash transactions, Peter relied on the Cistercians, or, for the Sicilian scheme, on Tuscan merchants. Although we only have occasional crumbs of evidence, it seems likely that Abbey Dore (the larger of the two Cistercian houses in the diocese of Hereford) played a major role in Peter's finances. It stored money from crusading taxation ready to be handed over to Peter's officials.[94] It helped Peter's underlings too: Master Peter of Ugine farmed his benefice of Bacton to the abbey in return for £10 payable in Hereford Cathedral each year to his representative.[95] Florentine merchants advanced money to Peter for a trip to Assisi in 1254,[96] while Sienese merchants lent money to Peter on the basis of void schedules for the Sicilian scheme.[97] There is only one instance of Peter dealing with a Jewish money-man, in the Fine Rolls of 2 January 1250, when Henry III gave him respite in repayment of his debt to Isaac of Worcester for the custody of the land and heir of an episcopal tenant, Richard of Bockleton, and here it is possible that the debt had been incurred by the Bockleton family before Peter took over the wardship of the heir.[98] Hereford's Jewish community had reached its financial peak under Hamo of Hereford, who had died in 1231; his son Ursellus, though influential, was less prominent, and by the middle years of Peter's pontificate Henry III's taxation was having a damaging effect on Jewish wealth.[99] But in any case for international money-movement the Cistercians, the Templars and Italian merchants were by now more obvious choices. Peter borrowed money from Italians in his work for Henry III.[100] He himself lent money to others, notably to Philip, formerly archbishop-elect of Lyons, who had managed to extricate himself from holy orders and become count of Savoy on the death of his brother Peter in 1268.[101]

Finally, Peter's entourage often had to act as bodyguards. The murder of Prior Bernard in 1252 was only the most violent in a sequence of attacks on Peter's supporters. He himself was set on by 'certain men horsed and on foot' in 1253,[102] had much damage inflicted on him by a clerk called Philip in 1255 and faced a forced entry into his episcopal palace in Hereford by the Montfortians early in

---

[93] Bannister, ed., *A Transcript of the 'Red Book'*, 19–20: 'Et debet deferre literas domini episcopi infra episcopatum ad mandatum domini episcopi vel eius ballivi'.

[94] *EEA*, xxxv. no. 49 of 23 June 1245.

[95] For the arrangement between Dore and Master Peter of Ugine, see TNA E326/409 of 24 June 1247. On 23 January 1257 we find Master Alexander of Savoy (i.e. Master Alexander de Acu) receiving the tithes of Bacton from Abbey Dore, evidently on Peter of Ugine's behalf (TNA E315/32, no. 182). For a roughly similar arrangement, see *EEA*, xxxv. no. 102, where Lire Abbey promised to pay an annual pension of 20 marks to Godfrey of Clermont, canon of Lyons, in return for renouncing the church of Fownhope, payable at the Temple in Paris.

[96] *CPL*, i. 300–1.

[97] Cf. TNA SC1/55/5; Pierre Chaplais, ed., *Diplomatic Documents*, i. *1101–1272* (London, 1964), no. 278.

[98] TNA C60/47, m. 15; http://www.finerollshenry3.org.uk/cocoon/frh3/content/calendar/roll_047.html

[99] On Hamo and his family see Joe Hillaby, 'A Magnate among the Marchers: Hamo of Hereford, his Family and Clients, 1218–1253', *Jewish Historical Studies* 31 (1988–90), 23–82; for Hamo's death, see TNA C60/31, m. 7; http://www.finerollshenry3.org.uk/cocoon/frh3/content/calendar/roll_031.html

[100] E.g. *CPR 1247–58*, 334, 358; Capes, ed., *Charters and Records*, 108–9; for Peter's own debts to Henry III see for example TNA C60/37, mm. 17, 15 and 8; http://www.finerollshenry3.org.uk/cocoon/frh3/content/calendar/roll_037.html; *CLR 1245–51*, 68; *CCR 1242–7*, 536; *CPR 1247–58*, 52.

[101] *EEA*, xxxv. nos 123–4; Peter says (ibid.), that other debts were owed to him, but without naming the debtors.

[102] Ibid., liv.

1262,[103] while in June 1263 they entered the cathedral and seized Peter and his Savoyard clergy, Sir Thomas Turberville grabbing hold of the bishop as he stood by the altar.[104] The parker on the large estate of Prestbury, in Gloucestershire, had an especially important job defending episcopal property from attack by neighbours in 1249, or, in the 1260s, by Montfortians.[105] Not surprisingly, Peter named manorial officials in his will and his codicil.[106] But Peter himself was quite capable of ordering his underlings to go on the offensive, especially when he was out of the country. In the summer of 1251 the under-miller of Sugwas provided flaming pitch to some other estate servants to set fire to the dean of Hereford's prebendal barns,[107] and in 1264 Peter's marshal, with a small private army, attacked villages around Hereford to threaten Montfortian supporters in the town.[108] Peter's absences from England did not mean that he was in any way neglectful of his responsibilities there. He simply sent the lads round to sort things out.

---

[103] *CCR 1254–56*, 236; *EEA*, xxxv. pp. lxi–lxii, citing *CPR 1258–66*, 232.

[104] *EEA*, xxxv.pp. lxii–lxiii.

[105] Ibid., pp. lxxix and lxi–lxii. Similarly, the bailiffs and men of Lydbury North were set on in 1258 by the men of John Fitzalan of Clun: *CPR 1247–58*, 644.

[106] *EEA*, xxxv. nos 124–5.

[107] Ibid., pp. li–lii.

[108] Ibid., p. lxiv.

Appendix
Recruitment into Hereford Cathedral Chapter during Peter's Pontificate[1]

Date	Savoyard or from the Bugey	English, Italian, Welsh and French
In or by 1241		Thomas Foliot II
		Master John Bacon
		Master Alexander Secular
By 1245		Huguicio, son of Peter Leo
By 1246	Master James of Aigueblanche	
In or by 1247	Anselm of Clermont/Conflans	
	John of Villargondran	
By 1247x1253		Master William de Montfort
		William of Ross
In or by 1249	Master Aimeric of Aigueblanche	Richard of St Albans
	John of Maurienne	
Before June 1252		Master Stephen of Anagni (resigned then)
		Master Peter of Radnor
Murder of Prior Bernard		
In or by 1253	Richard of Montvernier	Ralph of St Albans
	Master Peter of Ugine	
	Master John de Altasia	
In or by 1254	John of Ambléon, papal chaplain	Master Eustace de Lenn (of Lynn)
	Boso of Mâcot	John Foliot II
In or by October 1256	Master Peter of Sollières	
In or by 1258	William of Conflans	
	Master Martin of Gex	
In or by November 1258	Master Alexander de Acu/of Savoy	
In or by 1262	Master Stephen de Gurunville	
By 1262x1267	John of Aigueblanche	
	Aymo of Aigueblanche	
	Aimeric of Aigueblanche	
By January 1264		Adam Bevin
By January 1268		Master Ardicio de Comite
		Geoffrey the penitentiary
October 1268	Peter Eymer	
By December 1268	Aymo of Miolans	

[1] The material is taken from *Fasti*, viii. and *EEA*, xxxv. 192–6, though the Master Aimeric of Aigueblanche who occurs from 1249 onwards has here been identified as Bishop Peter's brother, and distinct from Aimeric of Aigueblanche (Bishop Peter's nephew), who occurs from the 1260s.

A Captive King: Henry III between the Battles of Lewes and Evesham, 1264–5*

Benjamin L. Wild

In 1242, the earl of Leicester, Simon de Montfort, quipped that his brother-in-law and monarch, King Henry III of England, should be locked up like Charles the Simple.[1] Recalling these words, the aphorism 'ever a true word is spoken in jest' comes instantly to mind, for some twenty years later, Henry III did become a prisoner, and Simon de Montfort was his jailer. For a period of fifteen months, between the crushing defeat of the royal army at Lewes on 14 May 1264, and Montfort's brutal murder at Evesham on 4 August 1265, Henry III lost control of his seal, his household and his kingdom as he was forced to accept the appointment of new officials at the centre and periphery of government.

This was not the first time in his long reign that Henry lost power over his kingdom. Between June 1258 and January 1261, the king relinquished the great seal to a group of fifteen barons, without whom he could not govern.[2] Between July and October 1263, the seal was taken from the king again.[3] However, on neither occasion were Henry III's authority and physical freedom severely restricted. Between November 1259 and April 1260, Henry circumvented baronial control through his prolonged absence in France to ratify the Treaty of Paris.[4] In 1263, restrictions on royal authority were removed when the king slipped from Montfort's grasp and joined his son and heir at Windsor castle.

Learning from past mistakes, the baronial reformers (Simon de Montfort in particular) made sure that Henry's loss of power between the battles of Lewes and Evesham was near total. From the Ordinance imposed in June 1264, which provided for the governance of the realm by a group of nine councillors, chosen by three electors (Simon de Montfort, the earl of Gloucester Gilbert de Clare and the bishop of Chichester Stephen Berksted), it is apparent that Henry had little control over his kingdom's precocious bureaucracy. The extent of the king's political emasculation can be gleaned from the chancery rolls. To perpetuate the fiction that the new council was fulfilling Henry III's mandate, chancery missives were issued in the king's name throughout his captivity, just as they had been during the period of baronial reform between 1258 and 1260. Nonetheless, the chancery rolls can tell

---

* I am grateful to David Carpenter and Huw Ridgeway for reading a draft of this paper and to those people who gave comments and criticisms in Paris. A version of this paper was also presented at the Institute of Historical Research, and thanks to those who offered further suggestions and improvements on this occasion. Muddles and omissions that remain are my fault.

[1] J.R. Maddicott, *Simon de Montfort* (Cambridge, 1994), 31–2; C. Bémont, *Simon de Montfort*, 1st edn (Paris, 1884), 341.
[2] R.F. Treharne, *The Baronial Plan of Reform, 1258–63* (Manchester, 1932), 82–101.
[3] Maddicott, *Simon de Montfort*, 228–47.
[4] D.A. Carpenter, 'The Meetings of King Henry III and King Louis IX', *TCE*, x (Woodbridge, 2005), 1–30.

us about the king's loss of authority in three ways. Firstly, the charter witness lists, which record the names of charter attestees, provide a tolerably accurate guide to the composition of the royal court between Lewes and Evesham. Secondly, because the close, patent and liberate rolls frequently record the name of the individual on whose authority a particular writ was issued, it is possible to gauge the influence of certain key people. Thirdly, by studying enrolments on the close, patent and liberate rolls systematically, we can ascertain who was in favour and who was trusted during the period of Henry's captivity.

What the chancery rolls show is that after the battle of Lewes virtually all of the people who served at the highest and most personal levels of Henry III's government were replaced. In June 1264, Montfort issued an ordinance whereby he, the earl of Gloucester and the bishop of Chichester would choose, and preside over, a body of nine councillors.[5] New appointments were also made to specific government offices. There was a new justiciar (Hugh Despenser), a new royal secretary (Roger of St John) and a new keeper of Henry III's wardrobe (Ralph of Sandwich). Within the royal household there were two new stewards (Adam of Newmarket and Walter of Crepping) and a new marshal (Stephen Soudan). Through these appointments Montfort gained control of the king's writing office, privy purse, household and knights.[6]

The new face of government is apparent from a letter close, enrolled on 8 January 1265, in which Henry, or rather Simon de Montfort, ordered robes to be distributed to twenty-four named individuals.[7] Those who received robes included six members of the council of nine (Peter de Montfort, Roger de St John, Ralph Camoys, Giles de Argentan, Adam of Newmarket and Humphrey de Bohun jr), the newly appointed justiciar (Hugh Despenser), wardrobe keeper (Ralph of Sandwich) and steward (Walter of Crepping).

So public a transformation at the centre of Henry's government could not go unnoticed. The king's submission at Lewes and subsequent captivity by Simon de Montfort is remarked on by various English chronicles.[8] It must be remembered, however, that the authors of these works, writing in the late thirteenth and early fourteenth centuries, knew of King Henry's eventual triumph.[9] This could not but affect their recollection and opinions. In some instances, the sympathy of certain chroniclers is plain. Consider the following extract from the chronicle of Thomas Wykes, a former administrator within the household of Richard earl of Cornwall, Henry III's brother. The hyperbole within Wykes's prose anticipates Montfort's brutal death at Evesham. Wykes wanted his readers to acknowledge that Montfort's nemesis was deserved:[10]

---

5   *CPR 1258–66*, 326.

6   For the reign of King John, Stephen Church has shown how the royal steward and marshal had responsibility for the household knights. Obtaining even the most nominal influence over the steward and marshal would surely have been a priority for Montfort. S.D. Church, 'The Knights of the Household of King John: A Question of Numbers', *TCE*, iv (Woodbridge, 1992), 151–65. For the duties of the knights, see idem, *The Household Knights of King John* (Cambridge, 1999), 39–73.

7   *CR 1264–68*, 11. Four people (Peter de Montfort, Adam of Newmarket, Humphrey de Bohun jr. and Walter of Crepping) received robes on behalf of others. Stephen Soudan received two robes, as did Mathias Bezill. In total, thirty-two robes were distributed to thirty people.

8   For continental chronicles, see B.K.U. Weiler, 'Henry III through Foreign Eyes – Communication and Historical Writing in Thirteenth-Century Europe', in *England and Europe in the Reign of Henry III (1216–1272)*, ed. B.K.U. Weiler and I.W. Rowlands (Aldershot, 2002), 146–8.

9   The chronicle of Hailes Abbey demonstrates this point well. BL MS Cotton Cleopatra D. III, fol. 43r.

10   Wykes did not always support or condone the actions of the king. Like many chroniclers, he tried to

And just as the tutor is accustomed to lead his pupil, so [Montfort] ignobly led the king through all the counties of the kingdom, and with the natural as much as the legal order inverted, he was not ashamed to rule the king, to whom he should be rightly bound; and he acted above himself, it was as though the name of the earl completely overshadowed the royal highness. What shameless things of unheard evil, such that he exceeded the pride of arrogant Lucifer![11]

Not all of the surviving commentaries of the period between Lewes and Evesham were compiled retrospectively. A letter composed sometime between 15 and 28 June 1265 by Geoffrey de Morley, and despatched to Henry de Maulay, shows that contemporaries were aware the balance of power in England had changed after the battle of Lewes, if vaguely:

For that reason, we tell you that Henry, king of England, and Earl Montfort are at Hereford, and we anticipate their coming to Gloucester soon with a great following, and we also expect the arrival of Lord Simon jr. from another part, with his men.[12]

Losing direct influence over his household and realm, King Henry's position looked decidedly bleak. But looks can be deceptive. For all that can be said about the restrictions that were imposed on Henry III's authority between the battles of Lewes and Evesham, I would like to suggest that a major theme of this period was, in fact, continuity. By using the, as yet unpublished, material from the royal wardrobe it is evident that appearances were kept up, and that despite great upheaval the splendour and ceremonial of the English royal court was maintained. In some instances it was enhanced.[13] There is a continuous sequence of wardrobe accounts enrolled on the exchequer pipe rolls from July 1258 to November 1272.[14] In addition, five wardrobe rolls survive from the period between 1 January and 6 August 1265, when control of the wardrobe was entrusted to the baronial partisan, Ralph of Sandwich.[15] The wardrobe material sheds new light on three particularly important

---

understand the violence of this period, to which royalists and rebels had both contributed. *Ann. Mon.*, iv. 194–5.

[11] '… et sicut tutor pupillum ducere consuevit, sic regem per omnes regni provincias ignobiliter circumduxit, et tam naturae quam juris ordine transmutato, regem suum regere non erubuit, a quo regi rectissime tenebatur, et se sic supra se extulit, ut nomen comitis celsitudinem regiam funditus obumbraret. O protervia scleris inauditi, quae superbiam arrogantis Lucifer sic excessit!' *Ann. Mon.*, iv. 153–4.

[12] *Royal Letters*, ii. 288. Another letter, enrolled on the patent rolls, responds to the challenge that 'the king's mandates do not issue of his own knowledge', *CPR 1258–66*, 429–30.

[13] For a full transcription and analysis of the wardrobe accounts of Henry III, see B.L. Wild, 'The Wardrobe Accounts of King Henry III of England, 1216–1272', 2 vols (University of London PhD thesis, 2008). I am currently preparing the thesis for publication by the Pipe Roll Society.

[14] For the wardrobe accounts that cover the period between Lewes and Evesham, see TNA E 372/113, rot. 2 and 2d (26 Jul. 1261 to 31 Dec. 1264) and TNA E 372/114, rot. 19d and 20 (1 Jan. to 6 Aug. 1265). For commentary on these accounts, see Wild, 'Wardrobe Accounts', i. 243–75, and for transcription, ii. 515–44.

[15] The rolls are as follows: alms and oblations (TNA E 101/349/30, m. 2), minute and necessary expenses (TNA E 101/350/4, which is badly faded), spices and electuaries (TNA E 101/350/1), hunters (TNA E 101/349/30, m. 1). The reason why more expense rolls survive from Ralph of Sandwich's keepership than for any other accounting period of Henry III's reign is probably that Sandwich was the only wardrobe keeper during the reign not to submit his account to the exchequer in person. Unable to question the wardrobe's keeper, the exchequer and wardrobe presumably went to greater lengths to preserve the written particulars from his time in office. For a fuller discussion of Ralph of Sandwich's wardrobe audit, see Wild, 'Wardrobe Accounts', i. 266–7.

areas; namely, the people who served the king during his captivity, royal expenditure and royal oblations. I shall consider each area in turn.

After Montfort's victory at Lewes, the chancery rolls show that many of the king's officials were replaced. The letter close that records the names of people who received robes from Simon de Montfort on 8 January 1265 is a veritable who's who of the new-look government. The writ deserves closer study, however, because not all of the beneficiaries can be considered sympathetic to the baronial cause. Mathias Bezill, steward of Queen Eleanor's household and castellan of Gloucester, who received two robes,[16] the justices, Gilbert de Preston, Nicholas Tower, William Bonquor and Hervey of Borham, and the three household knights, Robert Toyt, Gilbert son of Hugh and Alan Burnel, all of whom received a single robe, were hardly supporters of Montfort, and they were not directly involved in the business of the new government.

According to the close and patent rolls, many of these incongruously recorded men had been ordered to come to court in June 1264, presumably at the behest of Simon de Montfort, rather than of the captive king.[17] Mathias Bezill resisted till July, when he was given safe conduct to travel to court.[18] Michael Ray has suggested that at this point some form of rapprochement must have been reached.[19] In November 1264, Bezill received wine and money of the king's, or rather Montfort's, gift.[20] In May 1265, he was given custody of the manor of Woodhill.[21] Similarly, with regard to Gilbert Preston, Susan Stewart has noted that it was precisely around the time of Montfort's offering that this long-serving justice seemed inclined to temporize.[22] His fellow justices, who would have been aware of, and perhaps attended, Montfort's parliaments in June 1264 and January 1265, may have thought the same.[23]

It would appear, then, that Montfort's act of munificence in January 1265 was not solely conceived to reward his stalwarts. His largesse formed part of a complex process of negotiation by which the new administration tried to establish itself and sought to find a *modus operandi* with the senior figures in Henry's government; men on whom Montfort would need to depend if his rule were to last. The distribution of robes was perhaps conceived as a public gesture, but this was not the only offering that Montfort made. As well as gifts of money and wine, as noted in the case of Mathias Bezill, the patent rolls show that Montfort issued grants for markets[24] and hunting rights.[25] During the period of Henry III's captivity it is also interesting to note the increased reference to 'favour' and 'special favour', that is, nomenclature of a particularly royal nature, which Simon de Montfort appears to have adopted.[26]

---

[16] For Matthew's career, see M. Ray, 'Three Alien Royal Stewards in Thirteenth-Century England: The Careers and Legacies of Mathias Bezill, Imbert Pugeys and Peter Champvent', *TCE*, x (Woodbridge, 2005), 51–67.

[17] *CPR 1258–66*, 324.

[18] *CPR 1258–66*, 330.

[19] I am most grateful to Dr Michael Ray who has shared his notes and the transcript of a recent talk with me.

[20] *CR 1264–68*, 3; *CLR 1260–67*, 147.

[21] *CR 1264–68*, 52.

[22] I am most grateful to Dr Susan Stewart, who has discussed various points of detail with me. Susan was kind enough to send me a transcript of her paper, now published as, 'A Year in the Life of a Royal Justice: Gilbert de Preston's Itinerary, July 1264 – June 1265', *TCE*, xii (Woodbridge, 2009), 155–65.

[23] I refer to the transcript of a talk that Dr Susan Stewart gave to the Surrey Record Centre on 17 June 2006.

[24] *CPR 1258–66*, 49–50, 52, 53.

[25] *CPR 1258–66*, 344, 349, 352.

[26] The following is based purely on a study of the Close rolls. Before Henry's captivity, in the two

The tenor of the discussions that Montfort had with Henry III's officials in the months after Lewes cannot be known, but I would suggest that their results can. Included in the summons to court in June 1264 were nine serjeants-at-arms.[27] Like Bezill, these men had refused to attend court until the beginning of July 1264.[28] When they did arrive, it would appear that these nine men negotiated new terms of service. Evidence of these monetary arrangements survives in the form of a unique roll from Henry III's wardrobe (see Appendix). Under the name of each of the nine serjeants, the roll lists an almost identical list of six days and corresponding payments between April and August 1265.[29] As far as I can tell, the entries record payment for services on the recorded day.[30] Varying from 4s to one mark, the sums paid to these men are unlikely to cover multiple days of service, for two reasons. Firstly, there is simply no indication that the payments do cover multiple days. When payments were made for a period of service, wardrobe rolls always specify what this was. Secondly, the liberate rolls show that the king's serjeants were accustomed to receive between 6d and 12d daily. Whilst some figures on the roll are divisible by six and twelve, many are not.[31] What I therefore think the roll shows is that the nine serjeants were being paid more money for their service during Henry III's captivity. Quite what this service was, however, is unclear. While the heading of the roll states that these men were 'assigned to exchequer',[32] a corresponding entry on the enrolled wardrobe account says they were 'staying with the king'.[33] On one occasion, some of the serjeants were responsible for carrying money from the exchequer to the wardrobe, a duty they do not seem to have had prior to the king's captivity, or at least one that is not documented.[34] Further details are unfortunately lacking. Whatever duties these men did perform, the significant point is that they had rallied to Montfort's regime and continued to serve after Henry's captivity. In so doing, they took a different stance to another royal serjeant, Nicholas Tonny, who had refused to serve under Montfort.[35]

---

years and seven months between 28 October 1261 and 13 May 1264, 'favour' appears on 12 occasions, 'special favour' appears on 18. *CR 1261–64*, 23, 24, 25, 42, 43, 58, 60, 88, 102, 153, 218, 224, 232, 234, 274, 279–80, 280–1, 313–14, 319, 329, 332, 338, 343, 383–4, 384, 385. After the battle of Evesham, in the one year and one month period between 5 August 1265 and 27 October 1266, 'favour' appears 11 times, 'special favour' appears 16 times. *CR 1264–68*, 71–2, 76, 137, 144–5, 145, 146, 147, 152, 159, 160, 160–1, 166, 171, 174, 179, 180, 182, 187, 196, 200, 208, 209, 220–1, 228. During the fifteen-month period of Henry III's captivity, between 14 May 1264 and 4 August 1265, 'favour' appears 9 times, 'special favour', 12 times. *CR 1261–64*, 343, 362, 363, 393, 394–5; *CR 1264–8*, 11, 15, 19, 20, 21, 26, 29, 32–3, 35, 54, 55–6, 64, 82.

[27] Robert de Vilers, Garsye, Martin son of Peter, Robert Markeys, Henry de Roinges, Colin [sic] de Wincel, John Picard.

[28] *CPR 1258–66*, 324, 329, 330.

[29] TNA E 101/308/2.

[30] According to the Liberate rolls, on 22 April 1265, Robert de Vilers, Garsye, Martin son of Peter, Nicholas de Wincel and John Picard carried 500 marks to Ralph of Sandwich, for the expenses of the royal household (*CLR 1260–67*, 171). It is possible the payment of 4s, which each of these men received on 23 April, according to the roll, was payment for this duty. However, Henry de Roinges, who received the same sum of money on the same day is not mentioned in the liberate writ.

[31] *CLR 1226–40*, 379; *CLR 1260–67*, 146, 255.

[32] 'Denarii liberati servientibus ad arma assignatis ad scaccarium anno xlix tempore R. de Sandwico.' TNA E 101/308/2.

[33] 'Et in liberatione quorundam servientum equitum morancium cum rege per idem tempus.' TNA E 372/114. rot. 19d. Although the heading of the roll does not accord with what is written in the enrolled wardrobe account, the total sum of the roll exactly matches the sum that is recorded in the account, namely, £23 2s.

[34] *CLR 1260–67*, 152–3, 171.

[35] D.A. Carpenter, *The Reign of Henry III* (London, 1996), 323.

In the first few months after the battle of Lewes, it is apparent, then, that circumstances forced Montfort to be peaceable and pragmatic. Whilst some of Henry III's most important officials were replaced, it was neither practical nor politic to change all. By replacing the marshal and steward of the royal household, Montfort gained control over the household knights. The prospect of higher wages may have been sufficient to keep these soldiers in line.

Of course, the fact remains that Montfort was not willing to accommodate everyone. The removal of two officials from Henry III's household can be tracked in some detail. The first individual was Robert Aguillon. A steward whose service went unnoticed by Tout, Robert served between 1263 and 1264.[36] He was still active between 1266 and 1267.[37] It is clear, however, that Robert did not serve during the king's captivity. Indeed, the new regime regarded him with suspicion.

It would appear that Robert left court on or around 14 December 1264, when he was issued with a grant of simple protection until Easter 1265.[38] On the same day, John Mansel the elder was given protection on the proviso that he, like other royal clerks, was 'willing to reside at [his] benefices in England'.[39] The implication is that certain royal clerks were induced to leave the king's service, in return for a guarantee that their goods and property would remain intact. Whatever the terms of Robert's departure, the new government was unsatisfied. Almost as soon as Robert's simple protection had expired, on 21 April 1265, he was rounded upon for not having sworn an oath, 'that should be made to the king by certain persons'. Thomas son of Thomas, the mayor of London, and Master Thomas Piwelisdon were despatched by Montfort and the council to obtain Robert's oath. If he refused, they were told, he was to be arrested. But, even if Robert did swear, security was still to be taken of him and 'competent amends' had to be sought on account of his trespass and various suspicions against him.[40] The silence of the chancery rolls thereafter suggests Robert swore the oath. A wise decision. A mandate addressed to Master Thomas reveals that Robert was not the only individual to be targeted in this fashion. An ominous reference is made to the 'administering [of] the oath to others'.[41]

Richard of Ewell, chief buyer of King Henry III's wardrobe, suffered a similar fate. As far as I can tell, Richard had been in royal service since August 1257, when he replaced the recently deceased Roger the tailor.[42] Richard served with Hugh of the Tower until December 1263, apparently in a senior position as he is always mentioned first in joint communiqués.[43] Between December 1263 and November 1265, Richard does not appear in the chancery rolls as a royal buyer, although it is likely he continued to serve, at least till June 1264.[44] Richard was succeeded by Robert of Linton, in whose favour a writ *de intendendo* was issued on 28 June.[45]

---

[36] *CLR 1260–67*, 124, 135–7. T.F. Tout, *Chapters in the Administrative History of Mediaeval England: The Wardrobe, the Chamber and the Small Seals*, 6 vols (Manchester, 1920–33), vi. 38–41.

[37] *CLR 1260–67*, 200, 216, 263, 270, 277, 291, 294.

[38] *CPR 1258–66*, 394.

[39] Ibid.

[40] Ibid., 419.

[41] Ibid., 420. The mandates relating to Robert Aguillon are printed in *Foedera*, though under 11 April 1265.

[42] *CR 1256–59*, 89.

[43] *CPR 1258–66*, 304.

[44] On 7 January 1264, a 'Richard de Ewell' is described as 'serjeant'. He was serving with the king overseas. *CPR 1258–66*, 376.

[45] *CPR 1258–66*, 329.

Making his first appearance in the chancery rolls in 1250,[46] it is not until October 1254 that Robert is explicitly associated with the royal wardrobe, acting as a buyer.[47] For reasons that are not immediately apparent, Robert's service during Montfort's governorship displeased Henry III. In October 1265, Robert is listed on the patent rolls among various 'enemies' whose goods and properties were seized and divided between royal supporters.[48] By November 1265, Richard of Ewell had returned to his former position. I can find no further references to Robert of Linton in the chancery rolls of either Henry III or Edward I. If the dismissal of Robert Aguillon and Richard of Ewell reveal the extent of the control that Simon de Montfort exerted over King Henry between the battles of Lewes and Evesham, the king's anger toward Robert of Linton sheds light on how Montfort exploited his position to maintain a façade of continuity. The evidence is not explicit, but it would appear that under Linton's stewardship wardrobe buyers spent greater amounts of money in ways that appear to have been contrary to the king's wishes and not entirely to his benefit.

It is normally impossible to compare fluctuations in the quantity and cost of royal purchases from one year to the next because of the summary method in which the wardrobe accounts are enrolled on the exchequer pipe rolls. On this occasion we are more fortunate. The wardrobe account of Henry of Ghent, which covers the period between 26 July 1261 and 31 December 1264, distinguishes between the expenses of Robert of Ewell and Robert of Linton, that is, between purchases made prior to the battle of Lewes and those made during King Henry's captivity, and after. The costs of all of the purchases that were made for the wardrobe by Robert of Linton and Hugh of the Tower from June 1264 to January 1265 are itemized under a sub-heading.[49] Due to this quirk of enrolment it can be shown that wardrobe buyers were spending more money after Lewes than before. Furthermore, as the unit prices of victuals purchased by the wardrobe under Linton are comparable to those bought for the households of Eleanor de Montfort and Roger Leyburn over the same period, it is evident that Henry III's buyers were not paying over the odds for their goods. In short, the increase in wardrobe costs after the battle of Lewes can only have been caused by an increase in purchases.[50]

---

[46] *CR 1247–51*, 268.

[47] *CR 1254–56*, 239, 240, where Robert is described as a servant of the king's tailor, Roger Scissor. Robert is not referred to as a buyer of the wardrobe until 8 August 1264. *CR 1261–64*, 353.

[48] *CPR 1258–66*, 468. The king was not entirely implacable, though. In June 1267 he pardoned Robert for trespasses that had been committed in the wake of the earl of Gloucester's brief occupation of London, *CPR 1266–72*, 146.

[49] 'Et in subscriptis empcionibus factis per Robertum de Lynton' et predictum Hugonem de Turry a vigilia Assencionis Domini anno xlviij° usque ad festum Circumcisionis Domini anno xlix°'. TNA E 372/113, rot. 2 m. 2.

[50] The unit cost of the most frequently purchased items in the accounts of Henry III, Eleanor de Montfort and Roger Leyburn can be listed as follows: 1lb of saffron = Henry III: 9s–10s, Eleanor: 10s–14s; 1lb of Cinnamon = Henry III: 9d, Eleanor: 2d; 1lb of Peppar = Henry III: 10d, Eleanor: 10d–28d; 1 frail of raisins = Henry III: 10s–20s, Eleanor: 12s, Roger: 2d; 1 frail of Figs = Henry III: 2s 10d – 15s, Roger: 1½d; 1lb of sugar = Henry III: 18d–2s, Eleanor: 12d. For Henry III's wardrobe, see TNA E 101/350/4. For Eleanor de Montfort, a fragment of an account survives from 19 February to 29 August 1265. The account is transcribed in T.H. Turner, ed., *Manners and Household Expenses of England in the Thirteenth and Fifteenth Centuries* (London, 1841), 3–85; see also 'The Spice Account', in Margaret Wade Labarge's *A Baronial Household of the Thirteenth Century* (London, 1965), chapter 5. For Roger Leyburn, see A. Lewis, 'Roger Leyburn and the Pacification of England, 1265–67', *EHR* 54 (1939), 193–214 (at 211–14). The unit prices that were paid by these households may have been slightly higher because of the war, although they were not as steep as Thomas Wykes suggests in his chronicle, Wykes, pp. 157–8. That the households of King Henry, Eleanor de Montfort and Roger Leyburn did pay fractionally more for their goods during this period is suggested by the unit guide prices recorded in Beaulieu

To give some idea of the increased scale of the wardrobe's expenditure, during the final thirty-one weeks of Henry of Ghent's keepership, that is, after the battle of Lewes between 29 May 1264 and 1 January 1265, buyers acting under Robert of Linton spent £265 19s 8d on spices. In contrast, during the 148 weeks from the start of Ghent's keepership till Henry's capture at Lewes, wardrobe buyers had spent just £110 3s 3d. Similarly, where £543 6s 8½d had been spent on general purchases after the battle of Lewes, before, royal buyers had spent just £1,630 13s 2½d over much a longer period. The increase in expenditure after Lewes was due to the purchase of specific luxury items. During the last eight months of Henry III's captivity, wardrobe buyers bought 416 ells of *paonaz*, 120 ells of green cloth and 79 ells of *burnet*, 25 frails of figs, 5 frails of raisins, 115 pounds of cinnamon, 4¼ pounds of sugar, 56 pounds of ginger and 1 quart of almonds. If we consider that an ell of cloth measured 2¼m x 2¾m, that a frail could weight between 50 and 75 pounds, and that a quarter was equivalent to 8 gallons, we can appreciate the quantity of items that were purveyed.

The chancery rolls indicate that Simon de Montfort wanted to perpetuate the fiction that Henry III was still calling the shots after Lewes. This farce would have necessitated that the opulence of the royal court be maintained.[51] The caustic remarks of Matthew Paris regarding King Henry's decision to withhold the Christmas livery and various gifts of jewellery in 1250 show how easily changes in court ceremony and protocol were noticed, and discussed.[52] But this cannot be the whole explanation. After Lewes, the evidence of the royal wardrobe suggests the marvel that was Henry III's court was not simply maintained, rather, it was enhanced. According to a surviving roll that itemizes all of the purchases made under Robert of Linton between Ralph of Sandwich's appointment as keeper of the wardrobe on 1 January 1265 and Montfort's defeat at Evesham on 4 August 1265, at Easter (5 April), the king was given a set of matching garments fashioned from two otter skins. The clothes were finished with fur of *bis* and vair and cost £9 10s 4d. This outfit was far more elaborate than any of the Easter garments that were made for the king in 1235, for which we have a particularly detailed account, and were presumably more expensive.[53] Ralph of Sandwich's enrolled wardrobe account also records the purchase of a cameo brooch set with rubies, emeralds and pearls, costing £4.[54] This is the single most expensive piece of jewellery to be recorded in any of Henry III's enrolled wardrobe accounts, which cover almost thirty-five years of the king's 'personal rule'. The impression of 'conspicuous consumption' becomes sharper still if we consider that 700 pitchers (drinking vessels) were obtained for the celebration of Easter in 1265.[55] Whether or not the advance order of 700 pitchers indicates the expected number of celebrants, it is worth noting that 1,000 pitchers were acquired

Abbey's *tabula appreciatorum ad forinsecum faciendum* drawn up c. 1269–70. S.F. Hockey, ed., *The Account-Book of Beaulieu Abbey* (Camden Fourth Series XVI, 1975), 52–4.

[51] Similarly, Eleanor de Montfort supplied Richard of Cornwall with robes and raisins throughout his imprisonment at Wallingford. Turner, ed., *Manners and Household Expenses*, 14, 71.

[52] *CM*, v. 114, 199; F. Lachaud, 'Liveries of Robes in England, c. 1200 – c. 1330', *EHR* 101 (1996), 283.

[53] TNA E 101/350/4, m. 1. For Henry III's garment in 1235, see B.L. Wild, 'The Empress's New Clothes: A *rotulus pannorum* of Isabella, Sister of King Henry III, Bride of Emperor Frederick II', in *Medieval Clothing and Textiles*, vi, ed. G. Owen-Crocker and R. Netherton (Woodbridge, 2011).

[54] 'Et in uno firmaculo de precio cum rubettis, smaragdis, perlis et uno camahuto in medio iiij li.' TNA E 372/114, rot. 19d m. 2.

[55] *CLR 1260–67*, 210. According to the Liberate rolls, the Easter feast in 1265 cost £16 1s 3d. *CLR 1260–67*, 167, 169, 170, 210.

for the celebration of the feast of St Edward in January 1267, and that Rishanger comments on the size of this occasion, which involved archbishops, bishops, abbots, other prelates, earls and barons.[56] The point is that the Easter festivities in 1265 were evidently very large.

The list of victuals, wine and textiles that were purveyed for Christmas 1264 is also impressive. Total purchases for feast, as recorded on the chancery rolls, are £204 18s 9d. This is a larger sum than preceding and succeeding Christmas feasts.[57] In 1263, £101 15s 7d. was spent. In 1265, the total was £45 10s 10d. This last figure includes the purchase of 268 pitchers and 350 cups, which may suggest a rather modest gathering, despite the king's recovery of power after the battle of Evesham. Revealing though these figures are, they almost certainly underestimate the true cost of the Christmas festivities because the chancery rolls record only a portion of the items that were consumed on royal feasts. The majority of foodstuffs and textiles would have been purveyed by the wardrobe, and so be listed anonymously among various heads of expenditure on the enrolled wardrobe accounts. That said, when used in conjunction with the surviving wardrobe expense rolls, these figures do provide a tolerably accurate guide to royal expenditure.

The increased level of expenditure between the battles of Lewes and Evesham is of more than technical, and passing, interest because it reveals something of the dilemma that Montfort faced after his victory in May 1264; namely, what was to be done with the captive king? In the twelfth century, the then royal prisoner, King Stephen, had been incarcerated in chains.[58] By the thirteenth century societal values, particularly amongst the nobility, had changed. The ideas of *chivalerie* and *courtoisie* that were expounded in works like the anonymous *Ordene de chevalrie* or Ramon Llull's *Libre del ordre de cavayleria*, popularized by *chansons de geste*, and in England demonstrated by the *Histoire de Guillaume le Maréchal*, may well have induced Montfort to relent, and to treat his monarch, if not other members of the royal family (the king's brother, Richard earl of Cornwall, was incarcerated after Lewes, despite his coronation in 1257 as *rex Romanorum*[59]), with a degree of (public) respect.[60]

It may be, then, that the higher levels of expenditure after Lewes and Evesham were a means by which Simon de Montfort could demonstrate his enduring respect for King Henry. It may have even proved advantageous. By looking after his king, Montfort could have hoped to legitimize his regime. In truth, Montfort's intentions could not have been so straightforward. If he had wished to demonstrate his abiding adherence to Henry, maintaining levels of royal household expenditure would have surely sufficed. The fact that levels of expenditure increased after the battle of Lewes

[56] *CLR 1260–67*, 252; '… ubi festum Sancti Edwardi, sicut ei moris erat, pariter et devotionis, vocatis Archiepiscopis, Episcopis, Abbatibus, et aliis ecclesiarum praelatis, comitibus, baronibus, prout decebat regiam excellentiam, cum ingenti gaudio solemnizavit …', 'Chronicon Willelmi de Rishanger de Duobus Bellis apud Lewis et Evesham commissis', in *Ypodigma Neustriae, a Thoma Walsingham, quondam monacho monasterio S. Albani conscriptum*, ed. H.T. Riley, 7 vols (Rolls Series XXVIII, 1876), vii. 558. See also H.T. Riley, ed., *Willelmi Rishanger Chronica et Annales*, 7 vols (Rolls Series XXVIII, 1865), ii. 34.

[57] *CLR 1260–67*, 152, 153, 154, 156, 161, 162, 166; *CPR 1258–66*, 385. Christmas 1263: *CLR 1260–67*, 127, 129, 137, *CR 1261–64*, 318, 322. Christmas 1265: *CLR 1260–67*, 188, 191, 193, 194; *CR 1264–68*, 278.

[58] R.H.C. Davis, *King Stephen 1135–1154* (London, 1967), 53–4.

[59] A point I owe to Dr Adrian Jobson.

[60] M. Keen, *Chivalry* (London, 1984), 6–11, 31–3; J. Bumke, *Courtly Culture: Literature and Society in the High Middle Ages*, trans. T. Dunlap (Berkeley, 1991), 275–90, 301–21.

suggests something further, particularly in light of the following extract from the *Flores Historiarum*, which implies that it was Simon de Montfort, not King Henry, who celebrated Christmas with the greatest pomp in 1264:

> The king returned to his famous palace which is called Woodstock, where he held Christmas solemnly. But the earl, fortune smiling on all things he conceived, celebrated the same feast at his castle of Kenilworth, surrounded by many knights. For it was said that he had from his own household at least 140 stipendiary knights, beyond innumerable others, devoted to him, when he went on campaign.[61]

Although it can be shown that the king's buyers were spending more money under Robert of Linton, it may be a mistake to assume that this increase in expenditure was entirely to the king's benefit. The evidence is not explicit, but it is tempting to suggest that Montfort was using wardrobe money and wardrobe buyers, over which Robert of Linton exercised control, to obtain goods for the support of his regime, and perhaps even for his personal aggrandizement. This would certainly explain why Robert was to incur the king's wrath after Montfort's death in 1265.

It is possible that purchases were redirected from the king's household to Montfort's.[62] It is also possible, and equally unprovable, that Montfort encouraged the celebration of more opulent royal feasts during Henry III's captivity so as to create a sufficiently obvious role for himself as 'steward of all England'. Simon de Montfort became hereditary steward when he inherited the earldom of Leicester in 1239. Between 1258 and 1260, he had been eager to exert whatever authority this office conferred on him, so much so that Henry III complained.[63] Now that Montfort had the king under much tighter control, it would not have been out of character if he had chosen to exalt his position further. We know that, in April 1265, Montfort sought clarification about the rights of his office from Lorretta, the dowager countess of Leicester.[64] The description of the Christmas festivities in 1264, and the enrolment on the patent rolls of a licence that permitted Montfort to travel throughout the kingdom with arms and horses, when everyone else was prohibited from doing so, certainly indicates that he earl's sense of theatricality could be every bit as grand as that of his royal master.[65]

Whilst there is no explicit evidence that Montfort used Robert of Linton to procure goods for himself, the wardrobe accounts show that Montfort did make use of the department's resources in other ways. By studying Henry of Ghent's enrolled wardrobe account in conjunction with a surviving wardrobe receipt roll, it is possible to show that, in the period after Lewes, £27 10s was used 'to defend the coast against the coming of the aliens'.[66] The sum of money is not particularly large but it does show that revenue from King Henry's wardrobe was being used

---

[61] *Flores*, ii. 504. Maddicott, *Montfort*, 310–12.

[62] Thomas Wykes tells of how Montfort's son, Henry, seized wool from English and Flemish merchants for his own use. *Ann. Mon.*, iv. 158–9.

[63] H. Ridgeway, 'King Henry III's Grievances against the Council in 1261', *Historical Research* 61 (1988), 230, 241.

[64] *CR 1264–68*, 115. See, Maddicott, *Montfort*, 239–41, 277, 332–3; F.M. Powicke, 'Lorretta Countess of Leicester', in *Historical Essays in Honour of James Tait*, ed. J.G. Edwards, V.H. Galbraith and E.F. Jacob (Manchester, 1933), 266–7.

[65] *CPR 1258–66*, 337.

[66] 'Et de xxvij li. x s. receptis de remanenti decime assesse in diocesa Cicestr' et Roff' per comitem Leyc' et quosdam episcopos ad muniendum mare contra adventum alienigenarum anno xlviij°'. TNA E 372/113, rot. 2 m. 2. See also Maddicott, *Montfort*, 235–6, 238.

to counter the army of foreign mercenaries that had been assembled in Flanders by Eleanor of Provence.[67] The wardrobe receipt roll also shows that two loans to the value of £99 19s 11d were paid into the wardrobe by the baronial Justiciar, Hugh Despenser.[68] It is unlikely that one of Montfort's closest allies was supporting Henry III on the sly. Instead, Despenser's payments suggest that the wardrobe's coffers had become a pot into which Montfort dipped when his own funds were low. Montfort certainly seems to have turned to the royal wardrobe in the early summer of 1265 to stave off bankruptcy. Between 20 May and 27 July 1265, when John Maddicott has shown that Montfort was in danger of becoming insolvent, fourteen payments, amounting to £269 10s 8d, were paid into the wardrobe by the people of Hereford.[69] The majority of the payments came from ecclesiastics affiliated with the Savoyard bishop of Hereford, Peter de Aigueblanche, who had fled the kingdom in 1263 after being harassed by Montfortian soldiers.[70] It would appear their money was directed into the royal wardrobe to keep Montfort's military machine afloat.

Montfort's control over the wardrobe went further still. A surviving roll of messengers shows that he also exercised control over the king's couriers. When news of the Lord Edward's dramatic escape from captivity was announced on 30 May 1265, Simon de Montfort summoned the host in the king's name and despatched messages to all the counties of England.[71] A paragraph on the surviving roll of messengers, next to which is written 'summonitio exercitus', reveals that six messengers, each of whom had been assigned a specific circuit of counties, were charged with distributing the summons, and that the wardrobe footed the bill (£2 5s 6d).[72] The logistics of sending such a message so quickly helps to explain why Montfort harnessed the apparatus of the royal wardrobe.

The extent to which Montfort controlled King Henry III's wardrobe and used it for his own ends can be explored further by studying the king's personal devotions during the period of his captivity. It is serendipitous that the remarkable survival of wardrobe documents from this period includes a roll of alms and oblations.[73] The roll covers the period between 1 January and 6 August 1265, and is one of two alms rolls that survive from Henry III's reign. The other roll covers the period between 28 October 1238 to 7 May 1239.[74] Twenty-six years separate these rolls, but a comparison of identical weeks in which the feast of St Peter in Cathedra in Antio-

---

[67] M. Howell, *Eleanor of Provence: Queenship in Thirteenth-Century England* (Oxford, 1998), 212–17.

[68] TNA E 101/350/3.

[69] TNA E 101/350/3. Maddicott, *Montfort*, 336.

[70] Seven payments, totalling £172 5s 5d, were made to the wardrobe from people linked to Hereford cathedral: 20 May, from the keepers of the bishopric: £133 6s 8d, see also, *CPR 1258–66*, 426; 5 June, from the men of the liberty of the bishop and the chapter of the cathedral: £6 13s 4d; 12 June, from the men and chapter of Hereford: £9; 16 June, from a loan of the men of the bishop: £16 13s 4d; 18 June, from Amaury de Aigueblanche, precentor of the cathedral and evidently a kinsman of Peter de Aigueblanche: 6s 8d; c. 22 July, from two canons of the cathedral, for two cups of silver and one pair of bowls: 58s 9d; 23 July, from John, deacon of the cathedral: 66s 8d.

[71] The letters were despatched on 31 May, *CR 1264–68*, 124–5; *Foedera*, 455–6. For the implications of Edward's escape for Montfort, see Maddicott, *Montfort*, 333–9.

[72] TNA E 101/308/2. (1) Roscel: Cumberland, Lancaster, Westmorland; (2) John Long: Leicestershire, Lincolnshire, Nottinghamshire, Rutland, Warwickshire, Worcestershire and Yorkshire; (3) Robert Bigod: Bedfordshire, Buckinghamshire, Cambridgeshire, Northamptonshire, Norfolk and Suffolk; (4) Simon of Barnham: Essex, Herefordshire, Kent, Middlesex and Oxfordshire; (5) Robert Taylor: Berkshire, Hampshire, Surrey, Sussex and Wiltshire; (6) David Swen: Cornwall, Devon, Dorset and Gloucestershire. Three of the messengers (Simon of Barnham, Robert Bigod and Robert Taylor) are identified as 'valets of the lord king'.

[73] TNA E 101/349/30, m. 2.

[74] TNA C 47/3/44.

Table 1. Henry III's disbursement of alms and oblations, 1239 and 1265

TNA C 47/3/44	TNA E 101/349/30 mem. 2
Sunday 20 February 1239 Oblations: 8d Oblations after mass: 5s Alms: 4s 2d (on arrival at Sutton)	*Sunday 22 February 1265* **Feast of St Peter in Cathedra in** **Antiochia** Oblations: 2d Oblations after mass: 5s
Monday 21 February 1239 Oblations: 3d Oblations after mass: 3d Oblations for cross at Bermondsey: 13d Alms: 4s 2d (on arrival at Westminster) Offering to St Paul's, London *ad perdonum*: 13d	*Monday 23 February 1265* Oblations: nothing Oblations after a solemn mass for St Peter: 5s
Tuesday 22 February 1239 **Feast of St Peter in Cathedra in Antiochia** Oblations for two masses: 5d Oblations after mass: 5s	*Tuesday 24 February 1265* Oblations: nothing Oblations after solemn mass for St Matthew: 5s
Wednesday 23 February 1239 Oblations: 5d Oblations after mass: 13d	*Wednesday 25 February 1265* Oblations: nothing Oblations after solemn mass for St Milburga: 5s
Thursday 24 February 1239 Oblations: 5d Oblations after mass: 13d	*Thursday 26 February 1265* Oblations: nothing Oblations after mass: 15d
Friday 25 February 1239 Oblations: 4d. Offering for the relics of the great church: 13d	*Friday 27 February 1265* Oblations: nothing Oblations after mass: 15d
Saturday 26 February 1239 Oblations for two masses: 3d Oblations after mass: 5d	*Saturday 28 February 1265* Oblations: nothing Oblations after solemn mass for St Mary: 5s
£1 7s 1d	£1 7s 8d

chia fell in 1239 and 1265, can provide some indication of how Henry's personal devotions were affected by his captivity.

According to Table 1, for the week of the feast of St Peter in Cathedra, Henry III spent nearly the same amount of money in 1239 and 1265, but to very different effect.[75] In 1239, King Henry arranged for a mass to be said each day. On the feast day of St Peter two masses were performed, as they were on the following Saturday. Throughout the week, the king's daily oblations varied between 3d and 5d. Oblations offered after the mass varied between 5d and 5s. In 1265, the king continued to order a daily mass, however, on four occasions (Monday, Tuesday, Wednesday and Saturday) the alms roll refers to a solemn mass that was held in honour of a particular saint. If the references to solemn mass can be interpreted in a technical sense, that is, if most parts of the mass were sung, if incense were used, and if a

---

[75] For what follows, I am grateful to Professor Anne Duggan, with whom I have had many enjoyable discussions.

Table 2. Henry III's disbursement of alms and oblations at Easter, 1239 and 1265

TNA C 47/3/44	TNA E 101/349/30 mem. 2
Week beginning Palm Sunday (20–26 March 1239): £8 13s 11d	*Week beginning Palm Sunday (29 March – 4 April 1265)*: £4 6s 5d
Palm Sunday (20 March 1239) Oblations for two masses: 14d	**Palm Sunday (29 March 1265) [6s 1d]** Oblations: 13d Oblations after mass *in capella sua*: 5s
Maundy Thursday (24 March 1239) 300 tunics: 25s *[Remainder of entry lost because the roll is damaged]*	**Maundy Thursday (2 April 1265) [13s 4d]** Oblations: nothing Oblations after mass *in capella sua*: 5s 100 tunics: 8s 4d 1 piece of gold offered at the shrine of St Edward in Westminster Abbey
Good Friday (25 March 1239) *[Roll damaged]*	**Good Friday (3 April 1265) [£2 14s 6d]** Oblations for the adoration of the Holy Cross: 5s Oblations and alms visiting various churches in the city of London: 49s 6d; 1 piece of gold offered at Westminster Abbey for the Cross and 12 *obols. de murce'*.
Week beginning Easter Sunday (27 March – 2 April 1239): 43s 5d	*Week beginning Easter Sunday (5–11 April 1265)*: 43s 5d
Easter Day (27 March 1239) [8s 2d] Oblations: 19d Oblations after the mass: 5s Oblations sent for the mass in the great church [Westminster Abbey]: 19d	**Easter Day (5 April 1265) [8s 7d]** Oblations 'ad ressurectionem': 5s Oblations for the mass: 2s 10d Mass in conventual church at Westminster: 9d
Week beginning Sunday in the octave of Easter (3–9 April 1239): 19s 9d	*Week beginning Sunday in the octave of Easter (12–18 April 1265)*: 48s 6d
£11 17s 1d	£8 18s 4d

deacon and subdeacon officiated with the priest, the ceremony would have been longer and more visually and acoustically impressive than in 1239. The celebration of solemn masses was not confined to this week alone. According to the later roll of alms, between 1 January and 1 July 1265, the king ordered 100 masses and 69 solemn masses to be performed. In contrast, between 28 October 1238 and 7 May 1239, 197 masses were ordered. The earlier roll contains no reference to a solemn mass.

It is quite likely that the solemn masses performed in 1265 were votive, that is, they prayed for the king's deliverance. All but eleven of these masses were held in honour of a particular saint. The majority (21) honoured the king's patron saint, Edward the Confessor. In second place was Mary (11) and in third place, Thomas Becket (3).[76] Although the king only offered daily oblations on the feast of St Peter

---

[76] For Henry's devotion to Mary, see N. Vincent, 'King Henry III and the Blessed Virgin Mary', in *The Church and Mary*, ed. R.N. Swanson (Studies in Church History XXXIX, Woodbridge, 2004), 126–46.

in Cathedra in 1265, the increased scale of his offerings after the mass, which varied from 15d to 5s, not to mention the more ornate form of the mass itself, suggests that Henry was permitted a certain freedom in his religious devotions. Comparing Henry III's expenditure at Easter in 1239 and 1265 confirms this point.

Table 2 shows that, overall, Henry III spent less money on alms and oblations in 1265 than he had done in 1239, although the amount disbursed through oblations on Easter Day itself was comparable. There are also differences in practice between the two years. Two masses were said on Easter Day in 1239 and 1265, although only in 1239 were two masses also said on Palm Sunday. During the Easter period, the king's offerings were lower in 1265, and on Maundy Thursday no oblations were given. The king's customary distribution of cloths continued, but on a much reduced scale; where 300 robes had been given to the poor in 1239, 100 were given in 1265.

We should not create too austere a picture of the Easter celebrations in 1265. King Henry III may have distributed fewer cloths on Maundy Thursday, but on Good Friday the alms roll reveals that he visited various London churches, perhaps wearing his otter skin robes, and distributed £2 9s 6d in oblations. This itineration does not appear to have occurred in 1239, and I can find no evidence to suggest that it was customary. The reference to Henry III's visitations, which may have taken the form of a procession, along with the requisition of 700 pitchers, which have already been mentioned, may suggest that, despite a drop in the king's monetary and sartorial offerings, the Easter feast was celebrated in a very public, even festive, way.[77] What, then, of Simon de Montfort in all this? There is no explicit evidence that Montfort participated in the Easter celebrations, but as it was his appointees to Henry's household who acquired the provisions, at the very least he sanctioned them.[78]

In this paper I have argued that the extent of Simon de Montfort's control over King Henry III between the battles of Lewes and Evesham was considerable. The evidence is fragmentary and rarely explicit, but I have suggested that there is sufficient proof to show that Montfort used the apparatus and resources of the royal wardrobe to bolster his regime and to exalt his personal authority. A major finding is that Montfort appears to have gone to considerable lengths to maintain a sense of continuity. Whilst many of King Henry's ministers were replaced, many also continued to serve, some apparently under new preferential terms. The surviving wardrobe material also suggests that Montfort was keen to maintain, and in some cases enhance, the opulence of Henry's court through increasing expenditure and allowing the king to exercise a certain freedom in his religious devotions. However, whilst Montfort's shrewd concessions, dictated by current mores, may have helped to strengthen and legitimise his regime, it stoked the fires of the king's anger, which were given full vent after the battle of Evesham. The wardrobe account of Ralph of Sandwich, for example, refers to the belts of 'a certain enemy killed at Evesham' that were presented to King Henry. Considering the Latin refers to just one person ('cuiusdam inimici'), it is possible that this is an oblique reference to Simon de

For Thomas Becket, see P. Binski, *Becket's Crown: Art and Imagination in Gothic England 1170–1300* (London, 2004), 43, 139–40.

[77] On the significance of processions in the medieval period, see S. Bertelli, *The King's Body: The Sacred Rituals of Power in Medieval and Early Modern Europe*, trans. R. Burr Litchfield (Pennsylvania State University Press, 2001), 75–9, 130–1.

[78] Venison was delivered by the steward, Adam of Newmarket, who was to be captured at the battle of Evesham, *CLR 1260–7*, 167. The gold obols that Henry offered on Easter Day were delivered to Ralph of Sandwich on Good Friday, *CLR 1260–67*, 170. See also Maddicott, *Montfort*, 313–14.

Montfort. If this is right, by denigrating objects that had once belonged to his former jailer, Henry was making an unmistakable, and uncompromising, statement about his recovery and his power.[79] Within three months of his jailer's death, the king also initiated plans to invest his former stronghold, Kenilworth Castle. The resulting royalist siege, the longest in English history, lasted for 172 days and ended with the promulgation of one of the most fascinating documents of Henry's reign, the *Dictum of Kenilworth*, which casts royal authority as divinely sanctioned and all powerful.[80] In 1242, King Henry III had been the butt of Montfort's joke, which compared him to Charles the Simple. Ultimately, I think it was Henry who had the last laugh.

Appendix
Payments to Henry III's Serjeants at Arms, 5 April – 2 August 1265

(TNA E 101/308/2)

Denarii liberati servientibus ad arma assignatis ad scaccarium anno xlix tempore R. de Sandwico

Robert de Vylers	[5 Apr.] Sunday. Feast of St Ambrose at Westminster	20s
	[23 Apr.] Thursday. Feast of St George at Northampton	4s
	[6 May] Wednesday. Feast of John the Baptist *ante Portam Latinam* [no place recorded]	13s 4d
	[23 May] Saturday. Vigil of Pentecost at Hereford	13s 4d
		50s 8d
Garsye	[5 Apr.] Sunday. Feast of St Ambrose at Westminster	20s
	[23 Apr.] Thursday. Feast of St George at Northampton	4s
	[6 May] Wednesday. Feast of John the Baptist *ante Portam Latinam* [no place recorded]	13s 4d
	[23 May] Saturday. Vigil of Pentecost at Hereford	13s 4d
	[9 July] Thursday after translation of Thomas the Apostle at Abergevenny	2s
		59s 4d
Martin	[5 Apr.] Sunday. Feast of St Ambrose at Westminster	20s
[Son of Peter]	[23 Apr.] Thursday. Feast of St George at Northampton	4s
	[6 May] Wednesday. Feast of John the Baptist *ante Portam Latinam* [no place recorded]	13s 4d
	[23 May] Saturday. Vigil of Pentecost at Hereford	13s 4d
		50s 8d
Robert Markeys	[5 Apr.] Sunday. Feast of St Ambrose at Westminster	20s

[79] For the idea that objects could become imbued with meaning by virtue of past associations, see A. Weiner, *Inalienable Possessions: The Paradox of Keeping-While-Giving* (Berkeley, 1992), esp. pp. 36–40. Highly relevant, though largely overlooked, is the work of Percy Schramm, for which see 'Das Grundproblem dieser Sammlung: Die "Herrschaftszeichen", die "Staatssymbolik" und die "Staatsrepräsentation" des Mittelalters', in idem, *Kaiser, Könige und Päpste: Gesammelte Aufsätze zur Geschichte des Mittelalters*, 4 vols in 5 (Stuttgart, 1968), i. 30–58. For an English introduction to Schramm's work, see J.M. Bak, 'Medieval Symbology of the State: Percy E. Schramm's Contribution', *Viator* 6 (1973), 33–63.

[80] *DBM*, 316–37. I hope to study the *Dictum of Kenilworth* and the reassertion of Henry III's authority after Evesham on a future occasion.

	[6 May] Wednesday. Feast of John the Baptist *ante Portam Latinam* [no place recorded]	13s 4d
	[23 May] Saturday. Vigil of Pentecost at Hereford	13s 4d
	[25 May] Monday next at Hereford	12s
		58s 8d
Henry de Royngges	[5 Apr.] Sunday. Feast of St Ambrose at Westminster	20s
	[23 Apr.] Thursday. Feast of St George at Northampton	4s
	[6 May] Wednesday. Feast of John the Baptist *ante Portam Latinam* [no place recorded]	13s 4d
	[23 May] Saturday. Vigil of Pentecost at Hereford	13s 4d
	[9 July] Thursday after the translation Thomas the Apostle at Abergevennny	2s
	[2 Aug.] Sunday. Morrow of Peter *ad Vincula*	6s 8d
		59s 4d
Colin [sic] de Wync'	[5 Apr.] Sunday. Feast of St Ambrose at Westminster	20s
	[23 Apr.] Thursday. Feast of St George at Northampton	4s
	[6 May] Wednesday. Feast of John the Baptist *ante Portam Latinam* [no place recorded]	13s 4d
	[23 May] Saturday. Vigil of Pentecost at Hereford	13s 4d
		50s 8d
[Robert] Pychard	[5 Apr.] Sunday. Feast of St Ambrose at Westminster	20s
	[23 Apr.] Thursday. Feast of St George at Northampton	9s
	[6 May] Wednesday. Feast of John the Baptist *ante Portam Latinam* [no place recorded]	13s 4d
	[23 May] Saturday. Vigil of Pentecost at Hereford	13s 4d
	[9 July] Thursday after translation of Thomas the Apostle at Abergevennny	5s
	[2 Aug.] Sunday. Morrow of Peter *ad Vincula*	6s 8d
		67s 4d
Walter Archard	[5 Apr.] Sunday. Feast of St Ambrose at Westminster	10s
		10s
		£23 2s

The *Conflictus inter Deum et Diabolum* and the Emergence of the Literature of Law in Thirteenth-Century England

William Marx

The *Conflictus inter Deum et Diabolum* is a medieval Latin text whose principal subject is the theological doctrine of the Redemption of human kind, the central doctrine of Christianity.[1] The *Conflictus* is known to survive in three manuscripts, all of English provenance. The earliest manuscript, Oxford, Bodleian Library, MS Ashmole 1398, is described as written in a 'charter hand of the thirteenth century' which is one piece of evidence for locating the *Conflictus* to the thirteenth century and therefore making a discussion of the text and the issues it raises appropriate for this volume. The other two manuscripts are dated to the fourteenth century and the fifteenth century, which suggests an enduring, if fragile, textual history and continuous interest in the text.[2]

The *Conflictus* is not well known to modern scholarship and for this reason it will be useful to provide a brief summary. It is cast in the form of a legal dispute, and begins in this way:

> Videns itaque diabolus suam tirannidem expirasse quam diu in hominem exercuerat et se spoliatum homine quem longissimi temporis spacio sine contradictione possederat captiuum, frendebat sibi iniuriam irrogari et se illicita potencia non ordine iudiciario sed illegitime sua possessione expelli et priuari. In Christum itaque mouere querimoniam intendit et ei interdictum *Vnde vi* statim obicere proponit. Volens autem dominus ei satisfacere prefixit ei diem litis idoneum quo possit se suis rationibus premunire et sua instrumenta si haberet introducere. (ll. 7–14)

> (Seeing therefore that the tyranny that he had for a long time exerted over humanity had vanished and that he had been robbed of human kind whom he had held captive without objection for a very long time, the Devil complained that injury had been done to him and that he had been unlawfully deprived of his possession through the unlawful use of power, not through judicial procedure. The Devil therefore launched a complaint against Christ and proposed to invoke the interdict *Vnde vi*. The Lord God, wishing to treat the Devil fairly, fixed a suitable day for

---

[1]   William Marx, 'An Edition and Study of the *Conflictus inter Deum et Diabolum*', *Medium Aevum* 59 (1990), 18–40. All quotations are from this edition. See Carmen Cardelle de Hartmann, *Lateinische Dialoge 1200–1400: Literaturhistorische Studie und Repertorium* (Mittellateinische Studien und Texte 37, Leiden, 2007), 233–41 and 300–301. On the medieval doctrine of the Redemption and the *Conflictus* see: William Marx, *The Devil's Rights and the Redemption in the Literature of Medieval England* (Cambridge, 1995), 60–64.

[2]   London, BL, MS Lansdowne 379, from the fourteenth century, and Oxford, Bodleian Library, MS Bodley 52, from the fifteenth century. The three manuscripts are described in Marx, 'Edition and Study', 16–17.

the dispute when the Devil might make his arguments and introduce his documents, if he had any.)

Before the trial begins, the Devil is asked if he possibly regrets bringing the charge and if he might not consider withdrawing his action. The Devil replies:

Non penitet me litem mouisse sed paratus ad iudicium venio et pro qualitate litis rationes promtus sum allegare. Sed vnum est quod timeo ne, cum sis iudex ordinarius in causa que versatur inter me tanquam aduenam personam et filium tuum quod legibus nostris est contrarium, vereor ne inique lancis examine iniustum in causa presenti libretur iudicium. Et ob hoc qui sanum mihi prouident consilium arbitrantur esse sanccius ad maiorem si inueniri posset appellari presenciam. (ll. 23–9)

(I do not regret that I have initiated this lawsuit, but I come to the trial prepared and I am ready to present my reasons for the nature of the accusation. However, since you are the principal judge in this case between me, a foreigner, and your son, and since the case is hostile to our laws, I fear that an unjust judgement may be given in this case. For these reasons, those who advise me think it better to appeal to a higher judge if one can be found.)

After further argument, it is decided that the order of angels known as the Thrones should serve as judges in this case.

The Devil then sets out his accusation by first going through the principal events in the life of Christ; his account culminates with Christ's harrowing of hell and what he describes as the violent and forceful way in which Christ broke into hell and took away the Devil's possessions, that is, the souls of human kind. Having set the background, the Devil then proceeds to make his case:

Scio enim quod in omni causa ciuili vbi serie agitur, primo accio est edenda, qua edita, apparebit aduersario species litis future. Edita enim accio speciem litis demonstrat sicut in [*Digesto*] legitur, titulo *De edendo* cum in iudicium deducatur aut proprietas aut possessio, que certis interdictis expeditur. Ego possessorio interdicto experiri volens contra aduersarium meum intento interdictum *Vnde vi.* Hoc enim interdictum possessorium et restitutorium est et ideo per hoc interdictum peto michi restitui possessionem generis humani qua diutissime sum gauisus. Quod autem interdictum hoc michi efficaciter competat ex hoc liquet, per hoc enim interdictum vis cohercetur et ei proponitur qui vi de possessione eiectus est sicut legitur *Digesto*, ti(tulo) *De vi et vi armata*, l(ege) i. ... Aduersarius meus superueniens alligauit fortem et omnia mea diripuit ... Et hoc factum est contra omnem ordinem iudiciarium per quod maxime patet eum contra iura et leges fecisse et ideo nullo iuris debet gaudere subsidio. Ait enim lex quod frustra legis inuocat auxilium uel patrocinium qui contra leges venire non metuit, sicut legitur *Digesto*, ti(tulo) *De in integrum restitucione minorum*, l(ege) *Extat decretum*. Quod autem processerit aduersarius meus contra ordinem iuris ex hoc liquet, quia me non conuenit, non me in ius vocauit, nullam accionem edidit, nulla instrumenta produxit sed vsus fortitudine me possessione mea violenter eiecit ... (ll. 79–102)

(I know that in every civil action that follows the proper procedure, the action must be promulgated, and when it has been promulgated, the type of suit that has been brought will be apparent to the adversary. The promulgation of an action makes known the type of suit that has been brought, as we read in the *Digest* under the title *de edendo* when either ownership or possession becomes a matter for judgement. Such matters are settled by reference to particular interdicts. Wishing to launch an action using an interdict regarding possession, I propose to invoke the interdict *unde vi* against my adversary, for this interdict refers to matters of possession and restitution, and through this interdict I request that possession of the human race which I enjoyed for a very long time be restored to me. That this interdict supports my claim is evident from this: through this interdict, power is checked and the invocation of this interdict is granted to one who has been ejected from his property, as we read in the *Digest* under the title *et de vi et armata*. ... My adversary, coming upon me, bound me[3] and snatched away all my possessions. ... And this happened against the order of justice; it is clear that he did this against rights and laws and therefore he ought to have no protection of right. For the law says that in vain he calls upon the assistance or help of the law who does not fear to go against the law, as we read in the *Digest* under the title *de integre restitucione minorum*. Indeed, that my adversary went against the order of law is evident from this, that he did not bring an action against me, did not call me into a court, proclaimed no action, and produced no documents, but having used his strength, he ejected me from my property forcibly.)

The Devil's case is sophisticated, and these passages give a sense of the direction of its arguments. The striking feature of the text is the extensive use of principles of law and legal procedures drawn from the *Corpus Iuris Civilis*, the great compilation of Roman law undertaken by the Emperor Justinian I (483–565). This consists of four books, the *Code* (529), the *Novellae* and the *Digest* (533) and the *Institutes* (533).[4] The last of these is a handbook or textbook for students of law. Together these volumes form the *Corpus Iuris Civilis*, and in the Middle Ages they served as reference works for law. The *Conflictus* is rich in its references to and quotations from the *Code* and the *Digest*. The interdict or 'provisional decree' *unde vi* that is referred to frequently in the text embodies a principle of Roman Civil Law that can be invoked in a dispute. The *Institutes* provides a succinct summary of how the interdict *unde vi* can be used:

> Reciperandae possessionis causa solet interdici, si quis ex possessione fundi vel aedium vi deiectus fuerit: nam ei proponitur interdictum unde vi, per quod is qui deiecit cogitur ei restituere possessionem, licet is ab eo qui vi deiecit vi vel clam vel precario possidebat.[5]

> (It is customary to use an interdict in order to recover property if anyone has been ejected by force from the possession of land or buildings. To such a person the interdict *unde vi* is available, by means of which the

---

[3] The Latin for the reading 'bound me' is *alligauit fortem*. In this context (ll. 91–3) the text incorporates a paraphrase of Matthew 12.29 (Mark 3.27).

[4] Justinian, *Corpus Iuris Civilis*, ed. by G. Kroll, P. Krueger, T. Mommsen and R. Schoel (Berlin, 1869–95). The editions of the different parts of the *Corpus Iuris Civilis* that are used here are: volume I (*Institutes* and *Digest*), 20th edn (Dublin, 1968), volume II (*Code*), 14th edn (Dublin, 1967), and volume III (*Novellae*), 8th edn (Berlin, 1963).

[5] *Institutes*, IV, xv, 6 (p. 54).

one who ejected him is forced to restore the property to him even if
that one obtained possession from the ejector himself through force or
secretly or by sufferance.)

The author of the *Conflictus* is very much at home with the *Corpus Iuris Civilis* and
can incorporate material from it into this fictional construction of the Devil bringing a
case against Christ for the manner in which he redeemed human kind.

The Devil's case is persuasive, and it might seem that under the law Christ was
culpable. The implicit question is: could Christ's actions be sanctioned if they were
scrutinized in the light of the procedures and principles of the *Corpus Iuris Civilis*? The
overriding issue is whether the Redemption of human kind was legal. In the second
half of the text, Christ presents a strong response as he answers the Devil's case point
by point. One of his arguments is that the Devil has made a blunder in invoking the
interdict *unde vi*:

> Item proposuit interdictum *Vnde vi* sicut in exordio litis accio editur.
> Constat causam inutiliter edi, nisi efficaciter competat actori. Interdictum
> igitur *Vnde vi* quod ex parte aduersa propositum est loco accionis, in hoc
> casu locum sibi vendicare non potest et hoc ex ipso negocio declaratur.
> Homo enim de cuius possessione sibi restituenda aduersarius experitur,
> in numero rerum mobilium computatur cum sit de numero sese mouen-
> tium, sed pocius nomine rerum mobilium. Ad eos tamen pertinet qui
> de re solo herenti deiciuntur sicut legitur in *Digesto*, titulo *De vi et vi
> armata*, l(ege) prima, c(apitulo) ii. Cum ergo non agitur de re soli uel
> solo herenti, patet hic non esse locum interdicto *Vnde vi*. (ll. 180–89)

> (Then, in the way in which at the beginning of a dispute an action is
> proclaimed, he proposed to introduce the interdict *unde vi*. It is agreed
> that it is useless to proclaim a cause if one does not take into account the
> plaintiff. Therefore, while my adversary, for his part, has put forward the
> interdict *unde vi* as the basis for his action, he cannot claim a place for it
> in this cause and this is evident from what follows. For humanity, whose
> possession my adversary complains must be restored to him, is proved
> to be of the class of movables since human kind is of that class of things
> that have motion and is known by the name of movables. Nevertheless,
> the interdict *unde vi* pertains to those who have been dispossessed of
> land or real estate as one reads in the *Digest* under the title *de vi et vi
> armata*, law i, chapter ii. Since therefore the matter under dispute does
> not concern land or real estate, it is obvious that the interdict *unde vi*
> cannot be used here.)

The interdict *unde vi* can be invoked in the case of a dispute over property but only in
the sense of property as real estate or 'immovables'; whereas human beings, because
they have freedom of motion, are classified as 'movables'. Another line of argument
that Christ uses comes in his response to the Devil's accusation that Christ used illegal
force against him:

> Est et alia vis a principalibus constitucionibus cuilibet concessa puta
> aduersus publicos latrones, desertoresque milicie, nocturnes popula-
> tores agrorum uel publicorum itinerum possessores quos comprehen-
> dere cuilibet permissa est licencia vt ilico non expectato iudicio dignis
> suppliciis afficiantur. Nullus enim parcere debet militia cui telo obuiare

oportet ut latroni, ut *Codice, Quando licet vnicuique sine iudice se vindicare*, lege i. (ll. 201–206)

(There is another power granted to anyone by the principal constitutions against thieves, deserters of the army, those who plunder the fields by night and highwaymen. Anyone is allowed to seize them in order to bring them to punishment immediately without judgement. For no one ought to spare a soldier who comes at him with a spear, but should treat him like a thief. We find this law in the *Code* under the title *quando licet unicuique sine iudice se iudicare*.)

Here Christ invokes the law in the *Code, quando licet unicuique sine iudice se iudicare* (when it is permitted to someone that he himself judge without a judge present). This argument is drawn from the *Corpus Iuris Civilis*, but it had a counterpart in English Common Law: 'In certain circumstances or in particular areas, summary judgement could be carried out by individuals or groups on outlaws, traitors and "hand-having" thieves (those who were caught red-handed).'[6] Christ draws on other parts of the *Corpus Iuris Civilis* and rounds off his arguments by invoking a principle of law from the *Decretum* of Gratian, the compilation of Canon Law.[7] The Devil had argued that he had acquired ownership of human kind by *prescriptio temporis*, that is, the acquisition by use or possession over time (ll. 118–27). Christ's reply to this argument is in part:

Nec unquam obicienda est prescripcio temporis vbi necessitas inter-uenerit hostilitatis sicut legitur in Causa xvi^a, questione iii, capitulo *Prima accione* in fine et capitulo *Porro*. (ll. 261–4)[8]

(*Prescriptio temporis* should never be invoked when hostile force has been used, as we read in [the *Decretum*] *causa 16, questio 3, capit-ulus 'prima accione'*, in the latter part of this *capitulus*, and *capitulus 'porro'*.)

In the *Conflictus*, using Roman law and one citation to canon law, Christ proves that he is the more convincing advocate in the trial and can cite the law more effectively than the Devil.

The question that the *Conflictus* provokes is this: what aspects of medieval culture does the text grow out of and in turn address? In considering this question we can suggest four contexts for the *Conflictus*.

The first context is theological, specifically the medieval doctrine of the Redemption, and the idea or argument of what was known in the Middle Ages and in modern scholarship as the concept of the Devil's rights.[9] This idea goes back to early writing by the church fathers, most importantly St Augustine, and formed part of the formulation of the doctrine of the Redemption. The argument runs that under the terms of strict and universal justice, in freeing human kind from the Devil, God was obliged to treat the Devil justly. The implication of this argument was that, to use Abelard's phrase,

---

6 Anthony Musson, *Medieval Law in Context: The Growth of Legal Consciousness from Magna Carta to The Peasants' Revolt* (Manchester Medieval Studies, 2001), 94.
7 Gratian, *Decretum*, in *Corpus Iuris Canonici*, ed. Emil Friedberg, 2 vols (Leipzig, 1879; repr. Graz, 1955).
8 Gratian, *Decretum* c.13, C.xvi, q. 3 and c. 14, C.xvi, q.3 (i, col. 793). Here the *Conflictus* uses a passage from caput 13: 'Non enim erit obicienda prescripcio temporis, ubi necessitas intererit hostili-tatis'.
9 My monograph *The Devil's Rights and the Redemption* (see above, n. 1) is a history of these two concepts; what follows here is a brief summary.

the Devil had a 'right in possessing human kind', or a 'right of possession'. The word that Abelard and other writers used is the term *ius*, that is, 'right' or 'justice'. This is the theological basis of the argument of the *Conflictus*: the Devil is claiming that at the harrowing of hell, Christ violated his right to possess human kind and that Christ's use of force was contrary to *ius* or 'right'.

In the final chapter of his landmark book *The Making of the Middle Ages*, Richard Southern argued that the great contribution of Anselm of Canterbury (d. 1109) to the doctrine of the Redemption was his refutation of the idea that the Devil held a 'right of possession' over human kind.[10] This overturning of the concept of the Devil's rights appeared in Anselm's treatise on the Redemption, the *Cur Deus Homo* ('Why God became Man') completed in 1098.[11] Southern argued that Anselm's refutation of the idea of the Devil's right of possession was a watershed in medieval theology that had consequences for medieval culture as a whole. His interpretation was that this rejection of the idea of the Devil's rights removed the concept entirely from formulations of the Redemption; he remarked decisively: 'once rejected [the concept of the Devil's rights] disappeared for good'. In his view Anselm's *Cur Deus Homo* changed fundamentally how the Redemption was understood; it liberated the doctrine from a legalistic straight-jacket, and in turn freed medieval culture to conceive of Christ's role in history in more human and emotive terms. For Southern, Anselm was responsible for an entirely novel view of the Redemption. This change of direction, signalled in the *Cur Deus Homo*, in thinking about the Redemption made possible what we have come to call 'affective piety', that is, the more emotionally charged responses to the figure of Christ in his salvation of humanity. Christ the warrior is replaced by Christ the Man of Sorrows. This interpretation is attractive and has been accepted explicitly or implicitly by genera-tions of scholars. My argument is that Southern's hypothesis that Anselm's refutation of the idea of the Devil's rights entirely removed the concept from formulations of the Redemption, and that this was the principal cause for the attitude to the role of Christ in human history that emerges in the twelfth and thirteenth centuries, while it is compel-ling, is not supported by the evidence. Certainly in the twelfth and thirteenth centuries we see the growth of affective piety in medieval literature and visual arts, as well as theological writing. The pseudo-Bonaventure *Meditationes Vitae Christi* ('Meditations on the Life and Passion of Christ') is among the most well known and influential examples of the expression of affective piety in medieval European literature.[12] But, Anselm's treatment of the Devil's rights did not sweep away all discussion and debate about that concept in relation to the Redemption. Anselm had not so much refuted the idea that the Devil had a right of possession over human kind but had redefined it. The revised formulation that emerged following Anselm cast the Devil in the role of a jailor who was subject ultimately to the will and power of God. Theologians following Anselm continued to acknowledge and debate the issue of the Devil's rights, and the concept remained an aspect of doctrine on the Redemption.

The *Conflictus* is of interest in theological terms because Christ's arguments in the text reflect the views about the nature of the Devil's possession of human kind that

---

[10] R.W. Southern, *The Making of the Middle Ages* (London, 1953). Southern's discussion of the implica-tions of what he saw as Anselm's denial of the Devil's rights is set out in pp. 223–5. Southern returned to the issue in his later book *Saint Anselm: A Portrait in a Landscape* (Cambridge, 1990), 207–11.

[11] *Cur Deus Homo*, in *S. Anselmi Opera Omnia*, ed. F.S. Schmitt, 6 vols (Edinburgh, 1946–61), ii. 37–133.

[12] Iohannis de Caulibus, *Meditaciones Vite Christi*, ed. M. Stallings-Taney (Corpus Christianorum Continuatio Mediaevalis 153, 1997). See also the modern English translation: *Meditations on the Life of Christ*, trans. Isa Ragusa and Rosalie B. Green (Princeton, 1961; repr. 1977).

appear in the wake of Anselm's redefinition of the idea of the Devil's rights; whereas the Devil's accusations against Christ reflect fairly closely theological ideas before Anselm. The text neatly brings together the two traditions of thought about the nature of the Devil's rights. The author of the *Conflictus* is astute in that he dramatizes the historical debate, taking into account the arguments about the Devil's rights that were current in the twelfth and thirteenth centuries. A number of theological writers who post-date Anselm and have close associations with England can be seen to take up the question, for example Robert of Melun (d. 1167) who was born in England and succeeded Abelard at the school of St Geneviève, and late in his career became bishop of Hereford (1163).[13] Robert Grosseteste (1175–1253) dramatized aspects of the concept of the Devil's rights in his Anglo-Norman poem, the *Chasteau d'Amour*.[14] This then is one context for the *Conflictus*. The text successfully dramatizes theological debate.

The second context for the *Conflictus* is what we have come to understand as the 'growth of legal consciousness' in the Middle Ages and within medieval England. Anthony Musson's *Medieval Law in Context* is useful for locating the *Conflictus* within legal culture of the thirteenth century and indeed later.[15] The subtitle *The growth of legal consciousness from Magna Carta to the Peasants' Revolt* indicates the aspect of the history of medieval law that Musson seeks to address. He aims to investigate what he refers to as the 'intrusion' of law into different areas of medieval society and culture. At one point he discusses 'the politicisation of the law', that is, the 'intrusion' of the law into politics.[16] The *Conflictus* shows the 'intrusion' of the law into theology, or what we might term the 'theologicisation' of the law. Musson's book is most useful, but it is sketchy on how law can be seen to have affected theology and literature.[17]

The development that it is proposed to identify here – the 'intrusion' of law into theology – is in one way not unexpected. Theological writing of the twelfth and thirteenth centuries invokes the idea of Christ as 'advocate', a role drawn from the first epistle of John, chapter 2, verses 1–2.[18] Hugh of St Victor conceived of the Redemption as a 'causa hominis adversus Deum et diabolum'; in context *causa* has the sense of 'legal dispute'.[19] And, of course, *ius* ('right') and *iura* ('rights') have strongly legal connotations. It remained for one Latin writer, the author of the *Conflictus*, to develop the implications of this language into a full-scale dramatization of a legal dispute between the Devil and Christ. Two texts of continental origin from the mid to late fourteenth century and early fifteenth century show the principal features of the *Conflictus*,

---

[13] On Robert of Melun's treatment of the Redemption and the concept of the Devil's rights see Marx, *The Devil's Rights and the Redemption*, 34–8 and Appendix II, 146–53.

[14] On Robert Grosseteste's treatment of the Redemption and the Devil's rights in the *Chasteau d'Amour* and elsewhere see ibid., 65–79 and Appendix III, 155–9.

[15] Musson, *Medieval Law in Context*.

[16] Ibid., 28.

[17] On literature and law, mainly in the fourteenth century, see Richard Firth Green, *A Crisis of Truth: Literature and Law in Ricardian England* (Philadelphia, 1999). Green discusses the Devil's rights in the context of his chapter 'Bargains with God' (pp. 336–76); his formulations are problematic and need refinement. Green refers once to the *Conflictus* (p. 427 n. 13) but fails to address the range of legal arguments that are central to the text. See also Richard Firth Green, 'Medieval Literature and Law', in *The Cambridge History of Medieval English Literature*, ed. David Wallace (Cambridge, 1999), 407–31.

[18] 'Sed et si quis peccaverit, advocatum habemus apud Patrem, Iesum Christum iustum: et ipse est propitiatio pro peccatis nostris.'

[19] Hugh of St Victor, '*De Reparatione Hominis*', book I, part 8 of *De Sacramentis Christianae Fidei*, *PL* 176.305–18.

but the evidence that has emerged so far is that the *Conflictus*, from the thirteenth century, is the earliest instance of this type of 'intrusion' of law into theology.[20]

As has been demonstrated, the legal references that the *Conflictus* uses are drawn from the *Corpus Iuris Civilis* which is not the basis of the law that was used practically in England in the thirteenth century. But Roman law and, of course, Canon Law in the form of the *Decretum* of Gratian and other compilations, were taught in medieval English universities. They were referred to as the 'learned laws' and from the twelfth century were taught at Oxford. Canon Law, which draws heavily on Roman Law, was taught at Cambridge from the mid-thirteenth century. These 'learned laws' formed the basis for education in law and were known as a *ius commune* (a general common law).[21] We should not assume a sharp distinction between the 'learned laws' on the one hand and English Common Law on the other within a university context and programmes of teaching and training. Also, principles of Roman Law were cited in English Common Law, although the whole range of Roman Law did not operate in medieval England. We need to recall as well that in the period of the twelfth to the fourteenth century, the law was predominantly a clerical profession, and in this period only latterly became a lay profession. It is clear that the *Conflictus* would have had a context in England, namely among a university and university trained audience, and this hypothesis is supported by the evidence of the manuscripts in which the text survives.[22] The 'legal consciousness' of members of this audience would have included familiarity with the 'learned laws' – Roman Civil Law in the form of Justinian's *Corpus Iuris Civilis*.[23]

The third context for the *Conflictus* is what is known to anthropologists and social historians as 'misrule', that is, the inversion and transgression of the established order. This is manifest, for instance, in social situations, in rural and urban festivals and processions. It is also found in medieval art, for example, in the margins of illuminated manuscripts, and in medieval literature.[24] Indeed, this is how C.S. Lewis understood the *Roman de la Rose* which has at its centre the notion of a 'religion of love', with trappings and rituals borrowed from orthodox religion, but inverted, for example, in

---

[20] Bartolus of Sassoferrato (1313–57, Professor of Law at Pisa in 1339 and later at Perugia), *Tractatus quaestionis ventilatae coram Domino nostro Iesu Christo, inter Virginem Mariam ex vna parte, & Diabolum ex alia parte, vulgo dictus Processus Satanae contra D. Virginem coram Iudice Iesu*, in *Processus Juris Joco-serius*, ed. Melchior Goldast (Hanover, 1611), 1–36; and Jacobus de Theramo (1349–1417), *Processvs Lvciferi contra Iesvm coram Ivdice Salomone*, in *Processus Juris Joco-serius*, 37–366. On Bartolus and Jacobus see Hartmann, *Lateinische Dialoge*, 318–20, 721–2. I am grateful to Professor David Trotter for drawing my attention to a thirteenth-century Anglo-Norman text, the *Mirror of Justices* (dated, probably, as early as 1285–90), which is a literary text that combines, to a purpose different from that of the *Conflictus*, law and theology (drawn principally from the Bible). The compiler produced a moral text in the guise of a legal treatise. David Trotter, 'Language and Law in the Anglo-French Mirror of Justices', in *L'Art de la Philologie: Mélanges en l'Honneur de Leena Löfstedt*, ed. Juhani Härmä, Elina Suomela-Härma et Olli Välikangas (Mémoires de la Société Néophilologique de Helsinki 70, 2007), 257–70.

[21] Musson, *Medieval Law in Context*, 37.

[22] Marx, 'Edition and Study', 16–17.

[23] Musson, *Medieval Law in Context*, 9–15 and 36–83; also Leonard E. Boyle, 'The Beginnings of Legal Studies at Oxford', *Viator* 14 (1983), 107–31; Paul Brand, 'Legal Education in England before the Inns of Court', in *Learning the Law: Teaching and the Transmission of Law in England, 1150–1900*, ed. Jonathan A. Bush and Alain Wijffels (London, 1999), 51–84; James A. Brundage, 'The Canon Law Curriculum in Medieval Cambridge', in *Learning the Law*, 175–90.

[24] Michael Camille, *Image on the Edge: The Margins of Medieval Art* (London, 1992) and *Mirror in Parchment: The Luttrell Psalter and the Making of Medieval England* (London, 1998), chapter 5 (pp. 232–75). Also, the classic study: Mikhail Bakhtin, *Rabelais and his World*, trans. H. Iwolsky (Cambridge, MA, 1968).

the God of Love's 'Ten Commandments of Love'.[25] The *Conflictus* is an intellectually refined example of 'misrule'. In the most outrageous manner, the Devil brings a plausible although, as we later discover, a flawed law suit against Christ. For at least half of the text it would appear that Christ's redemption of humanity was illegal, at least under human laws. What are the implications of that for the medieval audience? On the basis of the Devil's argument only, it would seem that man-made or human laws are flawed because, if universally applied, they would deny the validity of the Redemption. The Devil is arguing that human kind was redeemed on a false premise and one's salvation is not, after all, safe or assured. Christ is a violent thug and did not obey the law. The way in which the Devil lays out his case against Christ transgresses and inverts the intellectual order and the central doctrine of Christianity, that is, the Redemption. Of course, as we have seen, the Devil's triumph is brief, and Christ puts forward convincing legal and theological arguments against the Devil's case. But, for a brief time, the edifice of Christian doctrine is called into question. The *Conflictus* reflects that characteristically human ability to hold two contradictory ideas at the same time. But, we may ask, why open the debate? We recall, of course, that Christ wins the arguments; he exposes flaws in the Devil's case and presents positive arguments for the Redemption. So, the legal and theological truth of this central doctrine of Christianity is safe. The function of the *Conflictus*, it is argued here, is to create an imagined situation in which the validity of the central doctrine of the Redemption is *tested* within the human legal framework. The effect – because of Christ's victory – is to strengthen for the audience the validity of man-made laws; in other words, the text is making a case for the law itself, which brings the right result in the highest court imaginable, the court of Heaven. In the end, the Devil's 'misrule' is safely confined and held in check by the law.

This leads to the fourth and final context for the *Conflictus*. A body of scholarship shows that through the thirteenth and fourteenth centuries, in European universities, including Oxford and Cambridge, there was a growing rivalry between the faculties of law and theology.[26] Those trained in the law were, it was assumed, more proficient at administration and so the number of clerical lawyers in positions of power gradually increased. Clerical lawyers were vying with theologians for power within the Church, not just administrative power but intellectual power as well. As R. James Long has shown, the first to address the question directly was the theologian Godfrey of Fontaines in the form of a *disputatio quodlibetalis* at the University of Paris in 1293: *Utrum iurista vel theologus plus proficiat ad regimen ecclesie* ('Whether a jurist or a theologian is more competent as a ruler of the church').[27] This *quaestio* was a response to an issue raised at a synod in Paris in 1290 at which Benedetto Caetani, who was to

[25] C.S. Lewis, *The Allegory of Love* (London, 1936); see chapters 1 and 3.

[26] John Scott, 'William of Ockham and the Lawyers Revisited', in *Rhetoric and Renewal in the Latin West 1100–1540: Essays in Honour of John O. Ward*, ed. Constant J. Mews, Cary J. Nederman and Rodney M. Thomson (Turnhout, 2003), 169–82 (at 174–8 and notes). See also Alan B. Cobban, 'Theology and Law in the Medieval Colleges of Oxford and Cambridge', *Bulletin of the John Rylands Library of Manchester* 65 (1982), 57–77; John M. Fletcher, 'Inter-Faculty Disputes in Late Medieval Oxford', in *From Ockham to Wyclif*, ed. Anne Hudson and Michael Wilks (Studies in Church History, Subsidia 5, 1987), 331–42; D.N. Lepine, 'The Origins and Careers of the Canons of Exeter Cathedral, 1300–1455', in *Religious Belief and Ecclesiastical Careers in Late Medieval England*, ed. C. Harper-Bill (Woodbridge, 1991), 87–120; Guy Fitch Lytle, 'The Careers of Oxford Students in the Later Middle Ages', in *Rebirth, Reform and Resilience: Universities in Transition 1300–1700*, ed. James M. Kittelson and Pamela J. Transue (Columbia, Ohio, 1984), 213–53.

[27] R. James Long, ' "Utrum iurista vel theologus plus proficiat ad regimen ecclesie": A *Quaestio Disputata* of Francis Caraccioli; Edition and Study', *Medieval Studies* 30 (1968), 134–62.

become Pope Boniface VIII (1294–1303), criticized theologians at the University of Paris for entering into the controversy over the mendicants. Benedetto Caetani's view was that the governing of the church was not the responsibility of theologians. It is plausible that the *Conflictus* grew out of this rivalry within university circles and the upper echelons of the church between theologians and lawyers, each insisting on their superiority. A question that the *Conflictus* generates for us is whether it is the work of a theologian who has appropriated legal ideas and legal arguments, or the work of a clerical lawyer who has set theological arguments within a legal framework. In favour of the theologian as author is that the central arguments and themes of the *Conflictus* are drawn from the historical theological debate about the Redemption; this is key to the dynamics of the text. In favour of the clerical lawyer is the thoroughness and precision of the legal arguments that the Devil and Christ use. The text is thick with legal arguments which suggest that the author had a thorough training in Roman Law and Canon Law.

In an earlier section we referred to what we might see as the 'intrusion' of the law into theology, here identified as the 'theologicization of the law'. It has been suggested in this essay that the *Conflictus* reflects the influence of the law on theology, that the law had intruded into the field of theology. But the alternative is possible, the 'legalization of theology', that is, that theology had intruded into the law and that lawyers were eager to show that their subject or their body of learning could be used to address and above all clarify significant theological issues. Unlike the *Conflictus*, in which the argument is resolved, the debate that this essay has opened up about the nature of the authorship of the text – theologian or lawyer – has no definite conclusion, and, as is the case with many medieval debate texts – for example *The Owl and the Nightingale*[28] – the question is left for the reader to decide.

---

[28] *The Owl and the Nightingale*, ed. Neil Cartlidge (Exeter Medieval English Texts and Studies, 2001).

Prosecuting Ravishment in Thirteenth-Century England

Caroline Dunn

Introduction

Three ravishment allegations from thirteenth-century court records tell very different stories. A 1208 record narrates the kidnapping (*abductione*) of the wife of Samson de la Pomerai in a case revealing the Latin antecedents for a modern criminal term.[1] A generation later, Maud daughter of Aylwine, came before justices at the Oxfordshire Eyre to complain of her rape (*rapo*) by Thomas of Fifield, who had violently deflowered her.[2] Here is a clear example of how the Latin *rapo* evolved into our modern English term for rape. Finally in 1290 Walter Lyppe instigated a civil lawsuit alleging that the priest Anselm of Hatfield had ravished and abducted (*rapuit et abduxit*) his wife Juliana.[3]

This last example might lead those uninitiated in the vocabulary that late medieval English scribes used for sexual and marital offences to conclude that Juliana was raped and abducted. Legal historians and literary scholars, especially those interested in what, exactly, the later authors Chaucer and Malory were charged with when they were accused of *raptus*, have demonstrated the ambiguity of that Latin term in the Middle Ages. It could refer to a woman's sexual violation, or it could denote her abduction – with or without her consent – and with or without sexual connotation. The first two examples given above date to the earlier thirteenth century, while the third mirrors the late thirteenth-century conflation of these two offences; a conflation most evident in the first and second statutes of Westminster (1275 and 1285). With these statutes, what were previously two offences became one under common law. This essay considers why this conflation occurred and what it meant for the women and their families who were affected by ravishment. Lawsuits based on the new pairing *rapuit et abduxit* proliferated after 1285. Juliana Lyppe's ravishment provides one of the earliest examples, and also highlights how prosecution narratives do not tell the whole story, for, according to jurors, Anselm had not forcibly raped or abducted Juliana; instead she had departed willingly from her cruel husband, and was having an affair with the priest.[4]

The study of ravishment, despite its ambiguities, illuminates the topics of women, family, law, and disorder in medieval England. It reveals relationships between marriage, kinship ties, and property, broadens our understanding of the

---

[1] *Pleas before the King or his Justices, 1198–1212*, ed. D.M. Stenton (Selden Society 84, 1967), no. 3509.

[2] PRO, JUST 1/695, m. 79; *The Oxfordshire Eyre, 1241*, ed. Janet Cooper (Oxfordshire Record Society 56, 1989), no. 810.

[3] PRO, KB 27/124, m. 55; *Select Cases in the Court of King's Bench under Edward I*, ed. G.O. Sayles (Selden Society 57, 1938), no. 8.

[4] Ibid.

role of women in the legal system (as victims and as prosecutors),[5] and provides a means for analysing male control over female bodies, sexuality, and access to the courts, as well as ways in which female agency sometimes rebelled against such controls. And although the vagueness of ravishment makes the topic more complex, its ambiguity is itself revealing of the motivations and practices lying behind legislation and litigation of medieval England.

The ravishment clauses found in the statutes of Westminster are not uncharted territory. Thirty years ago, J.B. Post's examination of the laws punishing the rape and abduction of women in thirteenth- and fourteenth-century England set a high standard for studies of female ravishment.[6] His argument that lawmakers conflated the dual offences of rape and abduction in order to punish consensual abductions (elopements), a conflation that diminished the right of recourse for genuine victims of sexual violence, has been widely accepted by historians and literary scholars alike.[7] Post's thesis has not been left unchallenged, however, as H.A. Kelly asserted instead that the ravishment statutes enacted by the English Parliament were designed to punish abduction, and not rape.[8] This essay reassesses the ravishment legislation, and offers a new synthesis that addresses Post's and Kelly's conclusions about the Westminster statutes in the context of numerous court cases.[9] Close analysis of the terminology used in the legal records, along with the types of cases prosecuted under the common law, aids our understanding of the intentions of lawmakers and the nature of ravishment prosecutions in medieval England.

The conclusions presented here are based on an analysis of 1,213 references to rape or abduction in England between the 1140s and 1515, and although the focus is on the 199 thirteenth-century references, later developments help to elucidate what was going on earlier. Cases were drawn from sources as diverse as manor court rolls, monastic chronicles, ecclesiastical courts records, and parliamentary petitions,

---

[5]   In theory, women were only allowed to appeal rape and homicide (and possibly personal assault), although scholars have found women appealing other wrongs. See *The Treatise on the Laws and Customs of the Realm of England Commonly Called Glanvill*, ed. G.D.G. Hall, 2nd edn (Oxford, 1993), 174, 176; *De Legibus et Consuetudinibus Angliae (Bracton on the Laws and Customs of England)*, ed. George E. Woodbine and trans. Samuel E. Thorne, 4 vols (Cambridge, MA, 1968) ii. 419; Daniel M. Klerman, 'Female Prosecutors in Thirteenth-Century England' (University of Southern California Law School, Olin Research Paper No. 00–13, 2000); <http://ssrn.com/abstract=241299> (21 January 2006), 19–20, 28–9, 32–5; C.A.F. Meekings, 'Introduction', in *Crown Pleas of the Wiltshire Eyre, 1249*, ed. C.A.F. Meekings (Wiltshire Archaeological and Natural History Society 16, 1961), 78–9; Patricia R. Orr, '*Non Potest Appellum Facere*: Criminal Charges Women could not – but did – Bring in Thirteenth-Century English Courts of Justice', in *The Final Argument: The Imprint of Violence on Society in Medieval and Early Modern Europe*, ed. Donald J. Kagay and L.J. Andrew Villalon (Woodbridge, 1998), 141–60. Susan Stewart ('Introduction', in *The 1263 Surrey Eyre*, ed. Susan Stewart (Surrey Record Society 40, 2006), 114) suggests that the rule limiting women's appeals was enforced with greater regularity from late in the reign of Henry III.

[6]   See J.B. Post, 'Ravishment of Women and the Statutes of Westminster', in *Legal Records and the Historian*, ed. J.H. Baker (London, 1978), 150–64; idem, 'Sir Thomas West and the Statute of Rapes, 1382', *BIHR* 53 (1980), 24–30. Post's argument is in both articles, but the present analysis concerns the more controversial Westminster statutes.

[7]   John G. Bellamy, *The Criminal Trial in Later Medieval England: Felony before the Courts from Edward I to the Sixteenth Century* (Stroud, 1998), 166–7; Christopher Cannon, '*Raptus* in the Chaumpaigne Release and a Newly Discovered Document Concerning the Life of Geoffrey Chaucer', *Speculum* 68:1 (1993), 79–82; Kim M. Phillips, 'Written on the Body: Reading Rape from the Twelfth to Fifteenth Centuries', in *Medieval Women and the Law*, ed. Noel J. Menuge (Woodbridge, 2000), 136–7; Corinne Saunders, *Rape and Ravishment in the Literature of Medieval England* (Cambridge, 2001), 62.

[8]   H.A. Kelly, 'Statutes of Rapes and Alleged Ravishers of Wives: A Context for the Charges against Thomas Malory, Knight', *Viator* 28 (1997), 398–410.

[9]   Both Post and Kelly looked at court cases, but not in the quantity examined here.

but the majority were obtained from royal legal records, including King's Bench files and Gaol Delivery rolls, Chancery petitions,[10] and the various Eyre, Assize, and Peace rolls available in print. Numerous incidents also appear in the royal pardons and special commissions of Oyer and Terminer calendared in the Patent Rolls, while the original manuscripts were consulted in order to glean the Latin vocabulary.[11] Naturally, choice of source can dictate the type of case revealed, and the types of sources available change over time.[12] This essay first briefly considers the situation in England prior to the promulgation of Westminster I and II. It then addresses the conflation of rape and abduction that occurred with the Westminster legislation, and the consequences of that conflation.

English prosecutions for rape and abduction before 1275

It is usually easy to discern whether texts written before the last quarter of the thirteenth century are referring to rape or abduction. When the twelfth- and thirteenth-century commentators Glanvill and Bracton outlined the procedure followed by a woman complaining of rape, they clearly used the Latin term *raptus* to describe sexual assault and not abduction. I provide only a simplified version of the procedure here because it has been well described previously and is not controversial among modern historians. A woman was responsible for raising the hue and cry and showing her wounds. Her second task was to initiate an appeal (private prosecution) alleging the rape. Third, the victim had to attend court to follow up her suit. Upon conviction, rape, at least the rape of virgins, was a felonious offence punishable by mutilation.[13] Although convictions were rare, this does not mean that rape was treated lightly, for not all alleged rapists who escaped conviction were acquitted; instead some were outlawed for failing to appear at court, while others settled privately with the victim by offering her either a financial settlement or marriage.

A standard procedure was in place for dealing with complaints of sexual assault by the thirteenth century, but this was not true of kidnapping. Some cases appear in the records of the king's courts before 1275, but only one statute, the 1236 Statute of Merton, provides official practices, and this legislation regulates only the abduction of heirs, both male and female, with no sexual connotation.[14] Wives and maidens who were not subject to underage guardianship had no official course of legal action

---

[10] Because of the extensive survival of late medieval material, I sampled records from four English counties (Bedfordshire, Devon, Northumberland, and London/Middlesex) chosen to explore local variation. All surviving Gaol Delivery rolls and Chancery petitions from these counties were examined. The voluminous KB 27 files, however, I sampled at five-year periods at the beginning, middle and end of each century, starting with their inception in the late thirteenth century and continuing to the end of the fifteenth century. The KB 26 rolls, in which eighteenth- and nineteenth-century archivists grouped together King's Bench and Common Pleas from the reigns of Richard, John, and the first half of Henry III, were consulted in the printed medium of the *Curia Regis Rolls*.

[11] I examined each volume of the Calendared *Patent Rolls* dating between 1216 and 1500, with cases from all counties included in my sample, and specific references tracked down in original Latin manuscripts. In total, the abovementioned legal and administrative sources provided 1,167 of the 1,213 ravishment references.

[12] Anthony Musson ('Crossing Boundaries: Attitudes to Rape in Later Medieval England', in *Boundaries of the Law: Geography, Gender and Jurisdiction in Medieval and Early Modern Europe*, ed. Anthony Musson (Aldershot, 2005), 84–90) provides an apt warning of the dangers of neglecting the multiplicity of law courts in medieval England, or of failing to comprehend crucial factors such as how the various courts differed procedurally and attracted diverse clientele.

[13] *Bracton*, ii. 414–15.

[14] *SR*, i. 3.

Table 1. Percentage of references using and avoiding *raptus*

	Rape cases		Abduction cases	
	Using *raptus*	Avoiding *raptus*	Using *raptus*	Avoiding *raptus*
13th century	82.1%	17.9%	30.6%	69.4%
14th century	89.4%	10.6%	78.6%	21.4%
15th century	90.0%	10.0%	61.0%	39.0%

Sources: see notes 10–11.

when they were stolen, nor did their male relatives. Some who could catch the king's attention through petitions or hearings before royal justices could have their cases adjudicated in this still informal era of legal process. Thus, Henry III took a personal interest in the theft of the noble widow Maud Longspee by John Giffard; indeed Henry 'several times commanded the said John to come to his court to purge his innocence or to cause [Maud] to be delivered without delay'.[15]

For most of the thirteenth century, the vocabulary used for prosecutions in the court records also suggests that authorities deemed rape and abduction to be two distinct offences. The argument presented here is based upon those prosecution narratives that provide additional vocabulary, beyond *raptus*, that enable classification of alleged offences as either rape or abduction. Thus cases like the one appealed by Maud daughter of Aylwine, outlined above, are clearly rape, whereas those using the term abduction – with or without *raptus* – have been classified as abduction cases. A number of prosecutions remain ambiguous, but nevertheless classification is possible in many. Looking closely at this terminology reveals how *raptus* was increasingly used to denote abduction as well as rape. Cases of sexual assault that use *raptus* remained steady throughout the thirteenth century and into the fourteenth; in each instance over 80 per cent of sexual violence allegations used the noun or verb form of *raptus* (Table 1). Abductions demonstrate a different trend, however, and increasingly use the Latin term *raptus* to explain what offence was being prosecuted (Table 1). Previously abductions had been denoted by the Latin terms *abduxit* or *abductione*, or other verbs of theft such as by *abstulerit* or *robauit*. By the end of the thirteenth century, *raptus* continued to mean rape, but it also increasingly meant abduction.

Legal and linguistic transformation: 1275–1285

Rape and abduction were clearly two distinct offences during the first two centuries after the Norman Conquest, but at the end of the thirteenth century our understanding of the offences and how they were prosecuted becomes murkier. The Westminster legislation has perplexed scholars seeking to know whether the new statutes regulated rape or abduction (or both), while conflation of the offences is evident in the prolific phrase, *rapuit et abduxit*, that emerges with the legislation. Before looking

---

[15] *CPR, 1266–1272*, 520. Some other early cases are at *CRR*, xi. no. 476 and *Select Cases of Procedure without Writ under Henry III*, ed. H.G. Richardson and G.O. Sayles (Selden Society 60, 1941), no. 103.

more closely at the new *rapuit et abduxit* cases, I offer first the texts and translations, and a short synopsis, of the relevant clauses of both Westminster I and II.[16]

First Statute of Westminster, Chapter 13

And the king prohibiteth that none do ravish nor take away by force
any maiden within age, neither by her own consent, nor without; nor
any wife or maiden of full age, nor any other woman, against her will.
And if any do, the party that will sue within forty days, the king shall
do common right; and if none sue within forty days, the king shall sue.
And such as be found culpable shall have two years' imprisonment, and
after shall fine at the king's pleasure and if they have not whereof, they
shall be punished by longer imprisonment, according to as the trespass
requireth.[17]

Second Statute of Westminster, Chapters 34 and 35
Ch. 34 (French text)[18]

It is provided, that if a man from henceforth do ravish a married woman,
maid, or other, where she did not consent neither before nor after, he
shall have judgment of life and member.

And likewise where a man ravisheth a woman, married lady, maid, or
other, with force, although she consent after, he shall have such judgment as before is said, if he be convicted at the king's suit, and there
the king shall have the suit.[19]

Ch. 34 (Latin text)

And of women carried away with the goods of their husbands, the King
shall have suit for the goods so taken away.

And if a wife willingly leave her husband and go away and live with
her adulterer, she shall be barred forever of the action to demand her
dower that she ought to have of her husband's lands if she be convicted

---

[16] These texts largely follow the transcriptions and translations available in the *Statutes of the Realm*,
but I am grateful to Dr Paul Brand for sharing his revisions with me. Post ('Ravishment of Women',
162–64) notes additional manuscript variations, but these are minor and do not alter their general interpretation.

[17] Et le Rey defent qe nul ne ravie ne prenge a force damoysele dedenz age, ne par son gre ne saun son
gre, ne dame ne damoisele de age, ne autre femme maugre seon; e si nul le fet, a la suite celi qe suiwera
dedenz les quarante jours, le Rey en fra comune dreyture: Et si nul ne comence sa suite dedenz quarante
jours, le Rey en siwera; e ces qil entrovera copables, si averont la prison de deus aunz, e puis serrunt
reinz a la volente le Rey. Et sil ne unt dount estre reinz a la volente le Rey, si seient puniz par plus long
prison, solum ceo qe le trespas le demande. *SR* (ii. 29).

[18] The lengthy Westminster II was written in Latin, with the exception of two brief clauses drafted
in French. Perhaps, as T.F.T. Plucknett suggested (*Legislation of Edward I* (Oxford, 1962), 121–2),
the French clauses were inserted when the rest of the statute was under discussion in Parliament. Post
('Ravishment of Women', 156–7) agrees that the French text was a late addition, 'almost certainly an
afterthought'. Kelly ('Statutes of Rapes', 370) disagrees that the French clauses were last minute addi-
tions, but offers no explanation for why they were not drafted in Latin. Unclear motives combine with
the vague terminology of the term used for the offence (French *ravie*) to ensure that this particular clause
remains worthy of debate.

[19] Purveu est que si homme ravist femme espouse, damoisele, ou autre femme desoremes,
par la ou ele ne se est assentue ne avaunt ne apres, eit jugement de vie e de member.
E ensement par la ou home ravist femme, dame espouse, damoisele, ou autre femme, a force, tut seit ke
ele se assente apres, eit tel jugement come avaunt est dit si il seit ateint a la suite le rei, e la eit le Rei
sa suite. *SR* (ii. 87–8).

thereupon, except that her husband willingly, and without the coercion of the church, reconcile her and suffer her to cohabit with him; in which case she shall be restored to her action.

He that carrieth a nun from her house, although she consent, shall be punished by three years' imprisonment, and shall make suitable satisfaction to the house from whence she was taken, and nevertheless shall make fine at the King's will.[20]

Chapter 35

Concerning children, males and females, whose marriage belongeth to another, taken and carried away, if the ravisher have no right in the marriage, though after he restore the child unmarried, or else pay for the marriage, he shall nevertheless be punished for his offence by two years' imprisonment. And if he do not restore, or do marry the child after the years of consent, and be not able to satisfy for the marriage, he shall abjure the realm, or have perpetual imprisonment.[21]

Each passage of Westminster II, saving the French text of Chapter 34, obviously legislates against abduction. Chapter 35 reveals continued concern about kidnapped wards, while thefts of nuns and wives (in both cases probably willing nuns and adulterous wives) are newly prohibited.[22] More ambiguous, however, are the Anglo-French texts of Westminster I and the brief French insertion at the beginning of Westminster II.

Westminster I's stipulation that no one may 'ravish nor take away' a woman against her will can be interpreted as a prohibition against both rape and abduction, or just abduction. It cannot, however, be interpreted to refer to rape alone, as some scholars have done.[23] Those who read the statutes solely as regulating sexual assault

---

[20] De mulieribus abductis cum bonis viri, habeat rex sectam de bonis sic asportatis. Et uxor, si sponte reliquerit virum suum et abierit et moretur cum adultero suo, amittat imperpetuum accionem petendi dotem suam que ei competere posset de tenementis viri, si super hoc convincatur, nisi vir suus sponte, et absque cohercione ecclesiastica, eam reconciliet et secum cohabitari permittat; in quo casu restituatur ei accio. Qui monialem a domo sua abducat, licet monialis consenciat puniatur per prisonam trium annorum, et satisfaciat domui a qua abducta fuerit competenter, et nihilominus redimatur ad voluntatem regis. SR, ii, 87–8.

[21] De pueris, sive masculis sive femellis, quorum maritagium ad aliquem pertineat, raptis et abductis, si ille qui rapuerit, non habens jus in maritagium, licet postmodum restituat puerum non maritatum, vel de maritagio satisfecerit, puniatur tamen pro transgressione per prisonam duorum annorum. Et si non restituerit, vel heredem post annos nubiles maritaverit et de maritagio satisfacere non poterit, abjuret regnum vel habeat perpetuam prisonam. SR, ii, 87–8.

[22] Clause 2, concerning unfaithful wives, at first bears little obvious relation to ravishment, but these wives frequently appear as consenting 'victims' of abduction, explaining why the text is sandwiched between two ravishment clauses. On the resulting dower cases see Paul Brand, '"Deserving" and "Undeserving" Wives: Earning and Forfeiting Dower in Medieval England', *Journal of Legal History* 22:1 (2001), 1–36. Kelly ('Statute of Rapes', passim) and Sue Sheridan Walker ('Punishing Convicted Ravishers: Statutory Strictures and Actual Practice in Thirteenth and Fourteenth-Century England', *Journal of Medieval History* 13 (1987), 238–39) also emphasize such consensual abductions. For more on nuns, see below, p. 75.

[23] See Barbara J. Baines, 'Effacing Rape in Early Modern Representation', *English Literary History* 65 (1998), 76–7, 82; John Marshall Carter, *Rape in Medieval England: An Historical and Sociological Study* (Lanham, MD, 1985); Sylvia Federico, 'The Imaginary Society: Women in 1381', *Journal of British Studies* 40 (2001), 180–1; Ruth Kittel, 'Rape in Thirteenth-Century England: A Study of the Common Law Courts', in *Women and the Law: The Social Historical Perspective*, ed. D. Kelly Weisberg, 2 vols (Cambridge, MA,1982), ii. 101–16; and *The Encyclopedia of Rape*, ed. Merril D. Smith (Westport, CT,

decry this text because they believe it downgraded rape from a felony to a tres-pass, for conviction at the king's suit required fine and imprisonment for two years, whereas previous commentators said that the punishment for the felony of rape was castration.[24] The Anglo-French addition to Westminster II then increased the punishment for ravishment, but it is likewise unclear whether the law was enacted to regulate rape or abduction (or both). This law states that a man convicted of ravishing a woman – wife, damsel, or other – against her will shall suffer judgment of life and limb. If the woman should consent to the ravishment afterwards, the king shall have suit.

According to Post, these statutes represent a late medieval transition from a defi-nition of *raptus* that emphasized sexual rape to one that increasingly focused on abduction. This process was initiated by the statutes of Westminster and finalized by a 1382 law.[25] The legislation conflated the two offences under the umbrella term of *raptus*, in which the abduction element of the *raptus* charge achieved primacy, and stemmed from enhanced tenurial concerns on the part of the male landowners of England who enjoyed a progressively larger role in lawmaking.[26] Conventions for the descent of property meant that the marriage of a daughter, especially an heiress, could have profound implications for both family fortunes and family honour. Because abduction was viewed as an assault on the lineage, the patrimony, rather than the well-being of the female victim, became the primary concern.[27]

If the landed elite feared the hazards that the theft of their daughters and wives posed to their lineage and affluence, elopement and adultery were equally threat-ening, and the statutes, Post argued, addressed these fears. The first statute of West-minster punished the abduction of consenting women, while the second prohibited the abduction of willing nuns and stated that wives who leave their husbands volun-tarily should not be allowed to obtain their dower. Westminster II stipulated that if a woman was found to have consented to her abduction afterwards, and declined to prosecute, then the king could sue.[28] A century later, the legislation of 1382 explic-itly condemned women who willingly left their families, stating that if a woman consented at any time – before, during, or after the abduction – their male relatives then enjoyed the right to prosecute the offenders and the woman was not allowed to receive any inheritance, dower, or jointure.[29]

---

and London, 2004), p. xiv. Early modern legal commentators recognized both the abduction and rape elements of *raptus* found in the laws. Edward Coke discusses rape in *The Third Part of the Institutes of the Laws of England* (London, 1817), 60, and abduction in *The Second Part of the Institutes of the Laws of England* (London, 1817), 434. Matthew Hale (*Historia Placitorum Coronae*) follows his consideration of rape (pp. 626–36) with a discussion of abduction (pp. 636–39). In the next century, William Black-stone (*Commentaries on the Laws of England* (Oxford, 1773), iv. 210) acknowledged that the definition of rape included forcible abduction. The three most prominent scholars of the subject in our lifetimes have all emphasized that the authorities who enacted these statutes were most concerned about abduction. Thus Post and Walker argue that they conflated rape and abduction, while Kelly states that they were exclusively designed to combat abduction. I emphasize below the arguments made by Post and Kelly because they focus on female ravishment, whereas Walker's research primarily concerns the ravishment (abduction) of male and female wards in the fourteenth century.

[24] See above, p. 69.

[25] Post, 'Sir Thomas West', 24–30.

[26] Bellamy, *Criminal Trial*, 166.

[27] Post, 'Ravishment of Women', 160; Post, 'Sir Thomas West', 24–5. See also Cecily Clark and Eliza-beth Williams, *Women in Anglo-Saxon England and the Impact of 1066* (London, 1984), 149.

[28] In practice the husband gained the right to sue the 'abductor' for civil damages, but this was not granted by the legislation.

[29] The 1382 ravishment law was likely a response to one specific abduction incident, the kidnapping for marriage of Eleanor West. Post, 'Sir Thomas West', 26–7; *SR*, ii. 27.

A revival of Roman law in medieval England assisted lawmakers in linking the new crime of abduction to the older charge of rape, for Roman law emphasized the abduction element of the Latin term *raptus*, whereas post-Conquest England had focused on sexual assault.[30] England already had a procedure in place for dealing with *raptus*, defined as forced sexual violence, but late thirteenth-century authorities were more concerned with departure – forced or willing – and the canonical tradition of merging the offences provided an expedient model for authorities wishing to supplement existing customs regarding rape with new laws designed to thwart abduction.

Lawmakers feared the kidnapping of their women, whether they were unwilling or compliant, and Roman law already had a tradition of defining *raptus* as abduction. The few abduction cases from earlier in the twelfth and thirteenth centuries reveal that the propertied classes had reason to be anxious about loss of women, even if such cases were not common. Three specific instances of abduction that are contemporary with the statutes and may have prompted the legislation also reveal how departure, rather than sexual violence, was the primary concern of lawmakers. Each of these three cases uses a novel phrase, *rapuit et abduxit*, to describe the alleged offence. Legal records documenting this lexical doublet stem from the writ purchased to initiate both wife- and ward-theft cases before King's Bench justices. Since such cases could not be heard until the Chancery writ was introduced, allegations employing the phrase *rapuit et abduxit* date almost exclusively from after the 1285 second statute of Westminster. Only four *rapuit et abduxit* references predate the 1285 introduction of the writ.[31] The writ would later become hugely popular (the pairing was the basis for 237 references (20 per cent) of all uncovered ravishment narratives).[32]

The ravishment of Amice, wife of William de Hotot, provides one of the earliest *rapuit et abduxit* pairings and Amice's 1274 capture may have provoked the anti-ravishment clause found in the 1275 first statute of Westminster.[33] Unknown foes had seized (plural *rapuerunt et abduxerunt*) Amice from the custody of the sheriff of Sussex when they were on the road travelling towards the king. Probably because it was Sheriff Hastings who complained about the offence, the editors of the *Calendar*

---

[30] Influential canon lawyer Gratian designated both offences to be *raptus*. See Gratian, *The Treatise on Laws (Decretum DD.1–20) with the Ordinary Gloss*, ed. and trans. Augustine Thompson and James Gordley (Studies in Medieval and Early Modern Canon Law, Washington DC, 1993), cases 27 to 36; James A. Brundage, 'Rape and Seduction in the Medieval Canon Law', in *Sexual Practices and the Medieval Church*, ed. Vern L. Bullough et al. (Buffalo, 1982), 142–4; James A. Brundage, *Law, Sex and Christian Society in Medieval Europe* (Chicago, 1987), 107. The conflation occurred in the Roman empire as well. See Judith Evans-Grubbs, 'Abduction Marriage in Antiquity: A Law of Constantine (CTh IX.24.1) and its Social Context', *Journal of Roman Studies* 79 (1989), 59–60.

[31] Three, as stated, are contemporaneous with the Westminster statutes and will be discussed below. The fourth is an early text from 1242–3, recorded in *CRR* (xvii. no. 53), in which it was alleged that John son of Knathou, with associates, seized and abducted (*rapuerunt et inde abduxerunt*) Katherine daughter of Keyndrek.

[32] Once the writ of ravishment became available to abandoned husbands, allegations of wife theft, using the *rapuit et abduxit* pairing, increased more than four-fold. The writ made it easier to prosecute the offence of ravishment in the king's courts, and so it is no surprise that more cases appear in the court records after its introduction, but I suggest that the reason it proved so useful for plaintiffs was that most husbands used it to publicize their wives' adulterous affairs. Not only did the 1285 statute put into writing an already held view that wife-theft was linked to illicit sexual behavior, but also the chapter of the statute prohibiting wives from inheriting dower provided husbands with an incentive to publicize their spouse's extramarital relationships.

[33] Post, 'Ravishment of Women', p. 154.

of Patent Rolls translated this ravishment as 'the rescue from their custody', rather than 'ravished and abducted'.[34]

A later lawsuit fortuitously provides details that reveal more than the inconclusive terminology found in the 1274 commission. Seven years later Hotot's husband William won a civil lawsuit after he prosecuted that Alexander le Sire had, with others, taken (*ceperunt*) Amice the wife of William de Hotot, and led her (*duxerunt*) away.[35] Defending his role in taking Amice, Alexander le Sire countered with a wife-theft allegation of his own, stating that Amice was in fact *his* wife, not William's, and that William had taken her away violently and against her will.[36] Two men are thus competing over the same woman, both arguing that they are legitimately married, and Amice's *raptus* experience was undoubtedly one of seizure and abduction (forced or consensual), rather than a prosecution sexual rape. Perhaps one should not discount the possibility that at some point during this drawn out marital triangle Amice suffered sexual assault, but that was not the offence being prosecuted. If Alexander le Sire had, upon retrieving Amice, consummated the betrothal, the act was not denoted by the verb *rapere* found in the judicial commission, because the plural form *rapuerunt* indicates seizure by multiple men, rather than sexual rape committed by one marital rival.[37]

If we accept that the contemporaneous Hotot capture prompted Westminster I, then abduction, and not rape, lay behind the legislation. A second case, the abduction of two nuns, has been linked to the clause of Westminster II prohibiting theft from convents, and this part of the statute was unambiguously legislating against departure (consensual or forced) rather than sexual violence. Logan proposes that the clause was based on Sir Osbert Giffard's theft of the two nuns Anna Giffard and Alice Russell from Wilton, where a cousin Juliana Giffard served as abbess, and was probably motivated by familial conflict rather than an adulterous liaison; there is certainly no evidence for sexual rape.[38]

A third early *rapuit et abduxit* coupling was contemporary with the 1285 Parliament that enacted Westminster II.[39] On 16 June 1285, the king issued a commission of oyer and terminer for three justices to hear Elias de Uddeston's accusation against William de Flamvill who had allegedly seized Uddeston's wife and goods.[40] The editors of the *Calendar of Patent Rolls* simplified the terminology used in this commission to speak of the 'abduction,' but the original Latin text reveals one of the first examples of the *rapuit et abduxit* formula.[41]

---

[34] PRO, C 66/93, m. 12d, and the calendared translation is at *CPR, 1272–1281*, 69.

[35] PRO, KB 27/60, m. 20.

[36] The *rapuit et abduxit* formula was employed by this later case, which states that: 'Hotot dictam Amiciam vi et contra voluntatem ipsius Amiciam rapuit et eam postea abduxit.'

[37] For more on this case see Sue Sheridan Walker, 'Free Consent and Marriage of Feudal Wards in Medieval England', *Journal of Medieval History* 8 (1982), 128. Hotot won the civil suit and received 200 marks in compensation.

[38] The kidnapping took place in the autumn of 1284, and the statute was enacted in the following summer, 1285. Description of the theft, which uses the *rapuit et abduxit* pairing, was found in the bishop of Worcester's Episcopal register, rather than in a strictly legal document, but Bishop Giffard (a cousin of the abductor) had been active in Edward I's legal circles and the phrase may have started to become well known. See F. Donald Logan, *Runaway Religious in Medieval England, c. 1240–1540* (New York, 2002), 87–8; *Register of Bishop Godfrey Giffard, 1268–1302*, ed. J.W.W. Bund, 2 vols (Worcestershire Historical Society 15, 1898–1902), i. 279–80.

[39] H.G. Richardson and G.O. Sayles (*The English Parliament in the Middle Ages* (London, 1981), 144) date the Easter Parliament from an opening of no later than 8 April to a closing date of 24 June or later.

[40] *CPR, 1281–1292*, 208.

[41] PRO, C 66/104, m. 16d.

Unlike the Hotot *raptus* case, the Uddeston ravishment provides scholars with no additional information other than recording the soon-to-be-standardized terminology. None of the (237) wife-theft cases that appear in the records after 1285 to prosecute the seizure and taking away of a wife with her husband's goods state or hint that an element of forcible sexual assault was responsible for the allegation. Indeed, many of these cases explicitly or implicitly involve either adultery, with a wife engaging in consensual sex and departing voluntarily with a lover, or consensual departure of a different nature, for example a wife abandoning her husband because of his abusive behavior. Unlike the *raptus* cases in which sexual rape was prosecuted, the victims in these ravishment cases were the abandoned husbands, even if their wives were the alleged sufferers.

The conflation of the offences of rape and abduction at the end of the thirteenth century makes it difficult for modern scholars to identify if the lawyers and justices were chiefly trying to prohibit and prosecute sexual violence or kidnapping, but the conflation was deliberate. The drafters of the Westminster statutes were more interested in drawing a line between cases of consenting and unconsenting ravishment than between abduction and rape. Westminster I implicitly differentiates between forced *raptus* (prosecuted and punished by appeal of rape), and consensual ravishment (prosecuted by the crown as a trespass after forty days). Westminster II is more explicit, using the general term of *ravist* but differentiating between cases 'where she did not consent', and 'although she consent after'.[42] Both Westminster I and the ambiguous Anglo-French portion of Westminster II, moreover, introduce the king's suit for instances when the woman seems to be consenting. Thus the 1275 law states that if the woman fails to initiate her own lawsuit within forty days, 'the king shall sue'. Ten years later, if the woman is ravished 'with force, although she consent after' then 'the king shall have the suit'.

Post's conclusion that lawmakers were increasingly alarmed by abduction – consensual or forced – is supported by evidence from both normative texts and the judicial record. Yet his hypothesis that genuine rape victims found their recourse to the common law limited is less valid. Post argued that the introduction of the king's suit caused a deterioration in women's status over the course of the later Middle Ages by preventing women from selecting their own partners through consensual ravishment, and that medieval legislators and court justices no longer exhibited concern or sympathy for the raped woman so that the laws of 1275 and 1285 transformed the judicial process for crimes of rape, and that 'the appeal of rape lapsed into insignificance'.[43] Yet although the new statutes did thwart the ability of women (and lovers) to arrange marriages by forging ravishment, they did not supersede standard rape appeal procedure, which continued as before, so that a true victim of sexual assault retained her right of recourse.

Women certainly maintained the right of appeal in both the fourteenth and fifteenth centuries. In 1391, for example, Johanna Swell appealed John Hawley of Dartmouth because he had assaulted her in London and 'carnally knew her against her will and feloniously deflowered her of her virginity'.[44] The assaulter of Elizabeth Jakes was accused *de appello de rapto et pace fracta* in 1490, over two centuries after the

---

[42] *SR*, i. 29, 87.

[43] Post, 'Ravishment of Women', 160.

[44] PRO, KB 27/522, m. 54. Mayor, MP and privateer John Hawley may have provided the model for Chaucer's shipman. See Stephen Pistono, 'Henry IV and John Hawley, Privateer, 1399–1408', *Reports and Transactions of the Devonshire Association* 111 (1979), 145–63; *The House of Commons, 1386–1421*, ed. J.S. Roskell, Linda Clark and Carole Rawcliffe (Stroud, 1992).

Westminster legislation.[45] Many convicted criminals, moreover, were pardoned for the rape of a women 'whereof he is indicted or appealed', thereby demonstrating the continued acceptance of the process of rape appeals, if not their actual operation.[46] The survival, into the late fifteenth century, of the appeal process for all crimes has also been documented.[47] Furthermore, legal commentators continued to refer to the appeal of rape; the compiler of the Year Book of 5 Edward II (1311–12) discussed two rape cases initiated by appeal.[48]

Evidence from the royal pardons in the Patent Rolls further suggests that some victims felt appeals remained valid resolutions to their experiences. These pardons indicate that women still enjoyed a private right to settle with their rapists, although the court records no longer reveal such private concords. Between 1334 and 1446, thirty-five men were pardoned specifically of the 'king's suit' thereby suggesting (and explicitly stating in six cases) that the woman could still implead, or threaten to appeal her rapist and bring him to trial.[49] The crown enjoyed the financial fruits of selling pardons for the royal suit,[50] but because rapists were pardoned only for the crown side of the rape prosecution, women could still appeal, and the initiation of such lawsuits may have resulted in private settlements favourable to the victim. Certainly the survival of appellee prosecutions into the fourteenth and fifteenth centuries indicates that women continued to believe that they had something to gain from the private suit, although they were probably aware that appeals rarely resulted in guilty verdicts.[51]

Post's assertion that the appeal 'lapsed into insignificance' is, however, more nuanced than simply declaring that rape appeals were superseded by the king's right to prosecute. Rather, he writes that appeals were increasingly rejected on technicalities, and that victims further lost their ability to settle privately when the king's suit was introduced. Admittedly, few post-1285 cases end in judgment, and I have found only one rapist receiving a guilty verdict.[52] However, this does not differ significantly from the thirteenth-century practice, when very few appeals led to convic-

---

[45]   PRO, KB 27/917, m. 44d.

[46]   I provide here only a few examples: *CPR, 1350–54*, 197; *CPR, 1370–74*, 86; *CPR, 1377–81*, 95. Note that the latest example comes over a century after the 1275 Statute of Westminster which supposedly rendered the appeal of rape obsolete.

[47]   Christopher Whittick, 'The Role of the Criminal Appeal in the Fifteenth Century', in *Law and Social Change in British History: Papers Presented to the Bristol Legal History Conference, 14–17 July 1981*, ed. John A. Guy and H.G. Beale (London, 1984), 55; Bellamy, *Criminal Trial*, 15, 36–7, 167.

[48]   *Year Books of 5 Edward II*, ed. W.C. Bolland (Year Book Series 12, Selden Society 33, 1916), 111, 134.

[49]   Examples can be found at *CPR, 1330–34*, 240; *CPR, 1338–40*, 110, 222, 232; *CPR, 1367–70*, 238.

[50]   A motive also noticed by Post, 'Ravishment of Women', 154–5.

[51]   Kelly also argued for the continuation into the fourteenth and fifteenth centuries of rape procedure existing in the thirteenth century. Yet although this claim is accurate, one of the points he offers in evidence is problematic. Kelly presents another statute, one dealing indisputably with sexual assault and not abduction, to support his position that the 1275 statute was not meant to alter the standard procedure of appeals for rape prosecutions. This Coroner's statute, which outlines the proper course of actions for a rape appeal, is unfortunately undated, and Kelly, following the editors of the *Statutes of the Realm*, ascribes it to 4 Edward I (1275–6). But *SR* is an imperfect edition of medieval laws; indeed Plucknett (*Legislation of Edward I*, 19) called it 'the most varied collection of apocrypha', and this particular 'statute' is one of those pieces of apocryphal legislation. The text was not a law enacted and promulgated, but rather an excerpt from Bracton that had been copied out into a medieval statute collection. Since the text comes from Bracton's early thirteenth-century work, it cannot be used to demonstrate that the crown and parliamentary authorities wished to maintain the status quo for rape prosecutions after 1275, even if the assertion that they accepted the persistence of the appeal remains valid.

[52]   PRO, JUST 3/15/4, m. 18 (1365).

tion and punishment.[53] The Westminster statutes do not serve as a turning point demarcating an era of easy prosecution for female victims from a time of hardship. Indeed rates of appeals declined for all crimes after the mid-thirteenth century.[54] The decline of the rape appeal in favour of royal prosecution by indictment should be seen as part of a wider trend concerning all appeals – made by men and women – and not as part of a deliberate attempt to curb female sexuality or female access to law courts.

According to H.A. Kelly, it makes more sense to conclude that these Westminster statutes were not at all interested in rape, and instead they reveal progressive anxiety about the problem of abduction, with lawmakers enacting increasingly stringent punishments for the offence.[55] The first written legislation targeting abduction, the 1236 Statute of Merton, considered the abduction of wards and made it a trespassory offence punishable by damages.[56] Kelly believes that Westminster I then expanded the legislation to encompass all women, as well as wards, but abduction remained a trespass, punishable by fine and imprisonment. The subsequent second statute of Westminster reveals that earlier anti-abduction measures had been ineffective, and the lawmakers thus strengthened the law even further. Abductors of wards, though still not considered felons, were threatened with abjuration and perpetual imprisonment, while the abduction of a woman – with or without her consent – was a felony, resulting in *jugement de vie e de member*.[57] The suggestion in Westminster II that a woman might be ravished with her consent convinces Kelly that we ought to translate *ravist* in this instance as abduction, and not sexual rape.[58] Scholars, including both Post and Kelly, then agree that the later legislation of the fourteenth and fifteenth centuries supplemented the law of abduction and were not concerned with rape. Thus, Kelly asserts, both of the late thirteenth-century statutes of Westminster should be placed within the context of expanding apprehension about the offence of abduction, while lawmakers intended that the felonious crime of rape, or sexual assault, should be prosecuted as before. Yet although Kelly is correct that the statutes were not enacted to transform the process of the rape appeal, but rather supplement it, and while he accurately protests that previous rape scholars should not have been translating *raptus* solely as rape, he nevertheless overreaches when he says that the clauses of the statutes should be translated as abduction only.[59]

In the first place, Kelly links abduction with consent, and rape with lack of consent.[60] Although he acknowledges the existence of forcible kidnapping, he does not allow for the opposing scenario – that some appeals of rape led to consensual settlements. Kelly thus rather simplistically hypothesizes that if the statutes mention the possibility of consent (as do both Westminster I and II) then they must in all cases be referring to the offence of abduction. By no means do I mean to argue that women were consenting to sexual assaults in the Middle Ages, but, as Post pointed out, wordings of consent in the statutes may in fact refer to the problem

[53] Kittel, 'Rape in Thirteenth-Century England', 109–10.
[54] Indeed lawmakers and crown justices of the thirteenth century followed a policy of preferring judicial settlements to private agreements. See Daniel Klerman, 'Settlement and Decline of Private Prosecution in Thirteenth-Century England', *Law and History Review* 19:1 (2001), 37–45, 58 <http://www.history-cooperative.org/journals/lhr/19.1/klerman.html> (26 July 2009).
[55] Kelly, 'Statutes of Rapes', 370.
[56] *SR*, i. 3.
[57] *SR*, i. 88.
[58] Kelly, 'Statutes of Rapes', 370–1.
[59] Kelly, 'Statutes of Rapes', 363.
[60] Kelly, 'Statute of Rapes', 366, 370.

of non-prosecuted rape appeals, that is, cases of sexual assault (or consensual sex) which the victim appealed, but then implicitly consented to by concluding a private concord before the case came to trial.[61]

Kelly therefore goes too far to correct the prevailing view that the Westminster statutes dealt with sexual assault when he continues to differentiate rape from abduction and counters that the legislation mainly concerned stolen women. He fails to acknowledge that lawmakers may not have wanted to draw a distinction, or that they might not have seen one. When Kelly does find cases of rape that refer to the statute of 1285, he has to stretch his argument by writing that this situation 'shows that the interpretation and observance of statute law, like other laws and procedures, is liable to be capricious'.[62] Yet this association of sexual assault with Westminster II is not an isolated incident in the courts, for I have found additional cases of what appear to be rape, as opposed to abduction, prosecuted for breach of that legislation.[63] While Kelly's position regarding the unpredictability of legal interpretation no doubt often holds true, it certainly is easier to accept that the 1285 statute covered both offences. That is what the vocabulary of the legislation states, and what we must recognize unless we find additional clues to the concealed intent of the lawmakers.

Just as Kelly has to concede that medieval courts interpreted the statutes as prohibiting sexual rape as well as abduction, he similarly faces the problem that the three contemporary legal commentaries (*The Mirror of Justices*, *Britton*, and *Fleta*) also understood the Westminster legislation in this way.[64] The anonymous author of *The Mirror* expressed displeasure that the term *rap* was 'by the arbitrary words of the statute' now being used 'for every forcing of a woman of whatsoever condition she may be,' that is, for both sexual rape and abduction.[65] The other two texts speak only of the offence of rape. Kelly handles this predicament unsatisfactorily; first by denouncing *The Mirror* as unreliable,[66] and then by asserting that the trial evidence needs to be examined more closely, although he fails to turn to the unpublished court proceedings himself.[67]

Although Kelly successfully draws attention to the significant role of abduction in the statutes, he fails to acknowledge the ways in which the legislation, particularly the Westminster statutes, conflated the offences of rape and kidnapping. One cannot successfully disentangle rape from abduction in the *raptus* clauses of Westminster I and II, and we can only know what the laws explicitly stated – that they differentiated between consenting and unconsenting ravishment, prohibited the ravishment of maidens, nuns, and wives, and formally introduced the king's suit in ravishment cases to work alongside the standard procedure of the rape appeal.

---

[61] Post, 'Ravishment of Women', 152–3, 160.

[62] Kelly, 'Statutes of Rapes', 418.

[63] See, for examples, *Year Book of the Eyre of Kent of 6 and 7 Edward II (1313–1314)*, ed. F.W. Maitland et al., 3 vols (Selden Society 24, 27, 29, 1910–13), i. 134–5 and PRO, KB 27/849, m. 138.

[64] Kelly, 'Statutes of Rapes', 384–7. *Britton*, ed. and trans. F.M. Nichol, 2 vols (London, 1865), i. 55; *The Mirror of Justices*, ed. W.J. Whittaker and F.W. Maitland (Selden Society 7, 1893), 28–9; *Fleta*, ed. and trans. H.G. Richardson and G.O. Sayles, 4 vols (Selden Society 72, 82, 99, 1955–84), iv. 5. Note that the first volume remains unpublished.

[65] *Mirror of Justices*, 28–9.

[66] Kelly, 'Statutes of Rapes', 384–5. On this point, see David J. Seipp, 'The Mirror of Justices', in *Learning the Law: Teaching and the Transmission of Law in England, 1150–1900*, ed. Jonathan Bush and Alain Wijffels (London, 1999), 85–112.

[67] Kelly, 'Statutes of Rapes', 388.

Conclusion

Defining *raptus* in the legislation and legal records of medieval England is far from easy, but it is imperative that scholars make the attempt before drawing conclusions about the theories or realities of rape and abduction. Even if imperfect, we can clarify the ways in which the legislation and litigation operated in medieval English society. Two conclusions about ravishment terminology emerge from this analysis of thirteenth-century abduction. First, the language used for abduction prosecutions was far more fluid in the thirteenth century than it would later become, probably because the terms were recorded from judicial sessions held at a time when the English legal system was still less settled. Moreover, chronological patterns emerge when cases are explored across the *longue durée*, so that whereas the term *raptus* was consistently employed in sexual violence cases, its association with abduction, elopement, and adultery allegations occurred only with the late thirteenth-century turning point.

The conflation occurred because it served a purpose for the propertied elite who were responsible for formulating laws and serving as royal justices. At the end of the thirteenth century they adapted existing terms and laws to address the particular problems of elopement and consensual abduction. Lawmakers were less interested in distinguishing rape from abduction; instead, as Post argued, they wished to curb consenting acts, whether comprised of fictitious rapes designed to thwart parental objections to marriage, or in the form of fictive abductions that allowed daughters, wives, and nuns to run away with lovers.

Those studying rape, abduction, or both offences in medieval England must be aware of changed prosecution processes as well as trends in terminology and legislation. The introduction of the king's suit, evident in the ravishment legislation but also in other aspects of English judicial procedure, changed, but did not supersede, how ravishment offences were constructed and prosecuted. Yet this investigation has highlighted how women continued to make appeals of rape after they had fallen prey to sexual violence, even after the Westminster statutes conflated the offences of rape and abduction as *raptus*. On the other hand, although Kelly countered Post's analysis with the argument that the new statutes dealt primarily with abduction, and that rape prosecutions continued to function as before, he overstepped when arguing that the legislation did not affect, or was not intended to affect, cases of sexual assault at all.[68]

Although the new laws were aimed largely at the issue of consent, and therefore, by extension, elopements by abduction, it is impossible simply to separate the offences and to debate whether the lawmakers were intending to combat abduction and not rape, or vice versa, because the offences were, from the perspective of the lawmakers, not entirely unrelated wrongs. From the viewpoint of the male relatives, men should be deemed guilty of theft whether their daughters or wives went along willingly or not, and furthermore abduction – whether consensual or not – often included an element of sex. We cannot uncover the emotions lying behind formulaic legal narratives, but we can speculate that the men left behind were not coldhearted and impervious when their daughters or wives were sexually assaulted, but in practice the consequence remained the same whether she was a forced or willing participant – he lost a marriageable daughter or his wife. Hence the laws do not consider the emotional or personal consequences for the woman, and have

---

[68] Kelly, 'Statutes of Rapes', 366, 390–1.

no need to distinguish between rape and abduction because they focus on familial consequences rather than the individual female perspective.

Finally, understanding the nuances of the statutes, and their preoccupation with consenting women, forces us to remember that, in most of the cases from court rolls, what has been recorded is merely an allegation, and not a positivist account of what really happened. That the legislators were increasingly concerned about consenting acts at the end of the thirteenth century underscores the fact that claims of violence should not be taken unquestionably at face value. Female plaintiffs, and the husbands and fathers left behind, might have exaggerated certain aspects of their ordeal to dramatize their plight and to capture the sympathy of juries and legal authorities. *Raptus* in the Middle Ages covered a diversity of experiences for the medieval woman and her family, from consensual illicit love affairs to the most horrific acts of violent rape, and lawmakers remained anxious to regulate and punish the whole array of ravishment offences.

John of Crakehall: the 'Forgotten' Baronial Treasurer, 1258–60[1]

Adrian Jobson

On 2 November 1258, John of Crakehall's appointment as treasurer of England was formally announced in a letter patent.[2] Chosen by the barons who had seized control of England's government from King Henry III during the previous summer, he was to serve for almost two years before dying in office in September 1260.[3] Exercising control over the exchequer, Crakehall was entrusted with the reformation of the king's finances. Yet despite of the importance of his position within the reformist project, John has been largely overlooked by historians of the period. John Maddicott, in his biography of Simon de Montfort, mentions him only three times.[4] In R.F. Treharne's influential study *The Baronial Plan of Reform*, the treasurer merits eighteen references, although several of these merely relate to his actual appointment.[5] Such is his general anonymity that, in his *Studies in the Period of Baronial Reform and Rebellion*, E.F. Jacob refers to him on just three occasions.[6] The aim in this paper is to place Crakehall firmly within the historiography of the baronial movement. After offering some thoughts on Crakehall's early career, the paper will propound a new analysis of the factors that lay behind his selection as treasurer before moving on to a discussion of the baronial exchequer and his personal contribution to the implementation of the reformist programme.

John's antecedents are somewhat shadowy but his use of the toponym Crakehall indicates that he hailed from either Great or Little Crakehall near Northallerton in the North Riding of Yorkshire. Exactly when he was born is unknown, although it must have occurred before 1210 at the latest. Uncertainty also surrounds John's parentage but he was probably the younger son of Ellis of Crakehall.[7] Peter, his older brother, had succeeded by 1240 while at least one unnamed sister had reached adulthood.[8] The family held land in Hornby, Patrick Brompton and Great Smeaton in Yorkshire as well as a share in the Lincolnshire manor of Holbeach.[9] These lands

---

[1]   The author would like to thank Dr Nick Barratt for his comments on an earlier draft of this paper.
[2]   *CPR 1258–66*, 1.
[3]   *Flores*, ii. 455.
[4]   J.R. Maddicott, *Simon de Montfort* (Cambridge, 1994), 171, 201, 252.
[5]   R.F. Treharne, *The Baronial Plan of Reform* (Manchester, 1971), 94, 118–19, 124, 124 n. 6, 131 n. 5, 179–82, 182 n. 5, 196 n. 3, 205, 211, 244, 369 n. 4, 372, 374.
[6]   E.F. Jacob, *Studies in the Period of Baronial Reform and Rebellion* (Oxford, 1925), 13, 93, 94 n. 2.
[7]   K. Major, 'The *Familia* of Robert Grosseteste', in *Robert Grosseteste: Scholar and Bishop*, ed. D.A. Callus (Oxford, 1955), 226. See also Appendix 1 below.
[8]   *Feet of Fines for the County of York from 1232–1246*, ed. J. Parker (Yorkshire Archaeological Soc. 67, 1925), 90–1 no. 985; *The Registrum Antiquissimum of the Cathedral Church of Lincoln*, vol. X, ed. K. Major (Lincolnshire Record Soc. 67, 1973), nos 2072–3; *Final Concords of the County of Lincoln, 1244–1272*, ed. C.W. Foster (Lincoln Record Soc. 17, 1920), 236 no. 42. This unidentified sister was the mother of William of Cadeby, who married Lucy, the co-heiress of the chief justice Gilbert of Thornton: see Appendix 3 below.
[9]   *EYC*, v. 276; *Fines for Yorkshire, 1232–46*, 90–1 no. 985; *Feet of Fines for the County of York, from 1216 to 1231*, ed. J. Parker (Yorkshire Archaeological Soc. 62, 1921), 35–6 no. 144.

had formerly constituted part of the fee held from the honour of Richmond by Conan son of Ellis. Conan, who could trace his lineage back to the Domesday tenant Landric, had been married four times but died without legitimate issue in 1218.[10] The fee was therefore partitioned between his three aunts, namely, Beatrice, Parnell and Ellis of Crakehall's mother Constance.[11] If John was indeed Ellis's son, he would have been related to several of the leading families in Yorkshire and Lincolnshire. Emecina, Conan's first wife, was a member of the knightly d'Oyry family from southern Lincolnshire.[12] Avice, his widow, was the sister of Isabella the ancestress of the Nevilles of Raby.[13] There was likewise a marriage connection to the Moultons of Lincolnshire as Avice had, shortly after Conan's death, wedded the son of the former rebel knight Thomas of Moulton.[14]

Crakehall's early years are equally shrouded in mystery. His later correspondence with the Franciscan theologian Adam Marsh, on diverse subjects including the performance of 'the most sacred ministry of the Gospel', would imply a solid grounding in theology while his subsequent administrative career indicates that he was literate.[15] If he had attended a university, however, it is clear that he never pursued his studies to master's level since there is no single surviving document according him the style *magister*. John was probably married in his youth as he had sired a daughter called Petronilla who later wedded the hereditary forester of Pickering, Alan of Kingthorpe. Neighbourhood ties may well have played a role in this match as the groom was a former ward of Robert de Creppinges, a future sheriff of Yorkshire.[16] Crakehall himself had invested considerable effort in ensuring that his daughter had a suitable dowry: over the course of several years he had acquired eight bovates of land at Fockerby near Scunthorpe while across the border in Yorkshire he purchased further property in South Duffield.[17]

The future treasurer was already in the service of the bishops of Lincoln at the time of his first appearance in the historical record. Hugh of Wells, who had held the see since 1209, prosecuted a suit for customs and services at Westminster against Margaret, the countess of Winchester, during the Easter term of 1231. The plea roll notes that Crakehall was acting as the prelate's attorney when proceedings were

[10] *Domesday Book: A Complete Translation*, ed. A. Williams and G.H. Martin (London, 2002), 813; *EYC*, v. 275; BL, Add. MS 40008, fol. 359; *RLC*, i. 368b; L.J. Wilkinson, *Women in Thirteenth Century Lincolnshire* (London, 2007), 75. Conan did leave an illegitimate son, William, who was rector of Holbeach, and a daughter who wedded William son of Simon of Holbeach.

[11] *EYC*, v. 276; P. Brand, 'Family and Inheritance, Women and Children', in *An Illustrated History of Late Medieval England*, ed. C. Given-Wilson (Manchester, 1986), 59; see also Appendix 2 below.

[12] Wilkinson, *Lincolnshire Women*, 69, 75; *EYC*, v. 275.

[13] *Complete Peerage*, ix. 493–6; *EYC*, v. 274–5.

[14] J.C. Holt, *The Northerners: A Study in the Reign of King John* (Cambridge, 1992), 54, 58, 97, 155–6, 172–3; N. Vincent, *Peter des Roches: An Alien in English Politics* (Cambridge, 1996), 332. She married Alan of Moulton.

[15] *The Letters of Adam Marsh*, ed. C.H. Lawrence (Oxford, 2006), no. 109. Both Hugh of Wells and Robert Grosseteste, the first two bishops he served, were concerned with the educational standards of their clergy and often rejected nominees on grounds in insufficient learning, see J.H. Srawley, 'Grosseteste's Administration of the Diocese of Lincoln', in *Robert Grosseteste*, ed. Callus, 169–70.

[16] *Final Concords Lincoln*, 236 no. 42; *CIPM*, ii. no. 111; *CPR 1232–47*, 223. See Appendix 3 below.

[17] *CRR 1242–3*, no. 622; *Fines of Yorkshire, 1232–46*, 114–15 no. 1074; *Final Concords Lincoln*, 236 no. 42. In October 1271, William of Cadeby, Crakehall's nephew, renounced his rights to these lands while Petronilla relinquished her rights to her cousin's tenements in Cadeby. John had also invested in a landed endowment for his nephew, see Lincolnshire Archives, FL 3028–36; *Reg. Antiquissimum*, x. nos 2872–3.

adjourned until June.[18] In the following term, he was named as an attorney in two pleas initiated at the Bench against Philip of Kyme and John of Stow.[19] He also became an established figure in the episcopal household. The earliest instance of his being in attendance upon the bishop dates from 29 March 1231, when at Fingest in Buckinghamshire he witnessed a letter of institution appointing Henry de Rand to Hargrave church.[20] Over the subsequent two years his presence continued to be intermittent but, from March 1233, the frequency gradually began to increase.[21] John's prominence within the diocesan administration was confirmed in the will made by the bishop in June 1233. Superseding an earlier one written in November 1212, he was named amongst the executors.[22]

On 7 February 1235, Wells finally succumbed to illness.[23] Six weeks later, Robert Grosseteste was unanimously elected bishop by the cathedral's chapter.[24] Approximately sixty-five years of age, he had acquired a formidable reputation as a theologian and scientist. Enthused with an almost messianic desire for reform, he immediately embarked upon a mini revolution in both the pastoral care and the administration of his see.[25] Amongst his first actions was to secure the 'help of capable and learned men to assist him in the work of his diocese'.[26] In Crakehall he found a man who possessed the administrative skills that he was searching for: within months the prelate had made him his chief steward.[27] Entrusted with the responsibility for administrating the episcopal estates in what was the largest diocese in England, this was an office he would hold for approximately fifteen years.[28]

Unfortunately, the lack of any surviving accounts from Crakehall's stewardship prevents the historian from undertaking an analysis of his effectiveness in office. In managing the episcopal estates he would nevertheless have followed the basic principles encapsulated in Grosseteste's *Statuta*.[29] Compiled by the bishop himself, these were intended to govern the conduct of his own household. Amongst its strictures was a ban on the acceptance of any gifts except for customary presents of food and drink while the levying of unjust demands was proscribed. Apart from outlining a general responsibility for the supervision and enhancement of his lord's property, rights and stock, the *Statuta* offers little advice that is specific to the steward's

---

[18] *CRR 1230–2*, no. 1314; *Bracton's Note Book*, ed. F.W. Maitland, 3 vols (Cambridge, 1887), ii. 413–14.

[19] *CRR 1230–2*, no. 1523.

[20] *The Acta of Hugh of Wells, Bishop of Lincoln 1209–1235*, ed. D.M. Smith (Lincoln Record Soc. 88, 2000), no. 334.

[21] *Acta of Hugh of Wells*, nos 349, 365, 367, 373, 393–4, 399, 422, 426, 430, 433; *Rotuli Hugonis de Welles, Episcopi Lincolniensis*, vol. 3, ed. F.N. Davis (Lincoln Record Soc. 9, 1913), 32. John witnessed twelve letters of institution, all of which were issued at Stow Park between March 1233 and October 1234.

[22] *DNB*, s.v. Hugh of Wells, 62; *Giraldi Cambrensis*, ed. J.S. Brewer, J.F. Dimock and G.F. Warner, 8 vols (RS, 1871–91), vii, Appendix G, 228–9; *Acta of Hugh of Wells*, no. 408.

[23] *CM*, iii. 306; *Wendover*, iii. 102.

[24] R.W. Southern, *Robert Grosseteste. The Growth of an English Mind in Medieval Europe* (Oxford, 1986), 249.

[25] For a detailed discussion of Grosseteste's desire to eradicate clerical abuses in his diocese and the spiritual wellbeing of the laity, see Srawley, 'Administration', 146–71.

[26] Srawley, 'Administration', 147.

[27] *Rotuli Roberti Grosseteste, Episcope Lincolniensis*, ed. F.N. Davis (Lincolnshire Record Soc. 11, 1914), 135. This is the earliest recorded reference naming Crakehall as steward.

[28] Major, '*Familia*', 225.

[29] *Walter of Henley and other Treatises on Estate Management and Accounting*, ed. D. Oschinsky (Oxford, 1971), 408–9.

office.[30] This lack of detail is partially remedied, however, in Grosseteste's *Rules*, a set of instructions based upon the *Statuta* that he later composed for the countess of Lincoln's use. It noted that the chief steward was to maintain a roll recording all the lord's 'rents, customs, usages, bond services, [and] franchises' in each manor.[31] After the harvest, he was to arrange for the securing of the granges while any accusations of tyrannical conduct made against his subordinates were to be investigated.[32] Given that John was the serving steward when these injunctions were created; he may have offered some practical advice during their drafting.

There are also occasional but tantalising glimpses of him performing the post's functions. In April 1242, a letter patent noted that at Winchester Crakehall had, by the king's order, paid a hundred marks to the earl of Norfolk. Rendered on behalf of Grosseteste, this sum represented the fine made by the bishop with the king for the custody of Idonea de Vipont's lands.[33] Adam Marsh, in an undated letter, sought Crakehall's assistance in support of an Oxford vintner named Warner who wished to recover certain lands in Thame.[34] In 1240, during the bitter dispute between Grosseteste and Lincoln cathedral's dean and chapter, it was the steward who explained to the bishop 'the secret machinations of devious cunning' that the canons would employ against him.[35] Active in both diocesan business and the bishop's personal affairs, it was not surprising that he was seen as one of the leading figures in the episcopal household.[36]

Quite when he resigned as steward is unknown but it occurred shortly before he accompanied Grosseteste to the papal *curia* at Lyons.[37] This trip in the spring of 1250 was partially intended to expose the *curia*'s corruption, the papacy having conferred benefices in the diocese of Lincoln on its constituent members as well as their relatives.[38] Unable to perform the pastoral duties attached to these livings, Bishop Robert believed that these papal nominees were damaging the provision of high quality spiritual care within his see.[39] On 13 May 1250, he denounced the *curia*'s venality in a series of statements submitted to Innocent IV and his cardinals.[40] Crakehall left for England immediately afterwards, where he appears in a final concord made at Lincoln on 29 May.[41] Whether he whole heartedly supported his bishop's position at Lyons is unrecorded but his presence in the episcopal entourage would suggest that, despite his recent resignation, he was still viewed as a faithful adviser and friend.

This close bond of trust and friendship continued until the prelate's death on 29 October 1253 at Buckden in Huntingdonshire. Amongst those present at his passing

---

[30] *Walter of Henley*, 409.

[31] *Walter of Henley*, 388–9.

[32] *Walter of Henley*, 390–1.

[33] *CPR 1232–47*, 283; TNA, C 60/38, m. 8.

[34] *Monumenta Franciscana*, ed. J.S. Brewer, 2 vols (RS, 1858–82), i. no. 132.

[35] *Roberti Grosseteste Episcope quondam Lincolniensis Epistolae*, ed. H.R. Luard (RS, 1861) [hereafter *Lincolniensis Epistolae*], no. 90. A detailed discussion of this dispute can be found in Srawley, 'Administration', 173–6.

[36] *CM*, v. 407–8. In c. 1240, for example, Crakehall witnessed the foundation of Mere hospital near Lincoln, see Cambridge University Library, MS Dowd 10/28, fols 77v–78r.

[37] Major, '*Familia*', 225; *Letters of Adam Marsh*, no. 99; W.A. Pantin, 'Grosseteste's Relations with the Papacy and the Crown', in *Robert Grosseteste*, ed. Callus, 209.

[38] Southern, *Grosseteste*, 276.

[39] Pantin, 'Grosseteste's Relations', 209–10; Srawley, 'Administration', 169–71.

[40] *DNB*, s.v. Robert Grosseteste, 83–4; Southern, *Grosseteste*, 276–81; Pantin, 'Grosseteste's Relations', 209–15.

[41] *Final Concords Lincoln*, 81 no. 102.

was the future treasurer, who subsequently described the event to the famous thirteenth-century chronicler Matthew Paris.[42] While the loss of the text of Grosseteste's will has meant that it is not possible to determine whether Crakehall was a beneficiary, it can be confirmed from other sources that he was one of the executors.[43] The next five years were spent in semi-retirement, with only an occasional foray into the public life of the diocese, despite his elevation in 1254 to the archdeaconry of Bedford.[44] Apart from an undated charter of Henry of Lexington, there is no other evidence of his having witnessed any episcopal grants or letters of institution.[45] He likewise only features occasionally in the public records at this time, usually in connection with the execution of Grosseteste's will. The memoranda roll for 1253, for example, notes that during the Michaelmas term John and his fellow executors acted as mainpernors for the payment of the bishop's debts to the king.[46]

The confidence that both Hugh of Wells and Robert Grosseteste had in Crakehall's abilities ensured that he received ample reward for his services. On 9 April 1231, less than three months after his first appearance in Bishop Hugh's service, he was collated to Somerton church in Oxfordshire. Probably his first ecclesiastical benefice, Somerton would remain in his possession until his death.[47] Greater preferment followed when the dean and chapter of Lincoln cathedral made him a canon between June 1233 and March 1234.[48] The location of his prebend cannot be determined although it may have been Milton in Oxfordshire: a foot of fine dated 3 May 1250 noted that certain lands in Milton-by-Thame had 'belonged to the prebend held by John of Crakehall'.[49] Shillington in Bedfordshire had been secured by 1240 while at an unknown date he had gained the rectory of Brington with Bythorne in Huntingdonshire.[50] On 24 April 1245, John was issued with a papal indult that allowed him to hold an 'additional benefice with the cure of souls'.[51] This dispensation may have been obtained to facilitate his presentation to Althorpe near Scunthorpe.[52] The

---

[42] *CM*, v. 401–2.

[43] TNA, E 368/29, m. 5d. Henry of Lexington and Mathew, the archdeacon of Buckingham, were his co-executors.

[44] *Fasti Ecclesiae Anglicanae, 1066–1300, III: Lincoln*, ed. D.E. Greenway (London, 1977), 43; *A Calendar of the Feet of Fines for Bedfordshire Fines preserved in the Public Record Office, of the Reigns of Richard I, John and Henry III*, ed. G.H. Fowler, 2 vols (Bedfordshire Historical Record Soc. 6, 1919), ii. no. 556.

[45] *CM*, vi. 264–5. Shortly after Grosseteste's death, Lexington had also written to Crakehall about a dispute between the dean and chapter and the archbishop of Canterbury.

[46] TNA, E 368/29, m. 5d.

[47] *Rotuli Hugonis de Welles, Episcopi Lincolniensis*, vol. 2, ed. W.W. Phillimore (Lincoln Record Soc. 6, 1913), 35. After Crakehall's death, there was a dispute over the appointment of his successor, see A. Jobson, 'The Oxfordshire Eyre Roll of 1261', 3 vols (unpublished PhD thesis, University of London, 2006), ii. no. 37; *Rotuli Ricardi Gravesend Episcope Lincolniensis*, ed. F.N. Davis (Lincolnshire Record Soc. 20, 1925), 215.

[48] TNA, E 315/62, fol. 6v; *Acta of Hugh of Wells*, nos 410, 422; Major, '*Familia*', 225.

[49] *The Feet of Fines for Oxfordshire, 1195–1291*, ed. H.E. Salter (Oxfordshire Record Soc. 12, 1930), 155 no. 10. If Milton was indeed his prebend, then it was worth £25 annually in 1254, see *Valuation of Norwich*, ed. W.E. Lunt (Oxford, 1926), 279.

[50] *Roll of the Justices in Eyre, 1240*, ed. G.H. Fowler (Bedfordshire Historical Record Soc. 9, 1925), no. 163; *Rotuli Gravesend*, 167, 190, 215.

[51] *Calendar of Entries in the Papal Registers relating to Great Britain and Ireland: Papal Letters, 1198–1304*, ed. W.H. Bliss (HMSO, 1893), 216.

[52] *Rotuli Roberti Grosseteste*, 148, 155–6; Major, '*Familia*', 225. The installation had occurred by 17 June 1245.

canon's ecclesiastical portfolio was finalised when, two years later, he came into the possession of Eddlesborough in Bedfordshire.[53]

Having explored in some detail the archdeacon's career before the baronial seizure of control in 1258, we will now analyse the reasons behind his elevation as treasurer. Of these, perhaps the most important was John's membership of the close circle of friends centred on Grosseteste. This clique provided several individuals who were to play a leading role in the reformist movement.[54] Simon de Montfort, the earl of Leicester, was the highest profile member of this network. One of the seven confederate magnates whose confrontation with the king in Westminster Hall in April 1258 forced Henry to submit to their demands for reform, the earl would eventually assume the leadership of the baronial movement.[55] Mutual friends and interests connected the magnate and the archdeacon although how close the relationship was is now uncertain. Montfort certainly knew Crakehall, the latter having mediated in a dispute between the earl and his men in 1249.[56] The archdeacon had likewise been part of Grosseteste's household when Leicester's sons, Henry and Aumary, were under the bishop's tutelage.[57] That Montfort had championed Crakehall's promotion to treasurer is suggested by the positive action taken in the earl's favour immediately after the latter's advancement. For several years, Simon had been unsuccessfully pressing his claims for a landed settlement of his wife's dower entitlement. Promised in 1253 an annual payment of 600 marks until lands of a comparable value were granted to him, Montfort's fee quickly fell into arrears.[58] Hopes of a final settlement had been temporarily raised by the baronial council's agreement to examine his claims, but the pressure of business had relegated them down its list of priorities. There matters rested until Crakehall became treasurer. On 4 November, just two days into his term of office, a writ of *liberate* for 300 marks had been issued 'in part payment of the king's debts' to Simon.[59] Three weeks later, Montfort was promised a further payment of £200.[60] Such a close correlation between the archdeacon's promotion and the immediate progress made in accommodating Simon's personal interests is unlikely to have been a mere coincidence.

These personal connections were not restricted to Grosseteste's circle. We have already seen that he had some dealings with Roger Bigod, the earl of Norfolk. A member of the baronial council, he had previously acted as the confederates' spokesman in April 1258.[61] Crakehall's probable kinsman, Robert de Nevill, was the newly installed keeper of the castles of Bamborough and Newcastle-upon-Tyne.[62] Nor were his contacts exclusive to the reformist movement: the king was also personally acquainted with the archdeacon. In the aftermath of the dispute over the prebend of Thame, it was the future treasurer who, acting as Grosseteste's emissary,

---

[53] Dunstable, iii. 175, 216; *Lincolniensis Epistolae*, no. 26. The canon had been interested in this particular living for several years, having lost a suit concerning the church in 1236.
[54] Maddicott, *Montfort*, 171, 251–2. Richard Gravesend, the newly appointed bishop of Lincoln, accompanied Montfort to France in November 1258 while Robert, the brother of Adam Marsh, was one of the baronial negotiators at Kingston-upon-Thames in November 1261.
[55] Maddicott, *Montfort*, 153, 225.
[56] *Letters of Adam Marsh*, no. 21; Maddicott, *Montfort*, 171.
[57] *Letters of Adam Marsh*, no. 25; Maddicott, *Montfort*, 95.
[58] Maddicott, *Montfort*, 122, 170.
[59] *CLR 1251–60*, 437.
[60] *CLR 1251–60*, 441.
[61] Tewkesbury, 164; *CPR 1232–47*, 283; M. Morris, *The Bigod Earls of Norfolk in the Thirteenth Century* (Woodbridge, 2005), 57–8.
[62] *DBM*, 112–13, clause 24.

begged the king that he 'remove a force that John Mansel, king's clerk, had applied to keep the prebend'.[63] Evidently Crakehall's advocacy of the episcopal position did not adversely affect his reputation with the king as he later received several marks of royal favour. In May 1251, for example, he was granted four oaks from Bernwood Forest.[64] Having imposed their own nominee on the king, the barons may also have calculated that, in selecting a man who had previously enjoyed his good opinion, their usurpation of the royal prerogative would be rendered marginally more palatable to him.

While personal bonds were an important factor in the archdeacon's nomination as treasurer, there were other considerations. Having recently dismissed Philip Lovel, a man with a reputation for both harshness and corruption, the barons were looking for someone with integrity to succeed him.[65] Their reasoning was outlined in their submission to Louis IX at Amiens in January 1264. It was, they realised, crucial that 'someone of approved fidelity and industry should be appointed by the council to undertake the care of the treasure and to keep it faithfully for the use of the king'. Once appointed, the new treasurer would 'correct the wrongs hitherto inflicted in the exchequer by the barons of the exchequer and others'. Of all the senior officials, the choice was of particular importance because 'even greater danger threatens from the abuse of his office'.[66] Under these criteria, the semi-retired archdeacon of Bedford proved to be their ideal candidate. The professional standards and behavioural restrictions placed upon officeholders in both the Petition of the Barons and the Provisions of Oxford would have been familiar to someone who had successfully operated within the boundaries prescribed by Grosseteste's *Statuta*.[67]

Fifteen years direct management of the finances of England's largest diocese would likewise have provided him with many of the administrative skills necessary to serve as treasurer. Whenever the bishopric's manorial accounts were audited, Crakehall would have played a leading role although whether he actually served as chief auditor is unclear.[68] The responsibility for the collection within the diocese of scutage payments had, before 1242, rested with him.[69] All manorial income would have been collected under his supervision and subsequently delivered to his master.[70] Serving as steward, John would have had direct personal contact with the exchequer although explicit references to his attendance at its sessions are sadly lacking. Given the frequency with which episcopal business appears in its rolls, he was probably a regular attendee and, over time, he would have become familiar with many of its procedures. While Crakehall may not have been formally schooled in the venerable traditions of the exchequer, the skills he learnt as steward were nonetheless sufficiently comparable to make him a suitable candidate for treasurer.

This practical administrative experience was combined with a reputation for competence. One incident from 1251 can serve to illustrate just how highly regarded were his skills. After John's resignation from the stewardship, there had been a significant delay in the appointment of a successor. Accounts were left unaudited and officials, lacking close supervision, had indulged in widespread embezzlement.

63 *CPR 1232–47*, 257; Srawley, 'Administration', 163–4.
64 *CR 1247–51*, 356, 439. For other gifts, see *CR 1237–42*, 418; *CR 1242–7*, 205.
65 Maddicott, *Montfort*, 171.
66 *DBM*, 260–1.
67 *Walter of Henley*, 408–9; *DBM*, 82–3, 106–9, clause 16.
68 *Walter of Henley*, 394–9.
69 N. Denholm-Young, *Seignorial Administration in England* (Oxford, 1937), 69.
70 *Walter of Henley*, 390–1.

Alarmed at the detrimental effect this was having upon the bishop's finances, Adam Marsh warned that the prelate was 'suffering considerable damage at the hands of some persons who have no compunction in violating their fealty'.[71] Eventually Robert de Easthale was installed but the fiscal mayhem continued unabated. Indeed, his use of unrealistic measurements and prices for the goods received from the episcopal manors actually exacerbated the situation. Urgent remedial action was needed to prevent further losses. The man to whom Grosseteste turned in this moment of crisis was Crakehall who, in conjunction with his successor, conducted a lengthy but comprehensive computation of the diocesan finances.[72] Widely respected, then, it was the acerbic chronicler Matthew Paris who described him as 'a venerable man, and amongst those surrounding the bishop, not of the lowest authority'.[73]

All the professional skills and experience that had recommended the archdeacon to the baronial council would be called upon during his two years in office. Since the early 1240s, the average annual cash income of the crown had fallen drastically. From a peak of £31,500 per annum in 1244/5, this had fallen to just £17,000 by the mid-1250s.[74] This revenue was derived from a combination of regular and variable sources. Regular income mainly consisted of the issues arising from the county farm and miscellaneous payments such as judicial amercements and fines. The king also received money from several lucrative but irregular revenue streams. Ecclesiastical vacancies were one such source. During the interval between a senior cleric's death and the election of a successor, all the income from their diocese or religious house was collected by its appointed keeper and paid into the exchequer. It has been calculated that some £18,000 had been raised from such vacancies between 1240 and 1244.[75] Only five bishoprics were vacant in the three years prior to 1258, however, providing the crown with a combined total of just £3,034.[76] Equally variable were the revenues derived from the king's feudal rights. If a tenant-in-chief died leaving an heir underage, for example, the custody of his lands along with the said heir's wardship and marriage, passed to the crown.[77] Several leading magnates had died during the 1230s and 1240s, benefiting the crown to the tune of £1,550 annually. Yet in the late 1250s, just £140 per annum was being raised from this source.[78] This deficit could have been offset by the levying of a tallage on the Jews, but the crown's insatiable demands for cash during the 1240s had effectively bankrupted the community.[79]

If the king had responded prudently to this drop in his income, there would have been sufficient funds in the treasury to cover his ordinary expenses. But the policies that Henry pursued during the 1250s ensured that he was ultimately unable to meet his fiscal obligations. Overly generous in his patronage of his Savoyard relatives and alien favourites, he often promised cash payments until lands of an

---

[71] *Letters of Adam Marsh*, no. 22.
[72] *Letters of Adam Marsh*, no. 27.
[73] *CM*, v. 407–8.
[74] R.C. Stacey, *Politics, Policy and Finance under Henry III, 1216–1245* (Oxford, 1987), 208–10; J.A. Collingwood, 'Royal Finance in the Period of Baronial Reform and Rebellion, 1255–1270' (unpublished PhD thesis, University of London, 1995), 24, 30.
[75] Stacey, *Politics*, 222.
[76] Collingwood, 'Royal Finance', 36.
[77] S. Waugh, *The Lordship of England: Royal Wardships and Marriages in English Society and Politics, 1217–1327* (Princeton, 1988), 8–9.
[78] Collingwood, 'Royal Finance', 39.
[79] R.C. Stacey, '1240–60: A Watershed in Anglo-Jewish Relations?', *HR* 61 (1988), 135–50; Collingwood, 'Royal Finance', 50–2; Maddicott, *Montfort*, 125–6.

equivalent value became available.[80] These fees were sustainable as long as there were enough lands, wardships and marriages falling into the crown's hands.[81] But the arrival at court in 1247 of Henry's uterine brothers, the Lusignans, had led to a new assortment of fees being awarded.[82] Even as these gifts were being bestowed, however, the windfall feudal revenues that subsidised them were drying up. Henry therefore had no alternative but to fund them from his own coffers. This profligacy was further exacerbated by the need to provide a suitable territorial endowment for the Lord Edward. Diverting valuable resources, its creation had left Henry 'a muti-lated kinglet'.[83] Meanwhile the crown's dwindling cash reserves were being raided to fund the king's unsuccessful attempt to place his younger son Edmund on the Sicilian throne. Henry had contracted to pay the pope a total of 135,541 marks.[84] The associated grant of a clerical tenth was intended to help defray the cost but it fell substantially short of what was needed.[85] Efforts at obtaining a parliamentary grant to cover the consequent shortfall were to prove futile as Henry refused to countenance the terms under which one was offered.[86] It was the treasury that was therefore left to pick up the bill. Such was the degree of indebtedness that when the Welsh under Llewylyn had invaded the Marches in 1257, the crown found itself incapable of bankrolling the counter-offensive.[87]

Stabilising the royal finances was thus the highest priority for the baronial regime and its newly appointed treasurer. Action was taken immediately to find a solution to the papacy's fiscal demands over Sicily. Envoys were sent to Rome to negotiate for less onerous terms while at home the council promised to support the granting of a 'common aid' from 'the community of the realm'.[88] Of equal import was the introduction of a systematic programme designed at reducing the crown's overall indebtedness. Its enforcement can be clearly seen in the treatment of the revenues arising from the crown's feudal rights such as marriages and wardships. Used mainly by Henry as a form of patronage, the potential income from these windfalls had been effectively squandered. The reformers, in contrast, usually sold these resources for a profit. Allowing them to extract the maximum gain, some of the proceeds were subsequently 'set aside' so as 'to reduce the king's debts'.[89] This policy was not always strictly enforced; it appears, for example, that none of the proceeds from a 1,200 mark fine made by William Latimer's were diverted to the settlement of old debts.[90] Crakehall was closely associated with this aggressive

---

[80] *DBM*, 276–7; M. Howell, *Eleanor of Provence: Queenship in Thirteenth-Century England* (Oxford, 1998), 30–1, 49–54.

[81] Collingwood, 'Royal Finance', 74–80.

[82] H.W. Ridgeway, 'Foreign Favourites and Henry III's Problem of Patronage, 1247–58', *EHR* 104 (1989), 590–610.

[83] *CM*, v. 450.

[84] F.M. Powicke, *King Henry III and the Lord Edward*, 2 vols (Oxford, 1947), i. 371; W.E. Lunt, *Financial Relations of the Papacy with England to 1327* (Cambridge, Mass., 1939), 266.

[85] B. Weiler, *Henry III of England and the Staufen Empire, 1216–1272* (Woodbridge, 2006), 149; Powicke, *King Henry III*, i. 371; Lunt, *Financial Relations*, 263–90.

[86] *CM*, v. 494, 623–4; Collingwood, 'Royal Finance', 49–50.

[87] D.A. Carpenter, 'The Gold Treasure of Henry III', in his *The Reign of Henry III* (London, 1996), 108, 123–5; Collingwood, 'Royal Finance', 65–6. Henry was forced to raid the store of gold treasure that he had accumulated since 1254.

[88] *DBM*, 104–5. The pope realised that Henry would not be able to fulfil his contract and the papal offer was subsequently withdrawn.

[89] *DBM*, 220–1.

[90] TNA, E 371/24, m. 1; *CPR 1258–66*, 60.

exploitation of the king's feudal rights as the responsibility for the sale of these resources rested with him and certain other named individuals.[91]

New rules governing the appointment and conduct of the county sheriff had been instituted by the Provisions of Oxford. Service was restricted to a year at a time while the incumbent had to hold land in the shire.[92] Nineteen new sheriffs were appointed during the autumn of 1258. Exactly how they were chosen is unclear but their selection would have been confirmed at the exchequer in the treasurer's presence.[93] In 1259, however, the method adopted for the selection of future sheriffs was enunciated in the Provisions of Westminster. The decision over who would serve as sheriff for the present year rested with the treasurer and his fellow barons of the exchequer. It was also provided that next year they would choose one of the four knights that were sent to the exchequer from each shire.[94] Crakehall similarly presided over the revision of the terms under which the sheriffs held their counties. Originally instituted in 1194, cash increments had been regularly imposed on the sheriffs.[95] Payable annually over and above the county farm, these were designed to extract any surplus profits that had been produced by the crown's traditional sources of revenue. These sums had risen steeply after 1250, however, leaving many sheriffs unable to meet their fiscal obligations without resorting to extortion. Thus, in 1258, the conditions under which they held their counties were changed. Instead of fixed increments, the sheriffs would answer at the exchequer for all the variable profits above the farm.[96] This policy was short-lived, the marked fall in receipts leading to the increments reappearing after just one year.[97] Enshrined in the Provisions of Oxford was the proposal that sheriffs would also receive a salary allowance. Compensating the incumbent for their official expenses, this remuneration was designed to prevent them 'taking anything from someone else'.[98] Evidently there was some confusion surrounding their introduction, since some sheriffs received an allowance while others did not.[99]

In the late 1250s, it has been argued, the exchequer was working at 'less than full effectiveness'.[100] Local officials were failing to fully discharge their debts upon leaving office. Owing substantial arrears, many had been allowed instead to make only minimal annual payments towards their outstanding balance.[101] Even when the exchequer had commanded a person's distraint for the arrears, the order was often repeated as the official was either unwilling or unable to enforce it.[102] The demand that all sheriffs should make their proffers in person at the twice yearly *adventi vicecomitum* was likewise ignored with only a minority putting in an appearance in any given year.[103] Considerable effort was therefore expended by Crakehall in the improvement of the exchequer's efficiency and the restoration of its authority.

---

[91] *DBM*, 152–3, clause 14.
[92] *DBM*, 108–9, clause 17.
[93] Treharne, *Baronial Plan*, 98, 121–4, 205–7; TNA, E 368/34, m. 3d.
[94] *DBM*, 154–5, clause 22.
[95] D.A. Carpenter, 'The Decline of the Curial Sheriff in England, 1194–1258', in his *Reign of Henry III*, 156–7.
[96] Treharne, *Baronial Plan*, 122–4.
[97] Collingwood, 'Royal Finance', 111.
[98] *DBM*, 108–9, 122–3, clause 17.
[99] Collingwood, 'Royal Finance', 129–36.
[100] Collingwood, 'Royal Finance', 92.
[101] *DBM*, 276–7.
[102] TNA, E 159/29, m. 1. Matthew son of Herbert's heirs, for example, were distrained to answer for the outstanding increment from 1227.
[103] *CM*, v. 588–9; TNA, E 159/29, mm. 30, 31; E 368/32, m. 32.

Shrieval issues were more vigorously collected: in 1258, for instance, twenty-four former sheriffs were recorded making repayments towards their arrears.[104]

Liberate writs were paid more promptly while a systematic investigation into unacquitted debts led to the formal quittance of sums already paid but not yet cleared in the audit process.[105] At the *adventi vicecomitum*, there was a small increase in the amount of money proffered between 1259 and 1261.[106] Shrieval attendance at the exchequer had likewise improved. At Michaelmas 1258, eighteen sheriffs had made an appearance at the lower exchequer but a year later this figure had increased to twenty-four. This compared favourably with the attendance rates during the two previous years, with twenty-two and eighteen respectively.[107] But the rate of recovery remained slow. The exchequer did not always insist upon the closing of the baronial sheriffs' accounts shortly after the end of their term in office. Some, such as Godfrey de Scudamore, did not clear their account until 1269, a full ten years after he stood down.[108] Guided by Crakehall, the baronial exchequer did make some progress in terms of efficiency although there was still significant scope for further improvement.

There was to be a systematic reform of the operations of the royal mints or exchanges in London and elsewhere. Often the subject of complaint, their management had been shrouded in allegations of corruption. Moreover, there had been sizeable variations in the level of exchange between the old and new currencies following the recent recoinage.[109] Corrective action, it was decided, would take the form of an enquiry that was to be undertaken by a high powered commission that included the bishop of Worcester.[110] Whether the treasurer himself was a nominated member is unclear but it is certain that he worked closely with the committee. William of Gloucester and Henry de Frowick, the keepers of the London mint, were commanded to appear before Crakehall and his fellow barons at the exchequer on 25 November 1258, where they were to answer for the coinage from their exchange.[111] Shortly afterwards, they were ordered to provide sufficient security for their 'good and faithful service' in operating the mint.[112] On 16 December, the custodians of the London mint were commanded to answer for their profits at the exchequer.[113] An award was later issued on some 'highly technical matters', but success still eluded the commissioners as further allegations of 'errors and defects' were to surface in 1261.[114]

Under the archdeacon's supervision, subtle changes in both format and layout were introduced into some of the records produced by the exchequer. This can be seen most clearly in the rolls of account for the county profits that were submitted by the sheriffs to the exchequer as part of the audit process. Fourteen such rolls have survived from the first year of Crakehall's treasurership. Of these, four follow a relatively simple format that consists mainly of long lists of receipts.[115] Sometimes the

---

[104] Collingwood, 'Royal Finance', 123. This compared to just nine at Michaelmas 1256.
[105] Collingwood, 'Royal Finance', 164–6; Treharne, *Baronial Plan*, 370–2.
[106] Collingwood, 'Royal Finance', 125–6, 168.
[107] M. Mills, '*Adventus Vicecomitum, 1258–72*', *EHR* 36 (1921), 492.
[108] TNA, E 372/114, m. 8.
[109] *DBM*, 96–7, 110–11; Treharne, *Baronial Plan*, 97.
[110] TNA, E 159/34, mm. 12–12d.
[111] TNA, E 159/32, m. 5; E 368/34, m. 3d.
[112] TNA, E 159/32, m. 5d; E 368/34, m. 4d.
[113] TNA, E 368/34, m. 4d
[114] Treharne, *Baronial Plan*, 97; *CPR 1258–66*, 77; TNA, E 159/34, mm. 12–12d.
[115] TNA, E 389/85; E 389/105; E 389/136; E 389/145.

clerk arranged the entries by wapentake or hundred while occasional subtotals were calculated at the end of each membrane. The remaining ten rolls were technically much further advanced.[116] Each session of the county and hundred courts formed a single dated section, within which the entries were arranged by vill and then by individual. Other profits including hidage and wardpenny were similarly segregated while subtotals were provided at the end of each subdivision. These stylistically advanced rolls employ formats similar to those found in the early 1240s, the last time that sheriffs had accounted as custodians, suggesting that the format had been imposed centrally.[117] The reasoning behind the simultaneous use of both formats is uncertain but it is likely to have been an administrative experiment, the trial enabling the exchequer to ascertain the exact level of detail required to effectively audit the shrieval profits.

Minor innovations were also made to the memoranda rolls produced by the lord treasurer's remembrancer. These improvements, found in the roll for Crakehall's first year in office, were probably designed to facilitate their ease of use. Each membrane in its *communia* section was numbered: this had not been the case in earlier rolls.[118] When the exchequer clerk drew up the year's *compoti*, he adopted a separate numbering sequence.[119] There was also a return to the practice of recording respites within the *communia*, a reversal of the previous year's experiment when these were enrolled on a separate membrane.[120] Under the treasurer's guidance, the exchequer's disbursement of money was now more closely monitored. From the first day of John's appointment, the clerks compiling the issue rolls began systematically recording the name of the individual into whose hands the money was actually being paid.[121]

The archdeacon's influence was probably behind a significant development in the receipt rolls. Mirroring earlier practice, two duplicate rolls had been started for the year beginning Michaelmas 1258. One of these rolls records the daily receipts for the whole term.[122] The other roll was never completed: the text ends abruptly midway down the final membrane. It is surely no coincidence that the last entry is 'die Sabbati', the Saturday in question being the day of Crakehall's appointment.[123] Exactly why this duplicate roll was discontinued is unclear; perhaps the treasurer was sending an unambiguous signal to the exchequer's personnel that the new reformist administration was now in control and intended to implement its own agenda. Equally, its termination may have been a calculated demonstration that the ultimate responsibility for the king's revenues rested with him. This policy of modest innovation did not extend to all exchequer records: there are no identifiable changes in the pipe rolls. Just how far this experimentation extended, however, is a question that can only be answered by further archival research.

John of Crakehall's term in office was markedly different in style to that of his predecessor. Whereas Philip Lovel had pursued a high profile career at court, the baronial treasurer adopted a more businesslike but much lower key role. This shift in approach was reflected in the number of royal charters they had respectively

---

[116]   TNA, E 389/46; E 389/68; E 389/79–80; E 389/88–90; E 389/123; E 389/128; E 389/146.
[117]   TNA, E 389/45. The Berkshire roll for 22/23 Henry III for example.
[118]   TNA, E 368/34, passim.
[119]   TNA, E 368/34, m. 18.
[120]   TNA, E 368/33, m. 30; E 368/34, m. 2d.
[121]   TNA, E 403/17B, m. 1.
[122]   TNA, E 401/39, m. 5. Crakehall's appointment was recorded in an annotation written on the following Monday.
[123]   TNA, E 401/38, m. 5.

witnessed while in post. Lovel, for example, featured in a total of sixty-one separate witness lists between 28 October 1256 and 27 October 1257. In the following year, he witnessed a further thirty-four.[124] This was in distinct contrast to the archdeacon of Bedford, who witnessed just eight royal charters during his first year as treasurer.[125] An analysis of the venues where these grants were issued likewise provides evidence of the careful attention he paid to the day-to-day responsibilities of the role. Unlike Lovel, every charter was, with just one exception, witnessed at Westminster.[126] This change in tone between the two regimes was echoed in the rewards that they both received whilst in office. Nineteen separate gifts were given to Lovel between 1253 and 1258 while just two were bestowed upon his successor.[127] An annual stipend of a hundred marks was also granted to Crakehall. It was disbursed in two instalments, namely fifty marks at Easter with the remainder being paid at Michaelmas.[128] This salary was intended to cover his official expenses.

After almost two years continuous service as treasurer, Crakehall died on Friday 10 September 1260 in London.[129] Undertaking official duties almost to the end, his last recorded appearance was in a letter close dated 18 August 1260.[130] Under the terms of the archdeacon's will, his body was interred at Waltham Abbey.[131] It was reported that he 'had left after him £18,000 intact'.[132] This immense financial legacy was probably an allusion, however, to the perceived state of the crown's finances at the time of his death.

In selecting as treasurer a former professional administrator with fifteen years direct experience of estate management, the baronial council had publicly signalled their intention to institute a root and branch reform of the exchequer. Free from the fossilised conventions of exchequer procedure, their appointee was a man of proven 'fidelity and industry'.[133] Charged with the replenishment of a depleted treasury, Crakehall was also entrusted with the correction of any injustice committed by the barons of the exchequer.[134] Adopting a more businesslike approach than his royalist predecessor, the archdeacon had embraced the obligations of his office with alacrity although his efforts at reformation only met with mixed results. Shrieval issues had been more vigorously collected while several sheriffs had made substantial payments against their arrears. In marked contrast, the flagship fiscal policy of accounting for all the county's variable profits at the exchequer had quickly foundered as receipts plummeted. Even with this setback, Crakehall nevertheless presided over a modest rise in the crown's revenues: £15,000 had been collected in 1259 compared to £13,000 in 1257.[135] Royal revenues therefore remained substantially

[124] *WL, Henry III*, ii., 101–21 passim.

[125] *WL, Henry III*, ii., 123–5 passim.

[126] *WL, Henry III*, ii. 109, 107, 113, 123–5; *CChR 1257–1300*, 22. The exception was the charter granted at Windsor on 6 August 1259 to the burgesses and merchants of Ghent. Amongst the various locations where Lovel appeared as witness were Woodstock, Chester and Merton.

[127] *CPR 1247–58*, 149, 263, 373, 406; *CR 1251–3*, 318, 326, 333, 367; *CR 1253–4*, 36, 84, 253; *CR 1254–6*, 87, 89, 261–2, 322, 354; *CR 1256–9*, 69, 163, 175, 193, 251, 388, 424. In May 1259, Crakehall received one tun of wine while he later was granted three deer from the forests of Essex.

[128] *CLR 1251–60*, 475; TNA, E 403/3115, m. 2; E 403/18, m. 1.

[129] *Flores*, ii. 455.

[130] *CR 1259–61*, 198–9.

[131] *Flores*, ii. 455; TNA, E 368/36, m. 13d.

[132] *Flores*, ii. 455.

[133] *DBM*, 260–1.

[134] *DBM*, 106–7, 260–1.

[135] N. Barratt, 'Finance on a Shoestring: The Exchequer in the Thirteenth Century', in *English Government in the Thirteenth Century*, ed. A. Jobson (Woodbridge, 2004), 75.

below the levels of a decade before. Some of this muted success was the result of the dismissal from office in November 1258 of several unnamed exchequer officials although the overall scale of the challenge facing him meant that it would take time to restore the institution to full efficiency.[136] The treasurer's conciliar masters tacitly acknowledged the difficulties the archdeacon faced when, in 1259, they ignored the limitations on tenure imposed in the Provisions of Oxford and allowed him to serve for a further year.[137] After his two years in office, slow but solid progress had been made in reforming the exchequer. Yet all this good work was negated by the baronial leadership's failure to address the two fundamental problems affecting state finance.

The crown remained dangerously reliant on the regular but dwindling revenues generated by the county farm. No attempt was made to identify a new and lucrative source of cash that would enable the royal coffers to be fully replenished. Without a more realistic income, the king faced the growing prospect of being locked into a vicious cycle of debt. This problem was only resolved in 1275 when his son secured a parliamentary grant of a tax on wool exports.[138] Nor did the barons use the opportunity provided by their seizure of power in 1258 to undertake a radical overhaul of the crown's financial administration. Ever since Henry's military expedition to Gascony in 1242, the royal wardrobe had gradually usurped the exchequer to become the king's 'preferred instrument of receipt and expenditure'.[139] Instead of being channelled through the lower exchequer, an increasing proportion of revenue was now being paid directly into the wardrobe.[140] The reformers opposed this development, declaring in the Provisions of Oxford that 'all revenues of the land shall come there', i.e. the exchequer.[141] Yet in direct contravention of this assertion, substantial sums continued to bypass the exchequer of receipt.[142] The exchequer consequently found it ever more difficult to perform efficiently its core functions of collection and audit. This created a potential risk that its 'traditional structure of business' would unravel which, in turn, could lead to a catastrophic collapse in the institution's authority.[143] Under a competent treasurer like Crakehall, there was little likelihood of such a situation materialising. Yet within three years of his death, the threat had become a reality as the internal administration of the exchequer ceased to function. Record keeping became chaotic as debts were left un-audited while payments at the lower exchequer had fallen dramatically.[144] The outbreak of civil war in 1264 occasioned further disruption and it was not until February 1270 that a thorough overhaul of the institution was begun. That this collapse had not occurred during his term in office is perhaps the greatest testament to John of Crakehall's effectiveness as the reformers' treasurer of choice.

[136] *CM*, v. 719–20. Thomas of Wyndmonham, for example, was appointed chancellor of the exchequer.
[137] *DBM*, 106–7; Treharne, *Baronial Plan*, 94; Jacob, *Studies in the Period of Baronial Reform*, 373.
[138] N. Barratt, 'Counting the Cost: The Financial Implications of the Loss of Normandy', in *TCE* x. 35;
M. Morris, *A Great and Terrible King: Edward I and the Forging of Britain* (London, 2008), 123–4.
[139] Barratt, 'Counting the Cost', 34.
[140] Barratt, 'Shoestring', 74.
[141] *DBM*, 106–7.
[142] Barratt, 'Shoestring', 75. The wardrobe received some £20,000 between 1258 and 1261, some of which included shrieval payments made in defiance of the provision.
[143] Barratt, 'Shoestring', 76.
[144] Mills, '*Adventus Vicecomitum*', 494; Barratt, 'Counting the Cost', 34.

Appendix 1. Conan son of Ellis

Landric
(fl. 1086)

Ruald the Constable

Tiffany   m   Ellis
(d. c. 1165)

Alan son of Landric
(d. before 1130)

Wigan son of Landric
(fl. 1145)

Beatrice

Parnell

Constance

Conan son of Ellis
(d.s.p.leg. c. 1218)

m(1) Emecina d'Oyry   m(2) Sybil   m(3) Ada   m(4) Avice de Neville

Geoffrey de Neville
(d.c. 1193)

Isabel de Neville
(d. 1254)

Nevilles of Raby

Appendix 2. The co-heiresses of Conan son of Ellis

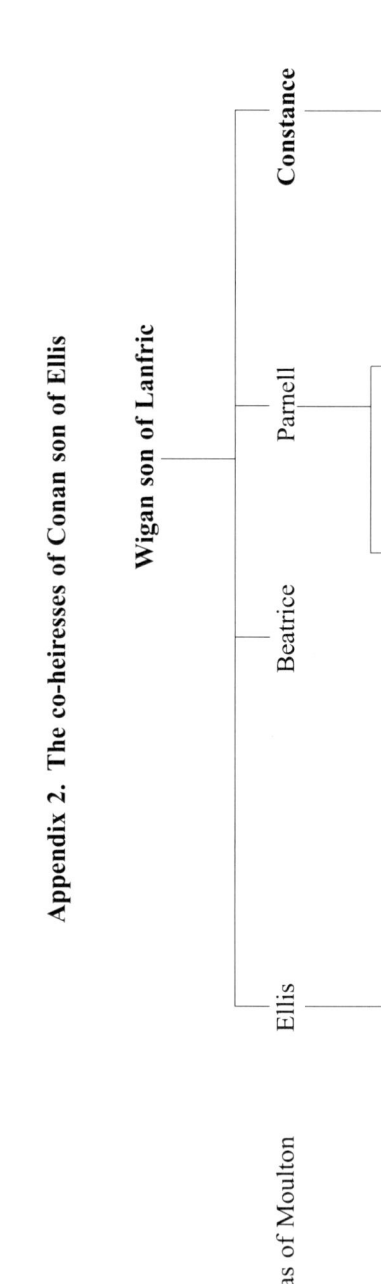

Appendix 3. John of Crakehall's descendants

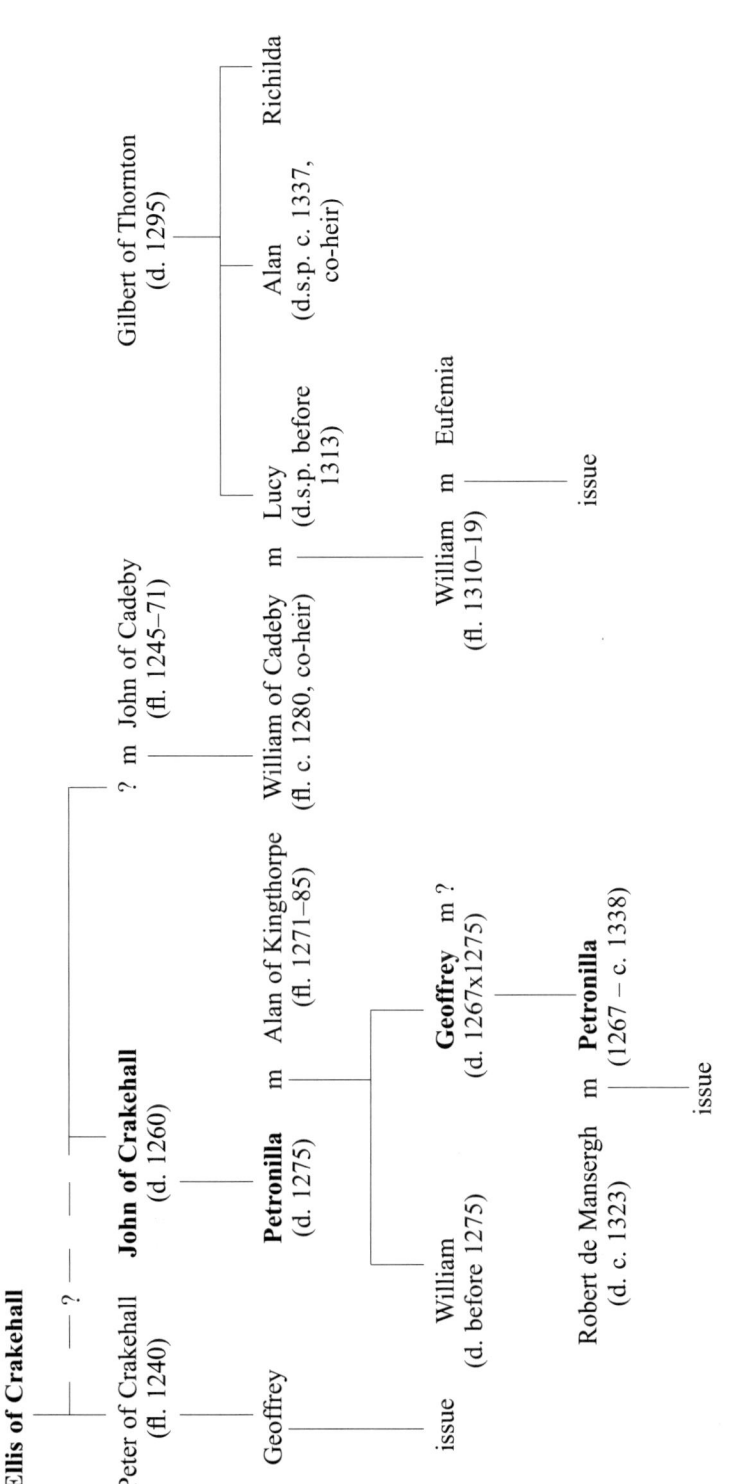

Credit Finance in Thirteenth-Century England:
The Ricciardi of Lucca and Edward I,
1272–94[1]

Adrian R. Bell, Chris Brooks and Tony K. Moore

The thirteenth century has been associated with a 'commercial revolution' and the beginnings of a money economy.[2] An important part of this was the increasing involvement of Italian merchant societies in trade and credit provision in Northern Europe and England.[3] The Lucchese were among the first Italians to break into the markets of Northern Europe, via the fairs of Champagne and then to London.[4] Lucca was famed for its silk industry and from the mid-1240s Lucchese merchants appear in the English sources as suppliers of silks and other fine cloths to the royal household, including members of the *societas Riccardorum*.[5] The frequent delays in securing repayment for these goods from Henry III's impecunious government effectively turned the Lucchese into royal creditors, but it was during the Lord Edward's crusade that the Ricciardi society began to play a more active role in royal finance. The Ricciardi advanced £6,000 to Edward during the crusade and later acted as intermediaries in repaying some of the other debts incurred by the king.[6] After his accession to the throne, Edward continued to employ the Ricciardi as his financial agents and, indeed, he incorporated them into the royal financial system. The relationship between Edward and the Ricciardi collapsed in 1294, but both Edward I and his son and grandson later developed ties to other Italian merchant societies, namely the Frescobaldi of Florence (c. 1299–1311) and the Bardi and Peruzzi (up to c. 1341), also of Florence.[7]

The essence of the 'Ricciardi system' was relatively simple.[8] The Ricciardi advanced sums in cash to the king or made payments to third parties at the king's

[1] This article is an output from the ESRC-funded research project 'Credit Finance in the Middle Ages: loans to the English crown, 1272–1340' (RES-062–23–0733). We are grateful to André Mansi for his assistance in creating figure 2.

[2] The classic statement of this thesis can be found in R.S. Lopez, *The Commercial Revolution of the Middle Ages, 950–1350* (Cambridge, 1976).

[3] A good introduction to the operations of the merchant societies can be found in J.B. Baskin and P.J. Miranti, *A History of Corporate Finance* (Cambridge, 1997), 29–54.

[4] T.W. Blomquist, 'The Early History of European Banking: Merchants, Bankers and Lombards of Thirteenth-Century Lucca in the County of Champagne', *Journal of European Economic History* 14 (1985), 523–30.

[5] For the origins of the Ricciardi society and their first appearance in England, see idem, 'Lineage, Land and Business in the Thirteenth Century: The Guidiccioni Family of Lucca (part 1)', *Actum Luce* 9 (1980), 9–19.

[6] TNA E 372/117, r. 6 m. 1d; *Accounts of the English Crown with Italian Merchant Societies, 1272–1345*, ed. A.R. Bell, C. Brooks and T.K. Moore (List and Index Society 331, 2009), 2–3.

[7] R.W. Kaeuper, *Bankers to the Crown: The Ricciardi of Lucca and Edward I* (Princeton, 1973); idem, 'The Frescobaldi and the English Crown', *Studies in Medieval and Renaissance History* 10 (1973), 42–95; E.S. Hunt, 'A New Look at the Dealings of the Bardi and Peruzzi with Edward III', *Journal of Economic History* 50 (1990), 149–62.

[8] The workings of this system are elucidated in Kaeuper, *Bankers to the Crown*, 80–131.

command. Most of these advances and payments were arranged through the wardrobe, the chief financial department under Edward I. In return, the Ricciardi collected the customs duty on exports of wool, hides and wool-fells imposed from June 1275, and, when necessary, this was supplemented from other sources of royal revenue, such as the proceeds of taxation and payments from the treasury. In general, the Ricciardi would have funded most of the payments that they made to the king or on his behalf either from the income that they had already received from the customs and other royal revenues, or else from their own resources, which they would charge against later receipts. The usual description of this arrangement is that the Riccardi's loans were secured against the granting of the customs revenue.[9] This alone would have been an innovative financial technique, with undetermined loans backed by long-term grants of customs duties. However, a better analogy would be with a modern current account, complete with extensive overdraft facilities. The relationship between the king and the Ricciardi was monitored by periodic accounts that, in effect, serve as royal bank statements. A summary of these accounts is shown on Table 1.

Table 1. Edward I's bank statement

Year[a]	Debits	Credits	Nominal balance[b]	Papal deposits[c]
1272–6	£54,540	£41,206	-£13,333	c. £5,000
1272–9	£201,478	£178,478	-£23,000	c. £10,000
1286–9	£107,485	—	—	—
c. 1290	—	—	-£54,180	c. £10,000
1290–4	£45,066	£80,321	-£18,925	c. £66,667

a *Accounts of the English Crown*, ed. Bell et al., 4–5, 14–15, 42–3, 48–51. The figures for 1289 and 1290 are not full accounts, but the first refers to the total amount advanced by the Ricciardi to the wardrobe between 1286 and 1289 and the second to the balance carried over to the account of 1294 from the preceding account, held c. 1290 but which has been lost.

b This is the outstanding balance at the end of the account and may have concealed an element of interest.

c W.E. Lunt, *Financial Relations of the Papacy with England to 1327* (Cambridge, Mass., 1939), 643–47. The significance of the papal taxation deposited with the merchants is discussed below, 111–13.

The following discussion will first provide an overview of the transactions between Edward I and the Ricciardi, including a reconstruction of the chronology of that relationship. Second, it will also try to assess the balance of the king's account with the Ricciardi, in other words, the state of the royal overdraft. The ideal method would be to compile a complete list of the value and date of all Ricciardi advances and receipts in order to calculate a running balance for Edward's account. Unfortunately, the gaps in the surviving source material, and the nature of those sources, means that such a detailed analysis is impossible. Instead, the methodology developed uses a combination of the figures given in the general Ricciardi accounts and the accounts of the keeper of the royal wardrobe, and the individual orders for payments recorded in the Chancery and Exchequer sources, especially the patent

9   M. Prestwich, *Edward I* (London, 1988), 99–100.

rolls and the liberate and issue rolls.[10] These are supplemented by some of the surviving wardrobe books and rolls, particularly for the king's sojourn in Gascony between 1286 and 1289.[11] This is similar to the approach adopted by Kaeuper in his study of the Ricciardi, but with one important modification. Kaeuper's figures for Ricciardi funding to the wardrobe were based on the sums that the keeper of the wardrobe recognised that he had received either from the Ricciardi *de mutuo* or from a specific individual or source of royal revenue *per manus mercatorum de Luka*.[12] These terms raise some questions of interpretation. The latter most likely refers to Ricciardi advances that had been repaid from an assigned source of royal revenue by the time that the wardrobe account was taken. The remaining uncleared Ricciardi advances were then described as *de mutuo*. Most of these *de mutuo* advances were subsequently allowed against the Ricciardi's next account for the wool custom.[13]

There was, however, an additional stream of Ricciardi funding, of which Kaeuper did not take account. The issue rolls of the Exchequer reveal that some of the sums described in the (heavily abbreviated) wardrobe accounts as having been received from the royal treasury by the hand of the treasurer and chamberlains were in fact paid to the Ricciardi on behalf of the wardrobe.[14] This can best be demonstrated from the arrangements for the funding of the king's extended stay in Gascony between 1286 and 1289. In total, block writs of *liberate* worth £77,000 were issued in favour of the keeper of the wardrobe, William of Louth, and the memoranda of issue rolls reveal that the Ricciardi received a substantial proportion of this sum.[15] For example, in Michaelmas term 1286–7, at least £4,364 was paid or assigned to the Ricciardi on a block writ of liberate for £10,000, issued on 26 April 1286.[16] The Ricciardi were also paid or assigned at least £8,755 on a writ of liberate for £12,000 during Michaelmas 1287–8 and Easter 1288 and, in the latter term, a further £5,472 out of a total of £7,775 charged on a second writ for £10,000.[17] In all, the Ricciardi received over £20,000 from the treasury during this period and this is certainly an under-estimate, since there are gaps in the sequence of memoranda of issue rolls and some of the surviving rolls are badly damaged. These Ricciardi receipts from the treasury must have functioned in the same way as the *per manus* entries discussed above. In short, the total Ricciardi payments into or on the orders of the wardrobe

---

[10]   The accounts submitted by the Ricciardi, with some ancillary documents, are edited in *Accounts of the English Crown*, ed. Bell et al., 2–52. The wardrobe accounts are enrolled in the Pipe and Chancellor's Rolls (TNA E 372 and E 352). The patent rolls are available in a calendared edition, but the liberate and issue rolls for Edward I's reign have not been edited and were consulted in the original (TNA C 62 and E 403).

[11]   *Records of the Wardrobe and Household 1285–1286*, ed. B.F. Byerly and C.R. Byerly (London, 1977) and *Records of the Wardrobe and Household 1286–1289*, ed. B.F. Byerly and C.R. Byerly (London, 1986).

[12]   Kaeuper, *Bankers to the Crown*, 125–7.

[13]   When the wardrobe account was compiled after the customs account was submitted, some Ricciardi advances, which would earlier have been entered as *de mutuo*, are now given as a *per manus* entry from the wool custom. For example, the wardrobe account for 1288–90 post-dated the Ricciardi account for the customs 1286–90, and the Ricciardi surplus of £22,812 19s 11½d on the latter account was entered as a *per manus* receipt in the former (*Accounts of the English Crown*, ed. Bell et al., 42–3; TNA E 372/138, r. 26 m. 2).

[14]   In fact, the roll of receipts for the fourteenth regnal year specifically states that these sums from the treasury were received 'on various occasions by the hand of divers people, both the clerks [of the wardrobe] and the merchants of Lucca' (*Records of the Wardrobe and Household, 1285–1286*, ed. Byerly and Byerly, 192).

[15]   TNA C 62/61, m. 2; /62, m. 2.

[16]   TNA E 403/51.

[17]   TNA E 403/55, /57.

in any one year can be calculated by adding up the receipts *de mutuo, per manus* and, where known, the proportion of treasury receipts delivered to the Ricciardi.

This new source for Ricciardi loans to the wardrobe suggests that Kaeuper's minimum figure of £408,972 for their total lending to Edward I should be revised upwards.[18] Based on the general and wardrobe accounts, it seems that the Lucchese advanced over £500,000 to Edward I between 1272 and 1294, although this may include an element of interest.[19] This represents an annual average of around £23,000, over half of the average wardrobe receipt each year.[20] The Ricciardi were clearly an integral part of the royal financial system. Moreover, these advances were not distributed evenly throughout the reign. Figure 1 uses the annual or bi-annual wardrobe accounts, including adjusted values based on the general accounts where these differ markedly from the wardrobe figures, to chart the changing pattern of Ricciardi lending over the course of the reign. The chronology of Ricciardi advances exhibits a jagged saw-tooth pattern, with periods of heavy borrowing followed by periods of retrenchment. For instance, the Ricciardi provided over £40,000 to the wardrobe during the sixth and seventh regnal years, much of which would have funded the first Welsh war in 1277.[21] The Ricciardi were even more heavily involved in funding the second Welsh war of 1282–3, advancing nearly £100,000 in the tenth, eleventh and twelfth years (1282–84).[22] No sooner had these advances been repaid than Edward again had to turn to the Lucchese to finance his prolonged stay in Gascony between May 1286 and August 1289.[23] The royal household in France was cut off from ordinary royal revenues in England and instead relied on the Ricciardi to pay the king's bills. In a letter obligatory of August 1289, Louth acknowledged receipts of £107,485 from the Ricciardi during the preceding three years.[24] These three periods account for nearly half of all the Ricciardi advances to Edward I. (See Figure 1.)

The important point to make about these figures is that the majority of the Ricciardi advances seem to have been rapidly cleared against specific sources of royal revenue (the *per manus* entries in the wardrobe account and payments from the treasury). Indeed, only £150,000 of the total Ricciardi advances were described as *de mutuo* in the wardrobe accounts, i.e. as un-cleared at the time of the account, and these were mostly covered by the customs income. For example, the £23,000 promised to the Ricciardi in November 1279 was cleared against the income

---

[18] Kaeuper, *Bankers to the Crown*, 128–31.

[19] This has been calculated from the expenditure stated by the Ricciardi in their general accounts covering 1272–79 and 1290–94, combined with Ricciardi advances during the second Welsh war, as reconstructed below, and the Ricciardi advances to the wardrobe in Gascony 1286–9, as acknowledged by Louth in 1289. The gaps have been supplied from the wardrobe accounts for 1279–81, 1284–6 and 1289–90, supplemented by known Ricciardi payments recorded elsewhere.

[20] The average annual wardrobe receipt, calculated from the same wardrobe accounts as above and including the special accounts for the Welsh wars, was £41,789.

[21] TNA E 352/72, r. 16 m. 2; E 372/123, r. 23 m. 1.

[22] This figure is based on the wardrobe accounts for the tenth and eleventh years, as well as the special accounts for the war of 1282–3, and some additional payments that seem to have been made outside the wardrobe. It thus includes some advances omitted by Kaeuper in his reconstruction. For the importance of the Ricciardi to Edward's success, see R.W. Kaeuper, 'The Role of Italian Financiers in the Edwardian Conquest of Wales', *WHR* 6 (1973), 387–403.

[23] For Edward's diplomatic efforts, see M. Morris, *A Great and Terrible King: Edward I and the Forging of Britain* (London, 2007), 196–221.

[24] *Accounts of the English Crown*, ed. Bell et al., 42–3. This was calculated using the standard exchange rate of £1 sterling to 4 *livres tournois*, although the account itself states that exchange was made at varying rates.

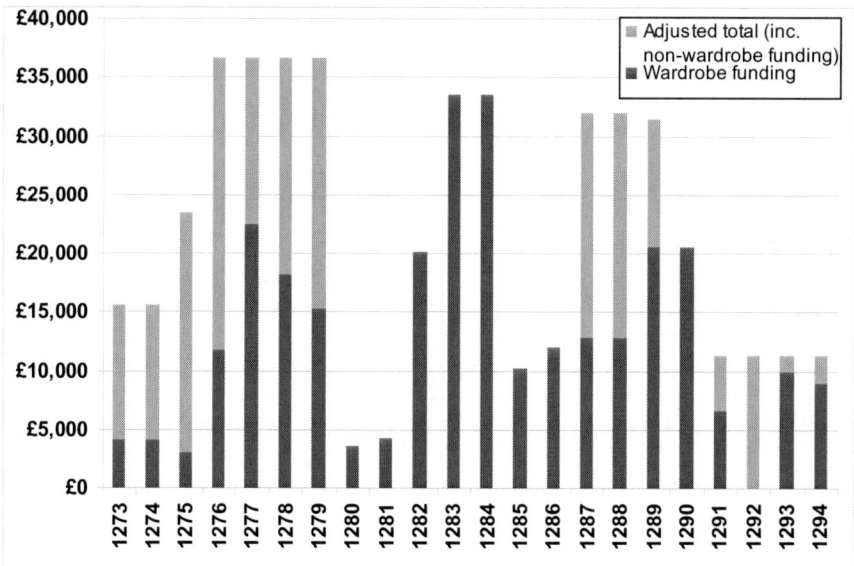

Figure 1. Ricciardi lending to Edward I

collected from the wool custom between Easter 1279 and Easter 1281, and the sums paid into the wardrobe by the Ricciardi between November 1281 and November 1285 were mostly allowed against customs revenue collected between Easter 1282 and Easter 1286.[25] Although the aggregate sums that passed through the Ricciardi's hands were huge, there was usually a rapid turnover of advances and repayments. This meant that the large debts accumulated as a result of the Welsh wars of 1277 and 1282–83 could be quickly cleared. Even the huge debt of £54,180 recognised by the king c. 1290, as a result of his expenses in Gascony, had been paid down to £18,925 by 1294.[26] Up to that point, at least, the 'Ricciardi system' seems to have worked smoothly.

This relationship had obvious benefits for both parties. It was more convenient for Edward I to use the balance transfer facilities and access to cash provided by the Ricciardi than to build up and maintain a large cash treasury, as his predecessors had done.[27] Moreover, the king could anticipate his revenues in order to smooth the seasonal fluctuations in royal income. Finally, Edward had access to a reliable source of credit in order to fund expensive projects, such as the Welsh wars or his diplomatic efforts in Gascony. The Ricciardi also derived considerable advantages from their connection to the English king. They enjoyed valuable but more intangible privileges, such as the ability to use the king's Exchequer courts to pursue their debtors and, perhaps more importantly, enhanced access to the English wool

---

[25] *Accounts of the English Crown*, ed. Bell et al., 16–17, 32–3.

[26] Ibid., 51–2.

[27] On his death in 1135, Henry I left a treasury of at least £60,000 at Falaise (M. Chibnall, ed., *The Ecclesiastical History of Orderic Vitalis*, vi (Oxford, 1978), 448). For the cash reserve accumulated by John before 1213, see J.E.A. Jolliffe, 'The Chamber and the Castle Treasures under King John', in *Studies in Medieval History Presented to Frederick Maurice Powicke*, ed. R.W. Hunt, W.A. Pantin and R.W. Southern (Oxford, 1948), 133–5.

market.[28] The latter point will be explored in more detail shortly. A key question is whether the Ricciardi received any direct financial return on their credit provision to the English crown. This is difficult to assess, in part because such benefits were often disguised in the accounts in order to avoid the appearance of usury but also because the sources that would allow us to look behind the general accounts do not survive.[29] The most that can be said is that there was certainly potential to disguise interest within the deficit acknowledged by the king at the periodic accounts. In particular, the fact that the accounts of 1276 and 1279 produced such round numbers hints at manipulation of the accounting process.

The preceding reconstruction of the provision of credit finance to Edward I by the Ricciardi raises a number of practical questions. The first involves the scale of the lending to the English crown, as set out above. It has been suggested that the king's account was usually in arrears by around one year's income from the wool custom, roughly equivalent to around £10,000. This was still a large sum of money for the Ricciardi to have tied up in government debt, but it would have been manageable. Furthermore, it will be suggested that much of this overdraft could have been funded from the papal taxes deposited with the Ricciardi.[30] At moments of crisis, however, Edward I needed large sums of money very quickly. On several occasions, especially in 1282–3 and 1286–9, Ricciardi advances to the king approached or exceeded £100,000. Even though the king's net debt to the Ricciardi, after deducting the royal revenues collected by or paid to them, would have been much lower than this, it is still difficult to see how the Ricciardi's own resources would have been sufficient to meet Edward's needs at these times.[31] Moreover, it would not have made economic sense for the Ricciardi to keep such vast sums of ready cash to hand in case of royal emergencies, when that money could have been productively invested in trade or loans. Instead, it seems that when larger sums were required, the Ricciardi acted as brokers, raising money from a cartel of their fellow merchant societies.[32] Table 2 shows loans contracted by the Ricciardi from other merchant societies in the late 1270s and early 1280s.

In effect, the Ricciardi could tap into the resources of the wider Italian community in England to expand the capital at their disposal. This could be compared to the interbank market today. It seems likely that the societies advancing such interbank loans would have required some form of return on their investment. The payment of interest was usually disguised in the accounts, but it can occasionally be identified.[33] Unfortunately, the question of whether the Ricciardi, like modern banks, took advantage of their easier access to such interbank lending and their good credit to borrow at lower rates of interest than they lent to the king, is impossible to answer given the surviving evidence. Alternatively, the merchant societies may have viewed such loans as an inevitable 'cost of doing business' for access to the English wool market.

A second question is how these Italian merchant societies were able to advance such large sums to the king and then repatriate their profits. After all, Lucca is over

[28] Kaeuper, *Bankers to the Crown*, 121–4.

[29] For difficulties in identifying interest in medieval sources, see A.R. Bell, C. Brooks and T.K. Moore, 'Interest in Medieval Accounts: Examples from England, 1272–1340', *History* 94 (2009), 423–7. Note that the discussion of the account of 1279 (ibid., 426) is revised in *Accounts of the English Crown*, ed. Bell et al., 14 n. 1.

[30] See below, 111–13.

[31] *Accounts of the English Crown*, ed. Bell et al., 38–43.

[32] Kaeuper, *Bankers to the Crown*, 201–7.

[33] For an example, see Bell, Brooks and Moore, 'Interest in Medieval Accounts', 416 n. 19.

Table 2. 'Interbank' lending

Society	1277[a]	1279[b]	1282–3[c]
Bardi of Florence	£3,333 6s 8d[d]	£1,000	£1,666 13s 4d
Cerchi of Florence	see Bardi	£1,333 6s 8d	£2,233 6s 8d
Falconeri of Florence	see Bardi	£751	£1,133 6s 8d
Frescobaldi of Florence	see Bardi	£1,116 13s 4d	£1,533 6s 8d
Mozzi of Florence	£800	£2,000	£2,000
Pulci of Florence	£666 13s 4d	£2,000	£1,666 13s 4d
Scali of Florence	£1,333 6s 8d	£2,666 13s 4d	£2,000
Bettori of Lucca	£666 13s 4d	£1,336 6s 8d	£1,133 6s 8d
Scotti of Piacenza	£2,000	£2,000	£2,000
Ammanati of Pistoia	£666 13s 4d	£2,000	£1,166 13s 4d
Bonseignori of Sienna	£666 13s 4d	£1,000	£1,666 13s 4d
Salumbeni of Sienna			£666 13s 4d

a *Accounts of the English Crown*, ed. Bell et al., 10–11.
b *CPR 1272–1281*, 358, 401. Technically, this loan was intended to provide the 'float' for the recoinage of 1279 and was paid directly to the keepers of the exchange and repaid from the profits of that exchange. However, Orlandino di Poggio of Lucca was joint-keeper of the exchanges, and it is likely that he used his Ricciardi connections when raising these loans.
c TNA E 372/130, r. 5 m. 2.
d The Bardi, Cerchi, Falconeri and Frescobaldi jointly contributed 5,000m.

720 miles away from Westminster as the crow flies. For a number of reasons, it is unlikely that this money was physically shipped from Italy to England. One pound sterling was one pound by weight of nearly pure silver and, moreover, for most of the period the highest denomination coin in circulation was the penny. £1,000 in cash would thus consist of 240,000 silver pennies and weigh nearly half a ton. There would therefore have been innumerable logistical problems involved in transporting the £20,000+ per annum loaned to the English kings by the Ricciardi from Italy to England and back again. The cost alone would have been prohibitive.[34] More serious were political problems as rulers, following what would later be termed Bullionist ideas, imposed restrictions on the export of precious metals and sought to restrict the use of foreign currencies within their territories. The English kings, in particular, sought to enforce the use of sterling and derived a sizeable income from the minting of new coins.[35] Moreover, transporting large sums of specie was inherently risky.

To overcome these practical obstacles, medieval traders developed sophisticated methods of credit provision to move the idea of 'money' from one place to another without having to physically cart about coins. In the most obvious case, a merchant with credit in one country could purchase goods, export them to another country and sell them there. This would, in effect, allow the merchant to transfer his money/

[34] Fryde found that the cost of transporting coin from England to the Low Countries was around 3–4% (E.B. Fryde, 'Financial Resources of Edward I in the Netherlands, 1294–8: Main Problems and Some Comparisons with Edward III in 1337–40', *Revue Belge de Philologie et d'Histoire* 40 (1962), 1186). The cost of transportation from Italy would have been significantly greater.
[35] For medieval attitudes to international transfers, in theory and in practice, see P. Einzig, *The History of Foreign Exchange*, 2nd edn (London, 1970), 90–110; and for England, see C.E. Challis, *A New History of the Royal Mint* (Cambridge, 1992), 130–2.

credit from one place to another, while also making a tidy profit. In the case of the Italian merchant societies and England, the main trading good was wool.[36] During the late thirteenth and early fourteenth centuries, English wool was mostly exported to feed the growing cloth industry in the Low Countries. Wool was sold in Flanders, probably on credit, and such credits could be transferred back to Italy by balance exchange via the Champagne fairs, or used to buy Flemish cloth, to be transported to Italy for sale.[37] Later, after the sea route between England and Italy was opened at the end of the thirteenth century, direct shipping of English wool to Italy became more common.[38] In both cases, English wool was the medium by which the Italian merchant societies repatriated their profits.

Some idea of the involvement of the Italians in the wool export trade can be gleaned from a number of sources, such as licences to export wool granted in the 1270s, the detailed customs accounts that survive from certain ports, and the 'Exchequer schedule' of 1294, listing some of the assets seized by the king after the outbreak of war with France, as shown in Table 3.

Table 3. Italian involvement in the English wool trade

Society	Export licences in 1273 (sacks)[a]	Export licences in 1277 (sacks)[b]	Exports from Boston, 1287–8 (sacks)[c]	Wool seized in 1294 (sacks)[d]
Bardi of Florence	700	200	559	99
Cerchi of Florence	400	1,500	125	651
Falconieri of Florence	620	25	41	
Frescobaldi of Florence	880	1,500	749	514
Mozzi of Florence[e]		100	210	414½
Macci of Florence	640			
Pulci of Florence		170	253	257½
Bettori of Lucca	700	550	97	35
Ricciardi of Lucca	1,080	n/a	340	413
Scotti of Piacenza	2,140	1,300		
Total	7,160	5,345	2,828	2,384

a These figures are taken from A. Schaube, 'Die Wolausfuhr Englands vom Jahre 1273', *Vierteljahress- chrift für Sozial- und Wirtschaftsgeschichte* 6 (1908).
b *Calendar of Chancery Rolls Various: Supplementary Close Rolls, Welsh Rolls, Scutage Rolls. A.D. 1277–1326* (London, 1912), 3–4, 7.
c Lloyd, *English Wool Trade*, 73–4.
d *Advance Contracts for the Sale of Wool c. 1200 – c. 1327*, ed. A.R. Bell, C. Brooks, and P. Dryburgh (List and Index Society 315, 2006), appendix I.
e In 1294 the Spini split from the Mozzi and, for comparability, their wool in 1294 is included in the Mozzi total.

[36] For a good introduction, see T.H. Lloyd, *The English Wool Trade in the Middle Ages* (Cambridge, 1977).
[37] For credit transactions and the Champagne fairs, see de Roover and Verlinden in *Cambridge Economic History of Europe, III: Economic Organisation and Policies in the Middle Ages*, ed. M.M. Postan (Cambridge, 1963), 42–69 and 126–37. For a more recent overview, see the chapter by Reynerson on 'Commerce and Communications' in *The New Cambridge Medieval History: Volume V, c.1198–c.1300*, ed. D. Abulafia (Cambridge, 1999), 50–70.
[38] R.S. Lopez, 'Majorcans and Genoese on the North Sea Route in the Thirteenth Century', *Revue Belge de Philologie et d'Histoire* 29 (1951), 1172–7.

These export figures can be used to provide a rough idea of the capital disposed of by the Italian merchant societies. There are numerous problems with valuing medieval wool, but using Munro's analysis of the Exchequer schedule of 1294, we can assess an average value of just over £9 per sack.[39] This would imply that the Italian merchants had very considerable sums tied up in the English wool market. The Ricciardi, for instance, expected to export around 1,080 sacks in 1273, with a potential value of nearly £10,000. The total value of Italian purchases of wool for export may have been around £50,000–£70,000 each year in the mid-1270s. Of course, it is possible that some of this wool was bought on credit, with only a deposit put down in advance, which would tend to reduce any estimates of the likely capital base of the merchant societies. On the other hand, at around this time, merchant societies began to enter into long-term advance contracts for wool with religious houses, paying large sums of money up front in return for guaranteed future deliveries of wool at a discounted price.[40] This would obviously have demanded a greater initial investment of capital, but would have promised a better rate of return. It is more difficult to assess the potential return on this investment from the wool trade, but a comparison between the figures given for the purchase price of wool in England and the sale prices in Flanders given by Francesco di Balduccio Pegolotti suggests that each sack could be sold for a profit of around £2, although this would be reduced by transportation and other expenses, as well as the customs duty.[41] In any case, even a small profit per sack would translate to a sizeable figure given the scale of the involvement of the merchants in the wool trade.

Indeed, one of the attractions of entering into a financial relationship with the English crown may have been to gain access to this lucrative market. For example, the Ricciardi were parties to nearly half of all the recorded forward contracts in wool with English producers between 1272 and 1294, when they were acting as 'bankers to the Crown'. Similarly, the Frescobaldi were involved in just under a third of all such contracts for the period 1294–1311, when they were involved in the large-scale provision of credit to Edwards I and II.[42] Finally, the 'super-company' of the Bardi derived just under half of their total profit between 1330 and 1332 from the wool trade, at which time they too were lending to Edward III.[43] Further, many of the same merchant societies from the above list of wool exporters also featured in the previous list of interbank lenders to the Ricciardi. This is not a coincidence. First, as explained above, it is likely that any merchant society with sufficient assets in England to be able to make loans to the king via the Ricciardi would also be involved in the wool trade. Second, the capital thus tied up in wool made the merchants vulnerable to royal pressure, whether direct or indirect. For

---

[39] This is based on Munro's calculations for average prices across England for wool from religious houses common to the Exchequer and Pegolotti lists in J.H. Munro, 'Wool-Price Schedules and the Qualities of English Wools in the Later Middle Ages c.1270–1499', *Textile History* 9 (1978), 131. These particular values have been chosen to provide the best indication of the potential profit for the merchant. The value of any particular wool could vary greatly from year to year and between different regions or producers. For more detailed discussion of these variables and a methodology to estimate changing wool prices, see A.R. Bell, C. Brooks and P. Dryburgh, *The English Wool Market, c.1230–1327* (Cambridge, 2007), 132–4.

[40] Ibid., 11–26.

[41] Munro, 'Wool-Price Schedules', 131.

[42] These figures have been calculated from *Advance Contracts for the Sale of Wool c. 1200 – c. 1327*, ed. A.R. Bell, C. Brooks, and P. Dryburgh (List and Index Society 315, 2006).

[43] E.S. Hunt, *The Medieval Super-Companies: A Study of the Peruzzi Company of Florence* (Cambridge, 1994), 165; E.B. Fryde, 'Loans to the English Crown, 1328–1331', *EHR* 70 (1955), 198–211.

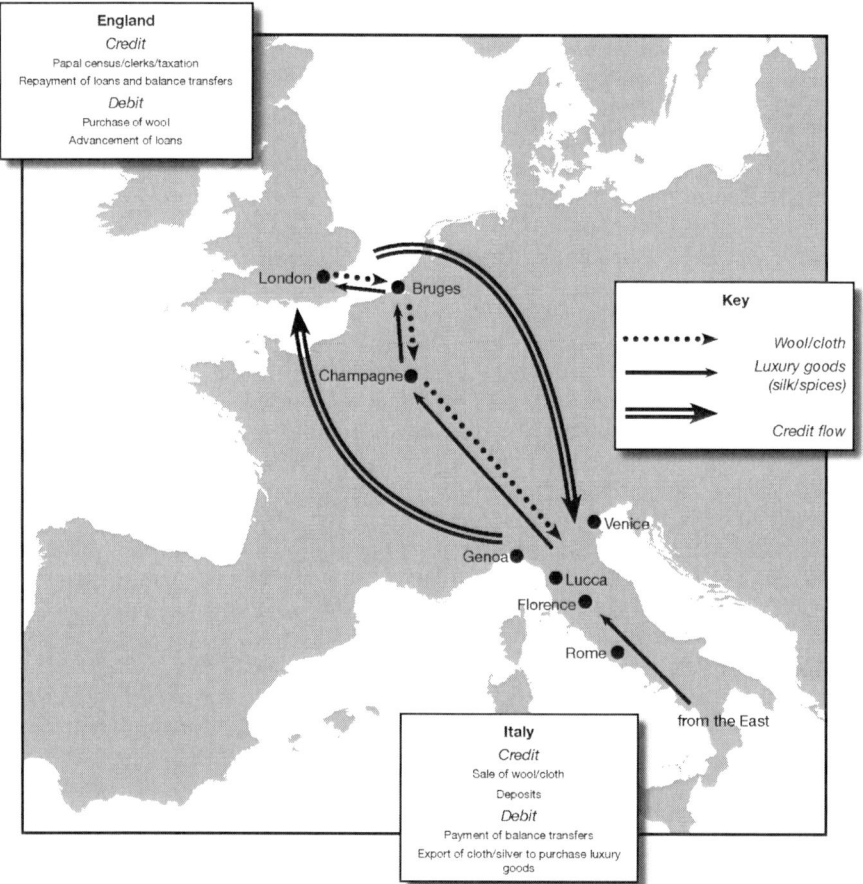

Figure 2. Flows of trade and credit between England and Italy in the thirteenth century

instance, many of the societies that agreed to loan money to the king in May 1277 subsequently received licences to export wool in June. Moreover, control over the granting of wool export licences was entrusted to the Ricciardi, who were themselves responsible for arranging and receiving loans from other merchants on the king's behalf.[44]

Direct trading could be a cumbersome and inconvenient method of transferring credit, however, and the merchants soon developed ways of utilising credit more efficiently. The most famous of these were bills of exchange.[45] In effect, the first party advanced a sum of money in one currency to the second party, in return for the promise of repayment in another place and in a different currency.[46] Merchant

---

[44] *Calendar of Chancery Rolls Various: Supplementary Close Rolls, Welsh Rolls, Scutage Rolls. A.D. 1277–1326* (London, 1912), 15–16.

[45] For a brief discussion of bills of exchange with examples, see *Medieval Trade in the Mediterranean World*, ed. R.S. Lopez and I.W. Raymond (New York, 1955), 162–7.

[46] For a contemporary example, see the suits brought against Lapus Philippi of the Clarenti society of Pistoia by English merchants relating to transfers between London and Antwerp (TNA E 159/79, m. 28).

societies could also transfer money from one branch to another through internal book-keeping. Although such instruments could be used for fictional exchanges as a means of hiding interest, they originated in trade. While developed as a convenience, the operation of bill of exchange still required that the first party, who wished to transfer his credit from place A to place B, had to find a co-party (or series of co-parties) who needed money at A and who had access to a surplus at the destination B. The operation of balance transfers between money-changers or merchant societies was more complicated, but still depended on the same basic needs. Trade remained the most common reason for the acquisition of a large sum of money or credit and the corresponding need for access to money or credit. In medieval Europe, as today, flows of credit and flows of trade were intimately linked, as represented on Figure 2.

A final question naturally arises from the above reconstruction of these networks of trade and credit: why did this massive Italian financial investment in English wool and government debt arise? Before 1272, the English kings had engaged in occasional dealings with Italian merchants, mainly in purchasing luxury goods for the household and arranging for balance transfers to Rome, but these interactions were on a much smaller scale than those of the Ricciardi and their successors as royal bankers, the Frescobaldi, and Bardi/Peruzzi.[47] Likewise, the Italians rapidly rose to a dominant position in the wool export trade in the early 1270s.[48] Now, once the system of credit finance described above was up and running, it could be largely self-perpetuating, since new loans could be funded from the repayments of previous loans, with additional profits repatriated to Italy via the wool trade. The same applies to the involvement of the Italians in the wool trade. In both cases, however, the merchant societies would have required a source of initial capital. Neither the volume of direct Italian trade in England earlier in the thirteenth century nor the repayment of loans advanced to Englishmen at Rome would seem likely to have provided sufficient capital accumulation for the scale of lending and the investment in the wool trade evident after 1272. It is therefore necessary to identify the trigger for the start of lending.

One possible candidate was the prolonged period of Anglo-French peace prevalent between 1243 and 1337. Although interrupted by wars in 1294–8 and 1324, this was a much more pacific century than the almost constant conflict between the Anglo-Normans/Angevins and the French kings in the twelfth century or the 'Hundred Years War' after 1337.[49] As should be clear from Figure 2, the key trade routes between Italy and England ran through Flanders, the fairs of Champagne and thence via south-east France. Any conflict between England and France would therefore have a disruptive effect on trade and thus on credit flows. The unusually good relations between England and France during much of this period should therefore be seen as a necessary prerequisite for large-scale Italian lending in England, if not perhaps a sufficient condition.

The most likely cause of the rapid growth in Italian investment in England, however, was the expansion of papal taxation in England during the second half of the thirteenth century. This started with the sums raised from the English church for Henry III's 'Sicilian business' in the 1250s, and continued with the crusading tenths

[47] For a brief overview of the activities of the Italians in England before the reign of Edward I, see R.J. Whitwell, 'Italian Bankers and the English Crown', *TRHS* new ser. 18 (1903), 187–97 and 224–9.

[48] Lloyd, *English Wool Trade*, 39–45.

[49] M.G.A. Vale, *Origins of the Hundred Years War: The Angevin Legacy, 1250–1340* (Oxford, 1996), 3–4.

imposed in 1274 and 1291. The first of these subsidies raised around £50,000 from the English church, the second as much as £130,000 and the third about £60,000.[50] This left the pope facing the same problem of getting this money back to Italy. It has been demonstrated that the physical transportation of such sums would have been fraught with difficulty. As a result, the papacy turned to the Italian merchant societies as a suitable vehicle for the transfer of the taxes raised in England.[51] The operation of this system can best be seen from the collection of the sexennial tenth imposed by the pope in 1274, to fund a new crusade to the Holy Land. By 1283 around £130,000 had been collected in England and the majority of this was deposited with a number of Italian merchant societies, as shown in Table 4.

Table 4. Deposits of the sexennial tenth with Italian merchant societies in 1283

Society	Value of tenth held in 1283[a]
Ricciardi of Lucca	£11,003 11s 5d
Scotti of Piacenza	£9,220 9¾d
Bonseignori of Sienna	£8,550 12s ½d
Bettori of Lucca	£7,114 9s 7d
Scali of Florence	£5,793 14s 6¼d
Mozzi of Florence	£4,575 11s ¾d
Ammanati of Pistoia	£4,570 13s 4½d
Cerchi of Florence	£4,454 12s 8d
Frescobaldi of Florence	£4,196 13s 5¾d
Pulci and Rembertini of Florence	£3,874 4s 6½d
Falconeri of Florence	£2,964 8s 9d
Bardi of Florence	£1,668 11s 10¼d
Cardellini of Lucca	£1,665 1¾d

a Lunt, *Financial Relations*, 641–65. Smaller deposits of less than £400 made with three other societies, the Getti-Honesti and Squarcialuppi of Lucca and the Reyner-Ardingelli of Florence, are omitted.

What distinguished the sexennial tenth from other papal taxes was the length of time for which the sums raised remained in the hands of the merchant societies. It was not until 1290 that Edward I finally agreed terms with the pope to lead a new crusade and, in return, was granted access to the proceeds of the tax in England.[52] The merchant societies had thus enjoyed the use of these deposits for over a decade. It is therefore not surprising that the same societies that held substantial sums in papal deposits also contributed to loans to the English crown and were prominent in the wool trade. For instance, the money from the papal tenth deposited with the Ricciardi would probably have covered much of Edward's 'overdraft' with them. In the same way, papal deposits could have funded the 'interbank' lending by other

[50] W.E. Lunt, *Financial Relations of the Papacy with England to 1327* (Cambridge, Mass., 1939), 289–90, 341, 356.
[51] Ibid., 599–603.
[52] Ibid., 337–41.

merchant societies to the Ricciardi. Edward I also occasionally 'dipped into' the papal taxes deposited at the New Temple or other religious houses to expand the reserves in the Ricciardi's hands.[53] It is also no coincidence that the start of the Italian hegemony in the wool export trade took place at this time. The long-term deposits may also have spurred financial innovation, as the Italian merchants sought to find new ways of putting this money to use, such as the advance contracts for wool discussed above.

Although doubtless extremely profitable for both king and merchant, the complicated system of credit finance described above proved equally fragile, as was demonstrated by the events of 1294.[54] At the start of the year, the Ricciardi finances appeared to be in a very healthy condition. In June 1291, after Edward and Pope Nicholas IV finally reached agreement on the terms of a future crusade to be led by the English king, the various merchant societies with whom the tenth was deposited were ordered to deliver a first instalment of 100,000 marcs [hereafter m] to the Ricciardi on Edward's behalf.[55] In the absence of surviving internal account books from the Ricciardi and other merchant societies, it is impossible to track particular money and credit flows, but we can advance a reasonable hypothesis. Crucially, it is unlikely that all of the money held by the other merchant societies was physically paid over to the Ricciardi, not least because no merchant society would have held such large sums in cash. It would have been more logical for the merchant societies simply to transfer their liabilities from the pope to the Ricciardi. On paper, therefore, the Ricciardi would have been credited with the extra 100,000 marks (less the share they already held). There is some explicit evidence to back up this interpretation; the Frescobaldi were still holding 5,000m of the tenth in July 1293, and the Bettori of Lucca and the Bonsignori of Sienna owed the Ricciardi £2,600 and £7,000 respectively in 1294.[56] The long-awaited grant of the sexennial tenth to Edward thus led to a complete reversal in the relative position of king and merchant. As we have seen, Edward's stated 'overdraft' in 1290 was £54,180, although, by 1294 he had paid this down to under £19,000. Even including the Ricciardi's loan of 25,000m (£16,667) to the king's brother Edmund of Lancaster in 1293–4, it would seem that, for the first time, Edward had a sizeable surplus on his account with the Ricciardi.[57]

Under the medieval system of fractional reserve banking, at any one time most of the capital of these merchant societies would have been committed in various ventures, both loans to governments and private borrowers, as well as investment in goods for trade. This was normally profitable, since this money was earning the merchants a good return, but it meant that they only retained a small buffer of liquid capital in hand. This left the merchant societies vulnerable should their deposi-

---

[53] In 1279, £5,000 was advanced to the Ricciardi from the tenth held at the New Temple (*CPR 1272–1281*, 305); at the height of the second Welsh war in 1283, Edward notoriously seized almost £30,000 from the portions of the tenth stored at various religious houses and delivered them to the Lucchese (Kaeuper, *Bankers to the Crown*, 200–1); and in 1286 the Ricciardi received a further £8,000 from the deposited tenth (*CPR 1281–1292*, 244).

[54] For the fall of the Ricciardi, see Kaeuper, *Bankers to the Crown*, 209–27 and I. del Punta, 'Il fallimento della compagnia Ricciardi alla fine del secolo XIII: un caso esemplare', *Archivio Storico Italiano* 592 (2002), 221–68.

[55] For the political context of the fall of Acre and Edward's intention to lead a crusade, see Morris, *Great and Terrible King*, 263–5. For the delivery of the first instalment of the tenth to the Ricciardi, see Kaeuper, *Bankers to the Crown*, 211–20. A second instalment of equal value was scheduled for June 1292 but it does not seem that this was ever paid.

[56] *CPR 1292–1301*, p. 33; TNA E 101/126/7, m. 26d; E. Jordan, 'La faillite des Buonsignori', in *Mélanges Paul Fabre: étude d'histoire du moyen âge* (Paris, 1902), 427–32.

[57] For the loan to Edmund, see TNA SC 1/12970.

tors seek to withdraw funds at short notice.[58] Unfortunately, this was precisely the situation that arose in 1294, on the outbreak of war between England and France. Edward now needed to raise money to fund his armies and, as before, he turned to the Ricciardi. Although, they should have been well-capitalised at that time, it seems that the greater part of their resources was tied up. This would not normally have posed a problem, since the Ricciardi could raise funds on the 'interbank' market, but in the early 1290s, there was a crisis of liquidity, as the pope called in the papal taxation deposited with the merchant societies and the French king Philip IV exacted large sums from the Italians in France.[59] This was significant because the merchant societies, like the Ricciardi, would have invested their shares of the papal taxation in loans or trade and therefore would not have had large sums in cash immediately to hand. As a result, they were either unable or unwilling to advance the necessary sums to the Ricciardi. This reveals a structural flaw in the medieval 'banking' sector; when one merchant society wished to raise money, they seem to have found it relatively easy to find credit from other merchant societies, either as loans or by selling assets. Problems arose when all of the merchant societies were seeking to raise money at the same time, particularly as there was no central bank that could act as a 'lender of last resort'.

All this meant that the Ricciardi were unable to provide Edward with the financial support that he desperately needed. Edward took typically decisive action; on 28 July 1294, he removed the Ricciardi from their position as collectors of the customs on wool, which effectively marked the end of the long-standing relationship between the Ricciardi and the English crown. Their assets (mainly wool but also debts owed by private individuals) were also confiscated.[60] The wool held by other merchant societies was also seized in both England and France. Since so much of the capital of these societies was tied up in wool, this made it impossible for them to raise cash from their chief assets, further freezing the 'interbank' market and compounding the liquidity crisis. These difficulties were exacerbated by the Anglo-French war, which disrupted communications between Italy and England, leaving the merchants unable to update their account books.

In response, the Ricciardi seem to have argued that their difficulties resulted from a short-term mismatch and that, overall, their assets matched their liabilities. In effect, the Ricciardi, like modern banks in 2007–8, claimed that they faced a crisis of liquidity, not of solvency. They sought to overcome this crisis through a series of what would be described in modern terminology as 'credit swaps' and 'netting' between their creditors and debtors; in effect, they petitioned Edward for a new audit of their account, in the belief that his 'overdraft', combined with Edmund of Lancaster's debts and the proceeds of their assets confiscated by the king, would cancel out the greater part of the papal taxation that they owed him. At the same time, the Ricciardi also owed money to the pope from the papal tenth for Sicily, and the merchants tried to persuade Boniface VIII to accept the debts owed to them

---

[58] For the structural weaknesses of medieval financial institutions, see R. de Roover, *Money, Banking and Credit in Mediaeval Bruges: Italian Merchant-Bankers, Lombards and Money-Changers: A Study in the Origins of Banking* (Cambridge, Mass., 1948), 209–10, 238–9, 317–21.

[59] The merchants themselves recognised that the calling in of the deposited papal taxes would reduce the availability of credit (from a Cerchi letter cited in E. Re, 'La compagnia dei Riccardi in Inghilterra e il suo fallimento alla fine del secolo decimoterzo', *Archivio della Società Romana de Storia Patria* 37 (1914), 101; R. Fawtier, *Philippe le Bel* (Paris, 1979), 189, 194).

[60] Kaeuper, *Bankers to the Crown*, 220–5.

in France and in Italy in lieu.[61] Unfortunately for the Ricciardi, they proved less persuasive than their counterparts today and failed to convince either Edward or the pope to support them. As a result, the society was gradually wound up.[62] Moreover, the Ricciardi were not alone as the disruptions to trade, possibly combined with counter-party risks as merchant societies and other debtors defaulted, caused a wider crisis in mercantile banking. In 1297, the Bonsignori society of Sienna also failed to secure a government bail-out and collapsed. They were joined by a number of Florentine societies and the Ammanati of Pistoia around the turn of the century.[63]

The case study of the Ricciardi of Lucca therefore provides evidence of a precocious, if doomed, experiment in government credit finance. Between 1272 and 1294, around half of all wardrobe expenditure, the chief financial department of Edwardian government, was channelled via the Ricciardi. For Edward I, the Lucchese proved highly competent, efficient and, for the most part, liquid money managers. He could take advantage of the Ricciardi's access to ready cash, both from deposited papal taxes as well as 'interbank' lending from their fellow merchant societies, and their ability to move money as part of an efficient system of cross-European trade and credit, in order to fund the smooth running of English governmental business. Expensive projects, such as the conquest of Wales, could be funded by Ricciardi credit and repaid over following years without the need to resort to politically sensitive means of raising revenue. In return, and even disregarding the probability of some degree of interest being disguised in the accounts, the position of the Ricciardi as collectors of the custom on wool exports must have provided them with a competitive advantage, partly by increasing the liquid funds at their disposal but also in building up a dominant position in the burgeoning forward market for wool. This relationship, however, came to an abrupt close in 1294, as the war between England and France disrupted international trade and credit networks, leading to a medieval 'credit crunch'.[64] The severing of ties between Edward and his bankers led to the effective collapse of the Ricciardi. The value of the merchants to the king, meanwhile, is clearly demonstrated by the financial and political difficulties that beset Edward after 1294, as he struggled to fund his armies, engaged in France, Scotland and Wales. Edward could only raise small 'payday' loans at punitive rates of interest and by pledging the crown jewels.[65] Denied access to credit, the English govern-

---

[61] An especially valuable source is a collection of internal Ricciardi business letters from the years following 1294 that survive in the National Archives (TNA E 101/601/5). These have recently been edited as *Lettere dei Ricciardi di Lucca ai loro compagni in Inghilterra,1295–1303*, ed. A. Castellani and I. del Punta (Rome, 2005). The Ricciardi's strategy during these years has been reconstructed in Kaeuper, *Bankers to the Crown*, 227–48.

[62] 'It is possible that such a declaration [of bankruptcy] was never made and that the company merely faded as the members died' (ibid., 246). The Guidiccioni family, however, continued to play a prominent role in Lucca in the later Middle Ages (T.W. Blomquist, 'Land, Lineage and Business in the Thirteenth Century: The Guidiccioni Family of Lucca (part 2)', *Actum Luce* 11 (1982), 32–4.

[63] The petition of the Bonsignori has been edited in *Medieval Trade in the Mediterranean World*, ed. Lopez and Raymond, 298–302. For the wider banking crisis, see R. Davidsohn, *Storia di Firenze*, 8 vols (Florence, 1955–68), iv. 297–304.

[64] For this analogy, see A.R. Bell, C. Brooks and T.K. Moore, 'Credit Crunch in the Middle Ages', *The Historian: The Magazine of the Historical Association* 100 (2008), 6–13.

[65] For example, Edward had to pay £35 in interest for a one-month loan of £265 from Albisso Fifanti of Asti, which is equivalent to an annualised interest rate of 145% (Bell, Brooks and Moore, 'Interest in Medieval Accounts', 426). For the pawning of the crown jewels, see *Documents Illustrating the Crisis of 1297–98 in England*, ed. M. Prestwich (Camden Society 4th ser. 24, 1980), 194–7. Significantly, the merchants of Asti were generally associated with pawnbroking rather than merchant banking (de Roover, *Money, Banking and Credit*, 101).

ment had to resort to imposing heavy and repeated taxation, which contributed to the political and constitutional crisis of 1297.[66] As a result, both Edward and the merchants of Lucca had cause to regret the way their relationship ended.

[66] A. Spencer, 'The Lay Opposition to Edward I in 1297: Its Composition and Character', *TCE*, xii (2009), 100–3.

(Socio)linguistic Realities of Cross-Channel Communication in the Thirteenth Century

David Trotter

The purpose of this article is to investigate how communication across the English Channel functioned during (at least mainly) the thirteenth century. I shall inevitably go a little beyond this chronological limit, since there is often better evidence from later on. Within this fairly broad field of investigation, I will be concerned principally with communication and contact between England and France. Part of the reason for this is simply linguistic: once other countries, whether the Low Countries or Spain, Portugal, Gascony, or Italy, are involved, then clearly different languages come into play. A second reason for restricting myself to England and France is that it fits more readily into the focus of this collection; and finally, it corresponds to the area in which I have some competence.

Those familiar with standard treatments of the history of the French language in England will have encountered the conventional outline of how things developed. This broad picture goes back to late nineteenth-century French philology, and to the origins of the study of Anglo-Norman at or shortly after the beginning of the twentieth century. The emerging disciplines of French medieval studies and of French historical linguistics were deeply imbued, from the outset, with a nationalist agenda within which, amongst other things, it was considered imperative to stress the continuity and purity of standard French. Anglo-Norman, as a visibly aberrant and indeed manifestly non-French variety in terms of geography, was, or would have been, problematic, had it not been marginalized and treated (to quote Gaston Paris) as simply 'une manière imparfaite de parler français'.[1]

Within the history of Anglo-Norman, the traditional approach was always (and until remarkably recently) to subdivide the history of the variety into two main phases: from the Conquest (1066) to 1204 (the loss of Normandy) was phase one. Phase two after the loss of Normandy (or its recapture from a French perspective) is typically characterized as a period of decline, degeneracy, barbarousness, wholesale contamination by and of English, and so forth.[2] This perspective owes more than a little to the parallel development within English philology of English nationalism, and is influenced by the narrative of the emergence of the heroic English language from under the tyrannical Norman yoke. It also reflects, in many ways, considerable ignorance by the so-called specialists of later Anglo-Norman documents, together with tangible distaste not only for the forms of the language, but for the types of document within which it was predominantly to be found. These are overwhelmingly not strictly literary, and thus, it seems, did not appeal to the founding fathers

[1] G. Paris and A. Bos, eds, *La Vie de Saint Gilles par Guillaume de Berneville* (Paris, 1881), p. xxxv.
[2] The history of this type of comment is reviewed in D.A. Trotter, '*Mossenhor, fet metre aquesta letra en bon francés*: Anglo-French in Gascony', in *'De mot en mot': Essays in honour of William Rothwell*, ed. S. Gregory and D.A. Trotter (Cardiff, 1997), 199–222 (at 199–200).

(and especially mothers) of the discipline of Anglo-Norman studies, brought up as they were on an overwhelmingly literary perception of language and culture. But the important point for my purposes is that the so-called decline of later Anglo-Norman is linked to the loss of Normandy in 1204.

Nowadays, this view of the history of Anglo Norman looks increasingly out of date and inaccurate.[3] That does not stop it continuing to exert considerable influence within histories of English and of English literature, a fact which is all the more surprising when we recall that the most important figure in the history of English medieval literature, Geoffrey Chaucer, was clearly fully conversant with French, and travelled extensively on the continent, often on royal business.[4] It goes without saying, too, that such a perception of Anglo-Norman, cut off from the continent, or more accurately, if in still more insular manner, presented as found on an island from which the continent was cut off,[5] is at variance with extensive historical records of all sorts, right the way through the Middle Ages and beyond. There simply was not a separation of England and France after 1204 and other contributions to this volume make that point extensively. Contact and communication across the Channel was extensive, constant, and probably increased throughout the period I am concerned with. Moreover, this involved people from very different walks of life, and was by no means the preserve of the aristocracy or of an educated elite. It took the form of diplomacy, war, trade, education, science and theology, continuing dynastic interests and connections. It is extensively recorded in treaties, private letters, diplomatic documents, military records, chronicles; in the continuing transfer from France to England of literary texts copied into insular manuscripts; and in the constant traffic of scholars and clerics to and from Paris and the various centres of learning of northern France. Trade in wine, woad, cloth, wool, tin, lead,

---

[3]   There is an abundance of evidence now available which supports the argument that linguistic contact across the Channel was real and persistent: Gilles Roques, 'Des interférences picardes dans l'*Anglo-Norman Dictionary*', in *'De mot en mot'*, ed. Gregory and Trotter, 191–8; and 'Les régionalismes dans quelques textes anglo-normands', in *Actes du XXIVe Congrès International de Linguistique et de Philologie Romanes, Aberystwyth 2004*, ed. D.A. Trotter (Tübingen, 2007), iv. 279–92; William Rothwell, 'Arrivals and Departures: The Adoption of French Terminology into Middle English', *English Studies* 79 (1998), 144–65; 'Sugar and Spice and All Things Nice: From Oriental Bazar to English Cloister in Anglo-French', *Modern Language Review* 94 (1999), 647–59; D.A. Trotter, 'L'anglo-normand: variété insulaire, ou variété isolée?', *Médiévales* 45 (2003), 43–54; 'Not as Eccentric as it Looks: Anglo-French and French French', *Forum for Modern Language Studies* 39 (2003), 427–38; 'Language Contact, Multilingualism, and the Evidence Problem', in *The Beginnings of Standardization: Language and Culture in Fourteenth-Century England*. ed. U. Schaefer (Frankfurt, 2006), 73–90; '*Oceano Vox*: You Never Know Where a Ship Comes From. On Multilingualism and Language-Mixing in Medieval Britain', in *Aspects of Multilingualism in European Language History*, ed. Kurt Braunmüller and Gisella Ferraresi (Amsterdam/Philadelphia, 2003), 15–33; '*Pur meuz acorder en parlance E descorder en variaunce*: convergence et divergence dans l'évolution de l'anglo-normand', in *Sprachwandel und (Dis-)Kontinuität in der Romania*, ed. Sabine Heinemann and Paul Videsott (Tübingen, 2008), 87–95; Richard Ingham, 'Syntactic Change in Anglo-Norman and Continental French Chronicles: Was there a 'Middle' Anglo-Norman?', *Journal of French Language Studies* 16 (2006), 26–49; 'The Status of French in Medieval England: Evidence from the Use of Object Pronoun Syntax', *Vox Romanica* 65 (2006), 1–22; 'Mixing Languages on the Manor', *Medium Aevum* 78 (2009), 80–97; 'The Grammar of Later Medieval French: An Initial Exploration of the Anglo Norman Dictionary Textbase', *Corpus* 7 (novembre 2008): *Constitution et exploitation des corpus d'ancien et de moyen français*, http://corpus.revues.org/index1506.html
[4]   M.M. Crow and C.C. Olson, *Chaucer Life-Records* (Oxford, 1966).
[5]   Frankwalt Möhren, 'Unité et diversité du champ sémasiologique – l'exemple de l'*Anglo-Norman Dictionary*', in *'De mot en mot'*, ed. Gregory and Trotter, 127–46; also Thera De Jong, 'L'anglo-normand des 13e et 14e siècles: un dialecte continental ou insulaire?', in *The Origins and Development of Emigrant Languages*, ed. H.-F. Nielsen and L. Schøsler (Odense, 1996), 55–70.

and more exotic materials all entailed cross-channel traffic and hence communication.[6] None of this is remotely compatible with the thesis that Anglo-Norman was
cut off from its continental roots, or that England itself was isolated.

Within the confines of this study, it will not, of course, be possible to consider
all of this. I shall concentrate on two aspects: **diplomacy**, above all, and to a
much lesser degree, **trade**. Diplomacy was alive and well in England and France
throughout the thirteenth century, even if, in the fullness of time, politics was to give
way to warfare. Diplomatic materials are readily available, and (because language
is so important in diplomacy) particularly instructive. Trade documentation, on the
other hand, is not as extensive as we might wish it to be for the thirteenth century:
customs systems at a national level did not emerge until the 1270s,[7] and some of the
more important trading partnerships (conspicuously, with Italian firms) date from
that period too. In some respects the thirteenth century is probably not typical of
the Middle Ages as a whole: there is more trade in this period with Picardy and
Flanders, less than there was to be later with southern Europe and especially Italy.
Documents are relatively scarce, probably simply because there was less documentation overall before 1300, and possibly also because its chances of having survived
are that much smaller than is the case for material from later periods.

What, then, were (both technically and theoretically) the linguistic possibilities
for cross-Channel communication? Obviously, several individual languages are
candidates: Latin, as the overarching language of correspondence, ecclesiastical and
state business, and scholarship, throughout Western Europe; French, as the second
most international language of the time; some (as yet undocumented, and indeed
unattested) form of trading *lingua franca*;[8] a type of 'semicommunication' which has
been identified in Scandinavia (medieval and modern), whereby the close proximity
of genetically-related but distinct languages makes possible communication using
more than one language, 'the use of the respective mother tongue together with the
willingness to accept and understand the neighbouring standard languages'.[9] A final
possibility, and one which other types of documentary record make more plausible
than might immediately appear to be the case, is some form of mixed-language

[6]   See, for discussion of cross-Channel trade, for example: C.M. Barron, *London in the Later Middle
Ages: Government and People 1200–1500* (Oxford, 2004), 84–117; M. Bateson, 'A London Municipal
Collection of the Reign of John', *EHR* 17 (1902), 480–511; E. Carus-Wilson, 'La guède française en
Angleterre: un grand commerce du Moyen Âge', *Revue du Nord* 35 (1953), 91–105; 'The Medieval
Trade of the Ports of the Wash', *Mediaeval Archaeology* 6–7 (1962), 182–201; *The Overseas Trade of
Bristol in the Later Middle Ages* (Bristol, 1937); P. Chorley, 'English Cloth Exports during the Thir-
teenth and Early Fourteenth Centuries: The Continental Evidence', *Historical Research* 61 (1988),
1–10; 'The Cloth Exports of Flanders and Northern France during the Thirteenth Century: A Luxury
Trade?', *EcHR* new ser. 40 (1987), 349–79; E.B. Fryde, 'Italian Maritime Trade with Medieval England
(c.1270–c.1530)', *'Les Grandes Escales': Recueil de la Société Jean Bodin* 32 (1974), 291–337; 'The
English Cloth Industry and the Trade with the Mediterranean c.1370–c.1480', in *Produzione, commercio
et consumo dei panni di lana. Atti della 'Seconda settiman di studio' (10–16 aprile 1970), Istituto Inter-
nazionale di Storia Economica 'F. Datini' Prato* (Florence, 1976), 343–366; *Peasants and Landlords in
Later Medieval England* (Stroud, 1996).
[7]   N.S.B. Gras, *The Early English Customs System* (Cambridge, MA, 1918).
[8]   By this I mean a *lingua franca* in the sense in which historical linguists (e.g. J.E. Wansbrough, *Lingua
Franca in the Mediterranean* (Richmond, 1996)) use the word, i.e. typically a hybrid/creole/pidgin of
some sort, based on but not synonymous with extant and identifiable language(s).
[9]   See K. Braunmüller, 'Semicommunication and Accommodation: Observations from the Linguistic
Situation in Scandinavia', *International Journal of Applied Linguistics* 12 (2002), 1–23.

communication of a type widespread in administrative and business use, and not unique to England.[10]

In considering the language choices open to medieval traders and diplomats, we need to bear in mind certain realities concerning both our knowledge of the situation and the limits of the evidence available. In the first place, however much we might wish it to be otherwise, we simply do not have direct, unmediated access to the spoken language or languages. As has been pointed out,[11] multilingualism was

> a necessary precondition for mastering the various tasks in everyday life [...] there is little evidence to be found in (written) sources which stresses the fact that a certain person was multilingual or that the command of a *lingua franca* like Latin or any other language for a specific purpose, was mandatory for a certain job. A lack of such linguistic skills would, by contrast, have been worth mentioning.

The Middle Ages were not encumbered by modern ideologies of nation-state and national language and we may assume that the boundaries between languages were more fluid (and porous) than they are now. This may explain why so little is said in medieval sources about linguistic problems. This absence of comment persists in situations far more complex (and for which Westerners were far less prepared) such as, for example, journeys to the Far East. Amongst accounts either of missionaries or of merchants, almost nothing is ever said regarding the linguistic difficulties which they must have encountered and which must have been very real. Thus, perhaps, it is hardly surprising, when dealing with the relatively straightforward situation of cross-Channel communication, that this should not be uppermost in the minds of those involved. The linguistic hierarchy of medieval Europe placed Latin firmly at the top, but Latin was not necessarily a language which was accessible to all those concerned in (for example) trade. The next language down, as it were, would have been French, 'douce francés, qu'est la plus beale et la plus gracious langage et la plus noble parlere aprés latyn de scole que soit en monde et de toutz gentz melx preysé et amee que nulle autre' (sweet French, the most beautiful and the most graceful language and after the Latin of the schools, the most noble form of speech in the world, and more prized and loved by all people than any other), as the *Manière de langage* of 1396 calls it.[12] I shall return below to some of the potential problems of different forms of French, and of the intercomprehensibility of different French dialects. Here, again, we have to be careful to remember that all our evidence is written, and that the bulk of the communication must have been spoken. English, I think, may probably be excluded as a possible language of communication between England and France, although the possibility remains that some form of Low German *lingua franca* was in the use between England and (say) the Netherlands. It has been convincingly argued that French operated as the normal maritime language in the Channel, with the proviso that in both London and Southampton, there must have been a considerable amount of activity (even more as the

---

[10] See e.g. G. Lüdi, 'Mehrsprachige Rede in Freiburger Ratsmanualen des 15. Jahrhunderts', *Vox Romanica* 44 (1985), 163–88; D.A. Trotter, '*Oceano vox*'; D. Vitali, 'Interférences entre le latin et la langue vernaculaire dans les chartes latines de Suisse occidentale', in *The Dawn of the Written Vernacular in Western Europe*, ed. M. Goyens and W. Verbeke (Leuven, 2003), 127–45; L. Wright, 'Code-Intermediate Phenomena in Medieval Mixed-Language Business Texts', *Language Sciences* 24 (2002), 471–89; 'The Records of Hanseatic Merchants: Ignorant, Sleepy, or Degenerate?', *Multilingua* 16 (1997), 337–49.

[11] Braunmüller and Ferraresi, *Aspects of Multilingualism*, 3.

[12] A. Kristol, ed., *Manières de langage (1396, 1399, 1415)* (London, 1995), 3.

fourteenth century advanced) in Italian, perhaps more precisely Genoese.[13] But that lies chronologically outside the scope of this study. Finally, it is hard to imagine that given the distance between English and French, any form of semicommunication on the Scandinavian model would have been a workable solution. Mixed language documents are a possibility (and customs accounts, port books, and other texts show considerable evidence of language mixing, particularly at the level of individual words), but it seems unlikely that this would have been a viable means of spoken communication (although we can probably assume that there was a fair amount of code-switching).

We are, then, almost certainly left with communication in French. This at once reinforces, and is supported by, the argument that Anglo-Norman, as a form of French, remained perfectly comprehensible in France, just as continental French (although perhaps by the thirteenth century recognizably different) would have been comprehensible in England. Hence the statement at the beginning of the (early fifteenth-century) All Souls 182 version of Donatus: 'les bones gens du roiaume d'Engleterre sont enbrasez a sçavoir lire et escrire, entendre et parler droit françois, a fin qu'ils puissent entrecomuner bonement ové lour voisins, c'est a dire les bones gens du roiaume de France' (the good people of the kingdom of England are aflame with the urge to know how to read, write, understand and speak correct French, so that they can communicate well with their neighbours, that is to say the good people of the kingdom of France). The author, John Barton, calls himself 'escolier de Paris, nee et nourie toutez voiez d'Engleterre en la conté de Cestre' (scholar of Paris, born and brought up however in England in the county of Chester) and explains that he is anxious to teach Englishmen 'la droit language du Paris et de païs la d'entour, la quelle language en Engliterre on appelle "doulce France" [i.e., Francé?]' (the correct language of Paris and the surrounding region, which language is in England called "sweet French" [if my emendation is correct; or possibly: (of) sweet France?]).[14] Despite this, his text, or manuscript, is clearly written in resolutely Anglo-Norman graphies. This is not without significance, precisely, I would suggest, because the differences would have been differences of pronunciation and accent, and experience confirms that very substantial differences of pronunciation can be accommodated by the majority of speakers. It is only when vocabulary diverges strikingly in either form or meaning that significant communication problems tend to arise. Finally, to quote Braunmüller and Ferraresi[15] again:

> Mastering two or more languages, however, does not mean that the persons in question were 'perfect' bilinguals who could manage all situations in their lives in any of the languages they knew. Receptive bilingualism, functionally restricted multilingualism or the command of a foreign linguistic variety as a *lingua franca* were absolutely normal. Nobody would ever have expected to know other languages 'perfectly' (whatever that may mean in detail). [...] The command of an academic language [i.e., the 'high' language, Latin] was a natural part of everyday life and guaranteed that one could master the various domains

---

[13] Rothwell, 'Sugar and Spice and All Things Nice'; M. Kowaleski, 'The French of England: A Maritime *lingua franca*?', in *Language and Culture in Medieval Britain: The French of England c.1100–c.1500*, ed. J. Wogan-Browne et al. (York, 2009), 103–17.
[14] T. Städtler, *Zu den Anfängen der französischen Grammatiksprache. Textausgaben und Wortschatzstudien* (Tübingen, 1988).
[15] Braunmüller and Ferraresi, *Aspects of Multilingualism*, 3.

of work, trade and religion without greater problems. The main point
was to achieve effective communication e.g. at the workplace and not a
'perfect' multilingualism in every respect.

We are, in short, in the world of practical reality, not academic perfectionism.
This was about communication, not grammatical elegance. One of those practicali-
ties was of course quite simply what the legal status of the English Channel itself
was.[16] To this question there were, it seems, several answers in the era prior to
the establishment of the English Court of Admiralty in the mid-fourteenth century.
Three admittedly fourteenth-century documents gathered together by Chaplais in
his invaluable *English Medieval Diplomatic Practice*[17] present no fewer than three
versions. The first, a petition presented by the proctors of the kings of England and
of the prelates to the English and also French commissioners at Montreuil-sur-Mer
in 1306, asserts that the 'English sea' comes under the exclusive jurisdiction of
English kings:

> Come les roys d'Engleterre par raison du dit roialme, du temps q'il
> n'y ad memoire du contraire, averoient esté en paisible possession de
> la sovereigne seignurie de la meer d'Engleterre et des isles esteans en
> ycele ... (I.i, no. 206)

> (as the kings of England on account of the said kingdom, as there is
> no contrary view since time immemorial, should have been in peaceful
> possession of the sovereign lordship of the English Sea and of the
> islands lying therein ...)

An alternative view is expressed twenty-five years later by the people of Guernsey
and Jersey in a petition enrolled in the Coram Rege rolls:

> pur ce q'ils [sc. the people of Guernsey and Jersey] sont enclos de la
> grant mer en la marche de toutes nacions (I.i, no. 207)

> (because they [sc. the people of Guernsey and Jersey] are surrounded
> by the great sea [ocean?] in the march of all nations)

Chaplais compares this in a note (ibid.) to the view (dating back to Justinian) that
seas are common ('naturali iure communia sunt illa: aer, aqua profluens, et mare,
et per hoc litora maris') (by natural law these are held in common: the air, flowing
waters, and the sea, and because of the sea, the shores of the sea); but this is not the
only possible reading of 'enclos de la grant mer en la marche de toutes nacions'.
Thirty years later, in a 1359 case brought before the admiral in London, it is asserted
that the sea (in the event, the Channel off Winchelsea) is a *marche*: 'la meer, q'est
marche entre les deux roialmes [sc. of England and France]' ('the sea, which forms
the march between the two kingdoms [sc. of England and France]') (I.i, no. 208).
Marche is not unambiguous in Anglo-Norman or for that matter in any Romance
language (FEW 16,522b–524a).[18] John of Garland uses it to gloss *meta* ('boundary')

---

[16] See also R. Ward, *The World of the Medieval Shipmaster: Law, Business and the Sea, c.1350–1450*
(Woodbridge, 2009) (although dealing with a slightly later period).

[17] P. Chaplais, *English Medieval Diplomatic Practice*: Part I, *Plates*; Part II, *Documents and Interpretation* (London, 1975, 1982).

[18] During the course of this article, the following dictionaries are referred to by their conventional
abbreviated titles: AND = *Anglo-Norman Dictionary*, ed. W. Rothwell et al. (London, 1977–92), and
now (together with a second edition A–L) online at www.anglo-norman.net; FEW = *Französisches
Etymologisches Wörterbuch*, ed. W. von Wartburg (Bonn/Leipzig/Basel, 1922 –2002); Gdf = F. Gode-

(AND **marche¹**) and a case in the reign of Edward II observes (of a dispute between two counties in south-east England) that 'le fil del ewe de Thamyse si est marche entre les ij countez' (the line of the river Thames is the boundary between the two counties) (YBB Ed II xxii 225). *Marche*, a derivative of Germanic *mark*, can mean (in the case of the Thames) '(line of a) boundary', or (probably in the case of the English Channel) 'boundary region'. What is particularly important here is that the claim (no. 208) that the sea is a 'march' between the two kingdoms of England and France is made by a Frenchman, as part of his defence against the accusation that he unlawfully captured a ship belonging to two Englishmen during the Anglo-French truce in March–June 1359. The document is more than likely to have been written down in the language of the proceedings. For that matter, and in just the same way, the document (no. 206) presented by the English proctors to English and French commissioners in France in 1306 would have been perfectly comprehensible to both parties, with the conceivable exception of the expression 'time immemorial' ('du temps q'il n'y ad memoire'), a particularly English formulation. These diplomatic documents, for that is what they are, demonstrate, in other words, the use of French as the obvious diplomatic language of both high- and low-level communication between England and France: state documents and local cases alike use it. They support, without a doubt, the argument that there was a linguistic continuum across the English Channel. In the same vein, the very first letter printed by Chapple in his unfortunately unpublished collection of London correspondence[19] is from the mayor of London to the Picard towns of Amiens, Corbie, and Nesle, encouraging them (in 1298) to resume their normal trading arrangements with London, despite the problems that the Anglo-Picard trade had experienced in the last quarter of the thirteenth century.[20] Here, too, the letter only makes sense if it made sense to its recipients. These documents, then, allegedly in degenerate later Anglo-Norman, were perfectly comprehensible on the other side of the Channel. No historian, I hasten to add, would ever imagine that they were not; but the implication (however absurd) of the orthodox position of historical linguistics is that they might not have been. In the same way, I have shown elsewhere[21] that diplomatic documents could perfectly well exist in different versions, with some element of local colour in the form of spelling variation, and that such spelling variation was not seen as problematic but was sometimes consciously used in order to make a political point. Thus, for example, an Anglo-Flemish agreement of 1296/1297 gave rise to at least six different documents: a draft (of English origin) in 1296, corrected by a Flemish scribe; an English version of the agreement with limited Anglo-Norman scribal features; letters patent sealed at Walsingham but written by a Fleming and heavily Picardized; a confirmation of the agreement, by Edward I, written by an Englishman but using Flemish diplomatic. This range of documents demonstrates (as Serge Lusignan has already done) that scribes were quite capable of varying their usage for particular political reasons, and

froy, ed., *Dictionnaire de l'ancienne langue française et de tous ses dialectes du IXe au XVe siècle* (Paris, 1880–1902); GdfC = ibid., *Complément*, in vols 8–10; TL = A. Tobler and E. Lommatzsch, eds, *Altfranzösisches Wörterbuch* (Berlin/Wiesbaden, 1925 –2002).

[19] G.F. Chapple, 'Correspondence of the City of London 1298–1370' (unpublished thesis, University of London, 1938).

[20] These three Picard towns were the key locations for woad-trading in the thirteenth century: see Carus-Wilson, 'Guède française', 93. Two-thirds of the 77 identifiable merchants bringing woad to England during the same century were from Amiens (ibid., 97) and substantial numbers of them were established, apparently more or less permanently, in English towns (ibid., 99–100).

[21] D.A. Trotter, '*Auxi bien dela come decea*: l'anglo-normand en France', in *Stvdia Lingvistica in honorem Mariæ Manoliu*, ed. S. Reinheimer Rîpeanu (Bucharest, 2009), 360–69.

that such variation cannot have been an impediment to communication.[22] In the case of these Anglo-Flemish documents, Picard scribal features seem to have been used to support the territorial claims of the English monarchy to land in Flanders. Language, in other words, as always, is not only a means of supposedly simple communication, but a political instrument: denotational meaning (in the form of the words of a document) is accompanied by connotations (in these cases, spellings characteristic of one variety of French or another). Similar practices are evident in two versions of the Treaty of Paris document itself, where a document dated in London is written (according to Chaplais) 'in a French hand from beginning to end – including the dating clause – without apparent interruption'.[23] It is possible that the work[24] was copied by a Frenchman residing in England, and there are spellings which imply that his native dialect may not have been Anglo-Norman (although here too there may be a deliberate disguise). The ratification of the document follows the French pattern, and in all probability directly and deliberately emulates Louis IX's ratification of the parallel French version. Again, what we seem to be dealing with here is a conscious attempt to model language features and diplomatic style on those of a document produced by the 'other side'. A peace treaty from Amiens in 1279[25] likewise displays French diplomatic, but written in an English hand. A prerequisite for practices of this sort is clearly a high level of scribal and diplomatic competence, but also what we might now regard as a stylistic or even sociolinguistic awareness of the relevance of such external features in the conduct of diplomatic affairs.

Another document in the Chaplais collection[26] makes the point in a different way. This is a confidential letter (?1330) by Edward III to Pope John XXII (Jacques Duèze of Cahors, who had studied in Paris), in French.[27] The king says that in future he will write with his own hand the words 'pater sancte' (holy father) at the end of letters to authenticate them, which indeed someone duly does on this letter. In the text itself, this formulation is written with the Anglo-Norman graphy -*aun*- ('pater s*aun*cte'), but that presumably is of no importance. More intriguing is that John XXII wrote in 1323 to the king of France, Charles IV, to say that a letter, also in French, had caused him problems and that his reply was delayed by the need to have it to translated into Latin 'ut earum valeremus percipere plenius intellectum' (in order that we should be able to perceive the meaning of it more fully).[28] Edward II of England had letters translated, conversely, from Latin to French in 1317, and Pope Innocent VI (Étienne Aubert from the diocese of Limoges) arranged in 1359 for an English notary available in Avignon to write to Edward III in French. Edward himself wrote in that language to Innocent VI in the following year. There was, in other words, a conscious decision to use these languages, even if it occasionally misfired because of wrong assumptions made about linguistic competence (although, in the case of John XXII and the king of France, there may also have been a political motive for the pope's claim to an implausible inability to understand the meaning of letters in French).[29]

---

[22] Trotter, '*Auxi bien dela come decea*', 362–3; S. Lusignan, *La langue des rois au Moyen Âge. Le français en France et en Angleterre* (Paris, 2004), 225–31.

[23] Chaplais, *English Medieval Diplomatic Practice*, II, 8 notes to pl. 4.

[24] Ibid., I.i, no. 289c.

[25] Ibid., I.i, no. 290.

[26] Ibid., I.i, no. 18.

[27] Ibid.

[28] Ibid., I.i, 21 n. 126, for all this section.

[29] For Anglo-papal relations during the Avignon papacy, see K. Plöger, *England and the Avignon Popes: The Practice of Diplomacy in Late Medieval Europe* (London, 2005), esp. 179–96 ('Means of Commu-

Material of this type further underlines the elementary point that those engaged in the drafting, copying, reading, and deciphering of diplomatic correspondence needed to be able to function in several languages, and clearly, in at least some cases, were conscious of the salience of language choices. That, in itself, does not necessarily tell us all that much about the reality of language use in non-written communication. However, throughout the section of Chaplais' collection which is concerned with embassies and similar processes,[30] there is substantial and quite consistent evidence that the documents which are preserved were guides for what was to be orally delivered, and in some cases, contain speeches which were to be read verbatim. This is important for a number of reasons. One, of course, is that there are (admittedly not very frequently) sections of documents, and in isolated cases virtually entire documents, which are thought to transcribe direct speech as a record of discussion, and which thus preserve the written version of the verbal account of events, rather than as being the starting-point of an embassy. Thus, for example, a 1300 document[31] appears to be what we would now describe as a *procès-verbal* of a meeting between Pierre Aimeri, the envoy of Edward I, and Pope Boniface VIII. The entirety of the document is in French, with substantial portions, much of it attributed to the pope, in direct speech. Boniface VIII was not a Frenchman: born Benedetto Caetani at Anagni, fifty kilometres south-east of Rome, he had nonetheless travelled to France as a papal legate and as a cardinal, and had been to England as secretary to Cardinal Ottoboni Fieschi in 1265–68 (to which visit he alludes in the document recording the discussions in 1300). It is not unreasonable to imagine that he spoke French, and to judge by the sections of the document claiming to reproduce his speech, he seems to have had a good command of the language, even if he gives free rein (perhaps for political reasons when faced with an English delegation) to anti-French prejudices:[32]

> E pensames la graunt coveitise des Fraunceys et ne veismes q'en altre manere ne poet estre mieultz fait au profit le roi d'Engleterre qe cele terre de Gascoigne ne fust mise en nostre main, qar soveraine covoitise est es Fraunceis. Ceo q'ils tiegnent une fois jamés ne volount lesser. Et pur ceo deit mult prendre garde qi ad affaire od Franceis, qar qi ad affaire ové Fraunceis ad affaire ové deable. A l'autre foitz, quant les ditz messages de Fraunce feurent cy, nous lor reprismes mult de lor coveitise et lor deismes: 'Merveillouse est vostre coveitise, car ceo qe vous tenez une foiz, ou en bone manere ou en malvese manere, jamés ne voletz lesser. Et ne vous devroit il trop suffire qe vous avez tollu au roi d'Engleterre Normandie, q'est si graunde chose, semble qe vostre entencioun est de forclore le roi d'Engleterre de quanque il a decea la mier'

> (And we thought [that this was] the great covetousness of the French and we could not see any other way to ensure that it would be more profitable to the king of England, other than for the land of Gascony to

nication'), and also B. Bombi, 'Petitioning between England and Avignon in the First Half of the Fourteenth Century', in *Medieval Petitions: Grace and Grievance*, ed. W.M. Ormrod, G. Dodd and A. Musson (York, 2009), 64–81 and P. Zutshi, 'Petitions to the Pope in the Fourteenth Century', in ibid., 82–98.
30 Chaplais, *English Medieval Diplomatic Practice*, I.i, 46–141.
31 Ibid., I.i, no. 149.
32 Chaplais notes that contemporaries found Boniface particularly sharp-tongued, an Italian cardinal going as far as to observe that 'cum dyabolo enim habemus facere' (we have to deal with a/the devil) (I.i, 271 n. 80); ironically, the formula is virtually identical to that used by the pope of the French. The text is on pp. 270–1.

be in our hands, for the French are royally covetous. That which they
ever hold once, they never wish to let go of. And for this reason anyone
who has dealings with the French should be careful, for he who deals
with the French, deals with a/the devil. On another occasion, when the
said French messengers were here, we reproached them greatly for their
covetousness and said to them: 'Your covetousness is astonishing, for
that which you once hold, rightly or wrongfully, you never wish to
let go of. And should it not be sufficient for you that you have taken
Normandy from the king of England, which is a great thing, it seems
that your intention is to get the king of England out of all which he has
overseas.')

This has the ring of a reliable and authentic reproduction if not of the pope's
ipsissima verba, at any rate of what would have been to readers, a plausible reconstruction. Graphies are Anglo-Norman but there is nothing in this which is otherwise specifically insular or linguistically problematic from a French perspective.
Elsewhere, the documents preserve the verbatim text of a speech which the envoys
are to make to the pope in 1311 ('les paroles que mons Henry Spigurnel et mons'
Johan de Benstede deivent dire', from 1307) 'les paroles qe l'evesque de Wyncestre
et mons' Thomas de Berkle dirront a l'apostle de par nostre seignour le roi' (the
words which my lord Henry Spigurnel and my lord John of Bensted should say; the
words which the Bishop of Winchester and my lord Thomas of Berkeley will say
to the Pope on behalf of our lord the king).[33] In both cases, the pope was Clement
V, born Raymond Bertrand de Got from Vilandraut in the present-day Gironde.
He, too, we may perhaps assume, would have understood French, and the direc-
tions to the envoys do seem to suggest that they should actually use these texts for
their speeches. Perhaps more problematic is the summary in French of a credence
entrusted to Pierre Galicien for exposition to James II of Aragon in 1321,[34] but it
may be that the formula adopted (wittingly or unwittingly) reveals that the language
choice here is less straightforward: 'Pierres Galicien [...] est chargé de returner a
meisme le roi od lettres de creaunce et de lui dire de par nostre seigneur le roi qe ...'
(Pierre Galicien is instructed to return to the king himself with letters of credence
and to say to him on behalf of the king that ...) (my emphasis).

Diplomacy needed documents, either as an aid to oral negotiations, in advance of
them, or to record the results, once agreement had been reached. Typically, therefore,
it is well-documented, at least relative to other activities (it is probably no accident
that the first 'French' document, the Strasbourg Oaths, is a diplomatic text). Diplomacy deals in words and thus it leaves documentary traces. Commerce, on the other
hand, deals in numbers, and numbers are, alas, less eloquent about the language in
which the negotiations took place. As a result, and also of course because much
of it is more ephemeral, trade, particularly at a fairly basic and local level, is less
dependent on written documents and is correspondingly less well recorded.

Throughout the thirteenth century, and well beyond, by far the most important
trade was in wool and cloth, with a number of additional commodities (notably
woad and alum) directly related to and essential for these two central elements
in the English economy. From the early twelfth century at the latest, there was a
thriving cloth industry throughout England, with thirteenth-century documentation,

---

[33] Ibid., I.i, no. 43c, and I.i, no. 41b.
[34] Ibid., I.i, no. 47b.

in particular of cloth exports to Italy and Spain.[35] The pipe rolls for 1210/1211 show that most southern and south-eastern ports were by then importing woad, and it was being traded in towns (not only ports) all over England by 1225–50.[36] It has been estimated[37] that the manpower required to produce all the cloth made in England in 1400 would have amounted to about 15,000 people, or 0.65% of the population; to this, presumably, needs to be added those involved in import and export trade, and also in agriculture. At the same time, Flanders and northern France constituted significant rivals throughout Europe and beyond. Wool and finished cloth went to France, Spain, and Italy; England imported woad from Picardy in the thirteenth century, and from Toulouse in the fourteenth and fifteenth centuries.[38] English international commerce revolved around wool and cloth. The question then is what traces it has left, ideally in a form which will allow us to comment on the language in which the trade was carried out.

Sources reveal the geographical diversity from which merchants came. To take just one example, the ancient custom of 1275 from Hull lists in the first few pages Lübeck, Ghent, Saint-Valéry, Amiens, Corbie, Abbeville, Bordeaux, Cahors, Bruges, Ypres, Gravelinge, Dieppe, Cologne, Provence, and Pourville in northern France.[39] Men are identified as being companions of the Cerchi, Frescobaldi, and the Bardi. The account (like, for example, the *Port Books* of Southampton, or parts of the Little Red Book of Bristol, including the oath sworn by woad-merchants[40]) is written in French, but that does not really tell us very much, because the information provided is so sparse. Elsewhere, in a pattern identified previously,[41] ships' names are quoted in French, even in documents otherwise compiled in Latin. For example, the 1323 accounts for wool, woolfells and hides exported from ports along the south coast of England between Weymouth and Plymouth mention a 'navis que vocatur La Gaynghebien de Teynghemutha exivit xx die Januarii …' (a ship called La Gaynghebien of Teignmouth left port on 20th January).[42] Later Latin documents amongst those assembled by Gras[43] often display the language mixing which has been found to be a characteristic of later medieval business documents in a variety of different countries.[44] Typically, and predictably, names of merchandise are given in languages other than the matrix language of the document, a practice evident in Flanders, in the *Port Books* of Southampton (with English and Italian words) and throughout the type of mercantile document (for purely English or international purposes) which has been so fruitfully analysed by Laura Wright.[45]

---

[35] Chorley, 'English Cloth Exports', 9.

[36] Carus-Wilson, 'Guède française', 92.

[37] E. Miller, 'The Fortunes of the English Textile Industry during the Thirteenth Century', *EcHR* new ser. 18 (1965), 64–82.

[38] Chorley, 'Cloth Exports of Flanders and Northern France'; Carus-Wilson, 'Guède française'.

[39] Gras, *Early English Customs System*, 225ff.

[40] Fryde, 'Italian Maritime Trade', 221.

[41] Trotter, '*Oceano vox*', 16; Kowaleski, 'Maritime *lingua franca*', 114.

[42] Gras, *Early English Customs System*, 253.

[43] Ibid.

[44] Examples include: M.C. Davidson, 'Code-Switching and Authority in Late Medieval England', *Neophilologus* 87 (2003), 473–86; T. Hunt, 'Code-Switching in Medical Texts', in *Multilingualism in Later Medieval Britain*, ed. D.A. Trotter (Cambridge, 2000), 131–47; H. Schendl, 'Linguistic Aspects of Code-Switching in Medieval English Texts', in ibid., 77–92; D.A. Trotter, '*Si le français n'y peut aller*: Villers-Cotterêts and Mixed-Language Documents from the Pyrenees', in *Conceptions of Europe in Renaissance France: A Festschrift for Keith Cameron*, ed. D.J. Cowling (Amsterdam, 2006), 77–97; Vitali, 'Interférences entre le latin et la langue vernaculaire'.

[45] Wright, 'Hanseatic Merchants'; 'Code-Intermediate Phenomena'.

The obvious language for communication regarding trade in wool, or cloth, or woad, between England and France and possibly also between England and Italy or Spain, was French. The international status and role of French is demonstrated not only by its deployment in high-level diplomatic documents and in literature, but also in 'international' (by modern standards) correspondence such as that in the letters and petitions in All Souls 182, whose recipients are by no means all French or English.[46] Thus the collection contains (for example) a letter (no. 217) from the duke of Milan to his brother-in-law, in French (or in what may be scribal Anglo-Norman). So, too, diplomacy and trade come together in discussions about merchants' rights and in attempts to resolve trade disputes. I conclude this short survey with three examples of material of this type, taken from the online National Archives (TNA) Ancient Petitions collection, all concerning north-eastern France and England.[47]

(A) TNA SC 8/312/E3 (c. 1280–96?)[48]

Driu Malerbe of Amiens and Southampton seeks to repossess his goods in Lincolnshire

[1] A nostre seignor le Rey moustrent les vallez Driu Malerbe bourgoys d'Amiens et de Norhampton com les biens l'avauntdit Driu fussent ares[2]tuz en Engleterre et les avauntdiz vallés eussent requis les biens a leur maistre par mainprise. E, Sire, de vostre grace et par la priere Sire Edmont [3] vostre frere comaundastes la delivraunce et ensivaunt leur bosoigne [4] furent venduez totes leur marchaundises fors .xvii. sacs de laine et [4] quatre toneus et .ij. quartiers de waide qe sont en le counté de Nicole et la unt trové les vallés .xxiiij. meinpernours obligés par escrit […][49] [5] le visconte de Nicole d'avoir la delivraunce. Et ad le visconte en sa garde les escriz et les biens et les vallés nient le plus que des biens, et sont[50] [6] les biens en perissaunt par defaute de garde; et ceo unt il moustré au Tresorier par plusours foyz, et nule remedie n'en voet faire. Par quei [7], Sire, il vous prient pur Dieu remedie, et q'il puissent avoir ceus biens qe sont demourés par la mainprise avauntdite.

(The servants of Driu Malerbe, burgess of Amiens and Northampton show to our lord the King how the goods of the said Driu were seized in England and the said servants had requested their master's goods as bail. And, Sire, of your grace and by the prayers of Sir Edmond your brother you commanded their release according to their needs; all the merchandise was sold except for seventeen sacks of wool and four barrels and two quarters of woad which are in the county of Lincolnshire and there the servants found twenty-four men who would guarantee in writing that they would stand as surety […] the sheriff of Lincoln would take delivery. And the sheriff has in his keeping the documents and the goods and the servants do not have the goods either, and the goods are perishing for want of being kept [properly]; and this they have shown to the Treasurer several times, and he does not wish to offer any

---

[46] M.D. Legge, ed., *Anglo-Norman Letters and Petitions* (Oxford, 1941).

[47] Documents are transcribed using the following conventions: line-numbers in the original are indicated by numerals in square brackets; manuscript contractions are expanded, and indicated by underlining; cedilla and acute accent (only) are used to indicate *ç* as in modern French, and tonic *e* (as opposed to mute *e*), whether it would bear a grave or an acute accent in modern French; word-division, capitalization, use of apostrophes and punctuation have been modernized.

[48] Dated in part by the mention of Edmund Crouchback, the king's brother, who died in 1296. See TNA online catalogue.

[49] The right-hand side of the document is dark and I cannot read the final word.

[50] Here too I have difficulty reading the document.

remedy for it. For which reason, Sire, they ask you in God's name for a remedy, and that they can have those goods which have remained as bail.)

(B) TNA SC 8/285/14241 (1300–30?)[51]

Amiens merchants petition the king for redress regarding goods in King's Lynn

[1] A nostre seigneur le Roi e a son conseil mustrent les marchantz de Amyens qe amenent diverses marchan[2]dises en la ville de Lenne sicome marchaundises de wadde, les queles q'i covent q'i y soint [3] assaez par teintures e qu'eles y[52] covent q'i çoent[53] mesurés venduz et tavernez[54] par mie leur [4] meyns e autrement nul homme les achateroit en gros e pur les queles y donnent leur custumes [5] deues e usueles au Roi; e pur les queles le meir e la communalté de Lenne leur maundent [6] tounu e ount destreint pur tounu doner; paront les ditz marchantz[55] [prient][56] a nostre seigneur le Roi q'il [7] voille commaunder as ditz meir e communalté par soen bref qe eux soient quites de tounu doner, [8] fesaunz au Roi ceo qe de dreit deyvent faire. E qe[57] la destresce qe sur eux est faite, leur [9] soit relessé qar il sount aliens e n'ount terres ne tenementz en Engleterre.

(To our lord the King and to his council: the merchants of Amiens show that they bring diverse merchandises to the town of King's Lynn such as quantities of woad, which it is necessary to assay for colour and and that it is also necessary that [the cloths] be measured, sold, and sold by them personally, and otherwise no-one would buy them in bulk, and for these goods they there pay the usual customs which are due to the King; and for which the mayor and town of King's Lynn demand taxes and have distrained their goods to oblige them to pay the taxes; by which the said merchants [ask] our lord the King that he will command by writ the mayor and town to exempt them from paying taxes, doing to the King what they should by law do. And that the distrained goods should be released, for they are aliens and have neither land nor property in England.)

(C) TNA SC 8/283/14137 (c. 1300–1325?)[58]

Spanish merchants petition the king regarding alleged mistreatment in Abbeville

[1] A tres excellent et tres poissant no segneur le roy d'Engleterre. Supplient les marchaans [2] d'Espaigne. Tres chiers sires, comme les dis marcaans ont usé de lonc tans de venir [3] en vostre vile d'Abbevile a tout leur marcaandises. Et puis .v. ans ennecha[59] nous funt [4] choses de coi nous sommes en damache: ch'est assavoir que li maires et li eskevin d'Abbevile nous [5] avoient otrié preju.gement que nous arions vij couratiers[60] de nos marcaandises tex que [6] seroient loiaux et a no volenté

---

51 The TNA online catalogue suggests this: 'tentatively dated on the basis of the hand and language'.
52 Written above the line with an insertion mark.
53 I.e., *soient*.
54 The verb can mean 'vendre en général', see Gdf 7,659a.
55 MS appears to read 'maunchantz'.
56 There is no verb in the MS.
57 Written above the line with an insertion mark.
58 The dating in the online TNA catalogue is based on a close rolls document (November 1313), a safe-conduct for Spanish merchants in Abbeville, to the circumstances of which this petition may refer (*CPR 1313–17*, 34).
59 Picard form of 'ença', Gdf 3,85b.
60 The word is in Gdf 2,312b in various quotations sub **correterie**; and cf. GdfC 9,228a; TL 2,845.

a droit. Et seur che[61] on nous a mis .vij. couratiers outre no vo[7]lenté dont il nous
vient grant damache. Et encore nous font[62] plus d'outrage li couratier que se [8] nous
vendons nos denrées a Arras ou a Amiens ou en le vile d'Abbevile et il n'i sont.
Si le nous font il pai[9]er le couratage[63] maugré nous ausi bien que s'il y fussent,
che qu'il n'est point acoustumé ne ainques ne fu en [10] nul pais lau[64] marcaans
repairent. Et le jour des frankes festes[65] que on nous souloit [11] doner le pois le
premier jour puis miedi en avant pour peser nos denrees, il le nous ont rete[12]nu[66]
et mis au secont jour dont nous y avons grant damage. Et se nous alons pour ches
choses[67] [13] ou pour autres outrages ou desonnors qu'il nous faichent par devant le
maire et les eschevins et le plus [14] mauvais ribaut de le vile nous fiert ou nous fait
autre vilenie, il sera crut et en sen dit [15] et nous serons mis en prison pour faire
nous couster du nostre. Chiers sires, si vous rekeurons par Dieu qu'il [16] plaise a
vostre haute nobleche de quomander au maire et as eskevins de le vile d'Abbevile
qu'il [17] nous ostent ches usages et qu'il nous tiegnent a droit et a raison, et que
vous nous fachiés metre en vostre [18] sauvegarde car autrement li dit marchaant
ne pourroient durer en le dite vile [19] d'Abbevile.

(To our very excellent and very powerful lord the king of England. The merchants
of Spain supplicate [as follows:]. Dearest Sire, as the said merchants have for a
long time been used to come to our town of Abbeville with all their merchandise.
And for five years they do to us things which have been damaging to us: that is to
say, the mayor and the aldermen of Abbeville allowed a prior judgement that we
would have seven agents for our merchandise who would be loyal and rightly act
according to our wishes. And thereafter they imposed on us seven agents against
our wishes, which has caused us considerable damage. And moreover, the agents
commit a further outrage against us if we sell our goods in Arras or Amiens, or in
Abbeville when they are not there. They then make us pay the agent's fees against
our wishes as though they had been there, which is not the custom and never was in
any country which merchants visit. And on the day of the annual market, when we
would normally take our goods to the balance on the first day, from noon onwards,
so that we can weigh our goods, they refused us it, and provided it on the second
day, which was greatly damaging to us. And if we go to the mayor and aldermen
regarding these matters or because of other outrages or disrespect that they show us,
and then the lowest ruffian of the town strikes us or does something similarly base,
he will be believed on the strength of what he says and we will be put in prison in
order to occasion us expense. Dear Sire, we have recourse to you in God's name,
that it might please your high nobility to instruct the mayor and aldermen of the
town of Abbeville to desist from these practices and treat us legally and resonably,
and that you should take us under your protection, for otherwise the said merchants
will be unable to continue in the said town of Abbeville.)

The word appears most frequently in north-eastern texts; the sense is 'agent', 'handling agent' (mod.
Fr. *courtier*).

[61] 'che' written above the line with an insertion mark.

[62] 'font' written above the line with an insertion mark.

[63] 'Le couratage' written above the line with an insertion mark.

[64] I.e., 'la ou'.

[65] *Feste* in TL 3,1773 has the sense 'Jahrmarkt', seemingly restricted to north-eastern France/Flanders.
Cf. FEW 3,483b, and n. 1: 'An diese wortzone schliesst nördlich an fläm. *feest*, "jahrmarkt"'.

[66] MS rete-lu.

[67] After 'choses', at the end of the line, crossed out and expunctuated, 'par devant' (the words are
instead used later in the same sentence, line 13).

What can we conclude from these three specimens, and more generally, about cross-Channel communication? The first document (A) is principally important in that it identifies a merchant as being simultaneously 'bourgoys d'Amiens et de Norhampton'. It is written with fairly consistent Anglo-Norman forms (notably -*aun*- for continental French -*an*-[68]). The second document (B) is intermittently but not consistently Anglo-Norman in its graphies: so, *marchaundises* but then *marchandises* in lines 1–2, *ount* and *sount* for continental *ont* and *sont* in line 9, Anglo-Norman *ceo* in line 8, but in a document the point of which is to emphasize that the merchants concerned 'sount aliens e n'ount terres ne tenementz en Engleterre'. It is of course perfectly normal for spellings to vary in medieval French and here (as is usually the case) the inconsistency extends to the variable use of 'dialectal' forms. (In fact, even decisively 'Anglo-Norman' documents, in terms of origin and language, never display absolutely consistent 'Anglo-Norman' spellings.[69]) The third document (C) is linguistically quite different from the other two and is strongly Picardized. Picard forms include *c* instead of central French *ch* (*marcaans* line 2, *eskevins* line 16), *ch* instead of central *c* (*ennecha* line 3; *ch'est* line 4; *faichent* line 13, *nobleche* line 16), *le* instead of *la* for the feminine definite article (lines 8, 16, 18) and lexical items such as *frankes festes* (line 10), *couratiers* (line 5) and *couratage* (line 9). But, again, these forms are not consistent: next to *marcaans* (line 2) is *marchaans* (line 1), the same word is spelt *damache* (line 4) and *damage* (line 12), Picard *ches* ('ces') qualifies non-Picard *choses* (line 12: Picard would spell it *coses*), the *eskevin* (line 4) are *eschevins* ten lines later (line 13). These are not differences that matter, and unless we are to imagine that one person would have pronounced the word differently in two or three places in the same short document, they cannot possibly reflect pronunciation: they are simply spelling differences of no importance whatever to the communication process.

Extrapolating from this, it might be argued on a more general level that the differences between Anglo-Norman (insular) and continental French (whether central or Picard) are unimportant. Petitions like these were read out loud,[70] so spellings which we now assiduously label as 'dialectal' would not really have mattered in the slightest, and this may have been true, too, of some of the more formal, higher-level diplomatic documents, where there is evidence that these too were variously the basis for, or the record of, oral exchanges. Purely orthographic differences like this are patently far less significant than the overwhelming similarities between the different forms of medieval French, and do not detract from the point that this is basically one language found on both sides of the Channel, right the way through the Middle Ages, and indeed long after.

---

[68] A. Kristol, 'Le début du rayonnement parisien et l'unité du français au Moyen Âge : le témoignage des manuels d'enseignement du français publiés en Angleterre entre le XIIIe et le début du XVe siècle', *Revue de linguistique romane* 53 (1989), 335–67; Trotter, '*Pur meuz acorder en parlance E descorder en variaunce*'.

[69] Trotter, ibid., 88–92.

[70] G. Dodd, *Justice and Grace: Private Petitioning and the English Parliament in the Late Middle Ages* (Oxford, 2007), 292.

The Priory of Deerhurst and the Treaty of Paris (1259)*

William Chester Jordan

In my recent book on Westminster and Saint-Denis I draw attention to the importance of the resolution of what I called *l'affaire Deerhurst* in improving the atmosphere surrounding the final negotiations of the Treaty of Paris.[1] Here I want to expand on my remarks in the book. The status of the priory of Deerhurst had brought the bishop of Worcester and the monastery of Saint-Denis into conflict. The priory was located on the River Severn in the county of Gloucester and geographically (though not juridically) in the diocese of Worcester.[2] From its foundation it constituted an alien priory, that is to say, it was a dependency of a non-English abbey, in this case Saint-Denis. It was Edward the Confessor who endowed the Capetian royal monastery at Saint-Denis with its initial grant of property in Deerhurst.[3]

Although not unique, Deerhurst was one of very few alien priories established before the Norman Conquest, the event which precipitated a flood of new endowments of such institutions in England, especially though not solely in favour of Norman abbeys.[4] Some of the English properties with which Norman houses were endowed, while called priories, remained merely income-producing holdings or franchises, administered by overseers sent from the continental owners. On some of the properties, however, either immediately or after more or less lengthy periods, real monasteries, dependent on the continental mother houses, came into being, real in the sense of being corporate communities (fictitious persons) with official seals. They could make contracts with the permission of their mother houses, and they followed the latter's monastic rules. These conventual priories, as they have come to be called, regularly sent payments, tokens of dependency, to their mother houses. Their priors were elected by the resident monks, subject to confirmation by the mother houses, or else chosen from among the monks in the mother houses and

---

* I am very happy to acknowledge the fruitful feedback from the audience for this paper at the Sorbonne in September 2009, especially the valuable remarks of David Carpenter and Nicholas Vincent.

1 William Jordan, *A Tale of Two Monasteries: Westminster and Saint-Denis in the Thirteenth Century* (Princeton, 2009), 55–9.
2 H.J.L.J. Massé, *Abbey Church of Tewkesbury with Some Account of the Priory Church of Deerhurst, Gloucestershire* (London, 1901) has some useful information, interspersed unfortunately with a great deal of misinformation. He suggests that the name translates as 'the wood or grove of wild beasts' (p. 105). This is possible, for *hurst* can and may originally have carried the meaning 'grove', but another early meaning (*OED*) is sandbank or ford, equally or perhaps more appropriate for a site on the lower Severn, where the river becomes estuarial.
3 *Gallia christiana in provincias ecclesiasticas distributa* [*GC*], 16 vols (Paris, 1856–99), vii. 364. Chester New, *History of the Alien Priories in England to the Confiscation of Henry V* (Chicago, 1916), 2.
4 Martin Heale, *The Dependent Priories of Medieval English Monasteries* (Woodbridge, 2004), 20, with references to detailed studies.

imposed without the necessity of formal consultation with the local inmates (which, of course, does not mean that consultation was never practised).[5]

It was not long after the Confessor endowed Saint-Denis with the Deerhurst properties that the French abbey dispatched monks to the site.[6] The mother house retained the right of appointment of Deerhurst's priors, who were chosen from Saint-Denis' community.[7] The Confessor's endowment was not for a term of years but permanent, as is revealed in a charter of 1059 ('donum in perpetuum sancto Dionysio').[8] To this extent the endowment was inalienable, except with the pope's permission as Saint-Denis' direct and sole ecclesiastical lord. Because Saint-Denis had no ecclesiastical superior but the pope, it enjoyed the status of what is known as exemption. The most resented feature of this status – the feature bishops most resented – was the grant of freedom from local episcopal authority that it implied.[9] Exemption typically attached to an exempt monastery's conventual dependants, so that in the case under discussion, that of Deerhurst, the English priory, except for its subordination to Saint-Denis and the pope, recognized no other ecclesiastical authority over it.[10]

As far as the evidence permits us to know, it would appear that the arrangement envisioned between Saint-Denis and Deerhurst and the exemption of Deerhurst from the jurisdiction of the local diocesan, the bishop of Worcester, perdured without any major complications for nearly two centuries. And the priory's parallel relations with the English crown were equally pacific. Without much complaint, it rendered both the aids it owed (or graciously offered) to the crown and other fiscal contributions arising out of the property it held by military service.[11]

Relations were different between Deerhurst and among the various powers in the immediate hinterland of the priory, at least with respect to those properties regarded as laic, secular or, to use contemporary language, temporal. Evidence abounds as to a large number of lords' (including the priory's) rights in the hundred, the half-hundred (fifty hides), the quarter hundred, the seigneurie, the liberty, and the manor of Deerhurst.[12] So complex were the fragmentation and ties of dependence in temporal properties that royal officials sometimes frankly confessed that they could not pinpoint the nature or dimension of the relationships ('nescitur pro quanto

---

[5]	In general, see New, *History of the Alien Priories*. Heale (*Dependent Priories*, 4–5) argues that the distinction between conventual and non-conventual alien priories, though adopted by modern scholars from late medieval administrative terminology, may be too hard and fast and thus may misrepresent the thirteenth-century situation in some instances, but the status of Deerhurst would fall into the category of conventual alien priory, either by New's (and late medieval administrators') or by Heale's definition.

[6]	New, *History of the Alien Priories*, 2.

[7]	Ibid., 37–9, 43.

[8]	*GC*, vii. 364.

[9]	William Jordan, *Unceasing Strife, Unending Fear: Jacques de Thérines and the Freedom of the Church in the Age of the Last Capetians* (Princeton, 2005), 4, 24, 40, 42, 45–7, 51–2, 54, 74–5, 78.

[10]	Cf. the argument about the limits on exemption of conventual dependencies of exempt houses retold in Jordan, *Tale of Two Monasteries*, 187–9.

[11]	Thus, the prior of Deerhurst, like the bishops and other heads of monastic houses, contributed to the aid given for the marriage of Henry III's eldest sister to Frederick II in 1235–6 and to the aid for the invasion of France in 1242–3; *Liber feodorum: The Book of Fees*, 3 vols (HMSO, 1920–31), i. 560; ii. 1134.

[12]	For a variety of references, see *Liber feodorum*, i. 51, 'Prior Derhustr' tenet 1. hidas de dono Regis Edwardi' in Gloucestershire (dated 1211–13); i. 626, a listing of those holding freely ('libere') of various abbots and priors, including Deerhurst's, in Oxfordshire (dated possibly around the time of the interdict); and *CR 1247–51*, 94 (reference to Roger de Derneford's holding of a quarter hundred of Deerhurst, 20 October 1248). See also London, Westminster Abbey Muniments [WAM], nos 32701–02, with later references to the fourth part of the hundred and the manor of Deerhurst.

feodo').[13] True, on occasion the king's claims in these properties might generate disputes with local elites.[14] But this was atypical. Ordinarily, when disputes arose, the adversaries, whether including Deerhurst or not, were almost uniformly local elites who had conflicting claims in the highly complex cluster of property rights characteristic of the area.[15] Did this make relations among Deerhurst Priory and other local landholders and possessors of franchises distinct from those elsewhere in the kingdom? To put it in the simplest terms possible, no. Deerhurst's history was like that of just about any other English monastic institution. Indeed, the fact that it was an alien priory does not seem to have mattered a fig. This status neither enhanced nor impaired its standing or affected its relations to any significant degree.

Then in the 1250s everything changed by a chain of events that is chronicled by Matthew Paris.[16] The monk of St Albans informs us that the king's brother, Earl Richard of Cornwall, visited Saint-Denis in 1250 and purchased Deerhurst Priory from the abbey. Richard had somehow managed to get papal endorsement and approval of his purchase while earlier traveling in Italy. This provided the legal basis for Saint-Denis' agreement to sell the priory; yet, it does not explain its decision to do so. Is it conceivable that the pope ordered the monastery to comply with Richard's wishes? The evidence one way or the other is wholly lacking.

In any case, after attaining 'title' to the property, Richard returned to England and, apparently without an iota of apprehension over how the monks might react, ran roughshod over them. A new prior, the Frenchman Robert de Tremblay, had entered upon his office by royal permission on 6 November 1251. The royal confirmation was accompanied by an order to the appropriate sheriffs assigning him the priory's temporalities in Gloucestershire, Oxfordshire, Worcestershire and Northamptonshire.[17] But this seems to have availed him and his monks nothing when they were faced with eviction by the earl soon after. Thus, they abandoned their home, and the earl set about making plans as to how best to transform the building complex, either by razing it or modifying parts of it, in order to erect a castle to protect trade on the Severn. While plans were maturing, the more vulnerable of the unoccupied and abandoned buildings began to sink into decrepitude, perhaps pillaged by locals.

No scholar, so far as I know, has disputed Noël Denholm-Young's opinion, expressed in his biography of Earl Richard, that this 'remarkable transaction never took full effect'.[18] The expelled monks probably found temporary refuge in one or more nearby monastic houses. When monks dispersed under other difficult circumstances, usually economic, it was customary for them to find lodging and

---

[13] See, for example, *Liber feodorum*, ii. 831–2, 'Prior de Derherst tenet utramque villam [Teinton' et Mor'] in liberam elemosinam, nescitur pro quanto feodo' (dated c. 1242–3).

[14] See the dispute over what was revealed to be the illegal taking of two malefactors apprehended in Westminster Abbey's liberty in Deerhurst to the king's prison (dated 9 April 1248); *CR 1247–51*, 38–9.

[15] See, for example, the dispute in the year 1249 between the earl of Gloucester and the prior of Deerhurst alluded to in the *CRR*, xix. *33 to 34 Henry III (1249–50)*, no. 2405. For an example of another institution enduring the same kind of locally based dispute, see the case of the abbot of Westminster and Roger de Derneford in 1249–50 concerning view of frankpledge in the quarter hundred of Deerhurst: *CRR*, xix. *33 to 34 Henry III (1249–50)*, nos 1297, 2025, 2404, and xx. *34 to 35 Henry III (1250)*, nos 243, 814, 1341, 1864.

[16] *CM*, v. 112, 118.

[17] *CPR 1247–58*, 118.

[18] Noël Denholm-Young, *Richard of Cornwall* (New York, 1947), 74 n. 2. Denholm-Young's is the standard modern biography, from which I have extracted the information that follows in this paragraph.

succour in neighbouring houses.[19] But what had happened to their rents and how were the tenurial relations between the priory and its tenants modified by the earl's purchase? Most likely Richard appropriated the rents as he must have intended to appropriate the priory's rights of patronage of six churches, and it is possible, in the first instance, that the tenants were indifferent as to whom they paid them as long as there was no change in the amount they owed and, in the second, that no opportunity arose soon enough to require the exercise of patronage.[20] There is no direct evidence on this point. Yet, the benefactors and heirs of Deerhurst would have been more concerned. We know that occasionally donors specified a reversion of rents to themselves or their heirs if, in the future, a house should not survive.[21] The point is that the possibility of the extinction of a priory like Deerhurst and the reallocation of its rents was certainly not a new issue, but it almost inevitably promised to be a contentious one. Men and women had confronted the possibility before, and it is plausible, albeit it is again undocumented, that Earl Richard and Deerhurst's donors and the descendants of its donors might have commenced a vigorous argument over the disposition of the rental income.

More difficult and far more troubling, at least in my mind, is the fact that some of Deerhurst's income was intended to support perpetual prayers and masses and the giving of alms. If the prayers were not being prayed and the masses were not being celebrated at Deerhurst's altars and if the alms were not being given, surely there must have been at least the potential for a real outcry. Or, and this is almost certainly the case, living donors and the heirs of donors whose souls were supposed to be honoured with supplications, anniversary masses and charity soon learned that the earl's whole project was being abandoned. For the monks and their patrons were fortunate in one respect. Richard could not successfully execute his plans for Deerhurst's transformation, because other matters of concern to him sapped his resources and occupied his time. He was pouring money into nearby Hailes Abbey, his most famous foundation (it was, like Deerhurst, also in Gloucestershire), and into a castle residence in Wiltshire. Negotiations about the possibility of his accepting the crown of Sicily and leading the papal war against the Hohenstaufen came to naught but put considerable demands on his time. He was eventually more successful in his equally time-consuming and certainly more costly negotiations to secure the kingship of Germany. The most emotionally draining, expensive and consuming issue in the decade of the 1250s was confronting the emerging baronial resistance to his brother's policies, in which his loyalty to his royal sibling was in a tense relationship with Richard's own sympathy with some of the barons' criticisms. He played a crucial role in every stage of this developing confrontation between King Henry and the magnates. In the circumstances, Deerhurst was saved.

After a relatively short period, then, the monks drifted back to their priory and reestablished their community. Since the earl let them be, they presumed that the situation had returned to the status quo ante. A seemingly routine royal order, dated 16 June 1253, permitting the prior to take thirty trees or big beams ('fusta') in his

[19] William Jordan, *The Great Famine: Northern Europe in the Early Fourteenth Century* (Princeton, 1996), 70–1, 84.
[20] On Deerhurst's rents and patronage (in addition to the six churches, the prior himself was parson of the parish church of Deerhurst), cf. *CIMisc, 1219–1307*, 156–7, no. 472.
[21] Anne Lester, *Making Cistercian Nuns* (forthcoming), provides evidence of this practice in the thirteenth century in northern France (the juridical environment of Saint-Denis which would have had to monitor gifts to Deerhurst), which she has kindly allowed me to cite before publication of her book. She has drawn it from the Archives Départementales of the Aube (Troyes), 3 H 3784, dated October 1224.

(the prior's) own woodlands, which fell within the bounds of the king's forest of Wychwood (Oxfordshire), testifies to this general understanding of the new situation.[22] This would suggest that the displacement of the monks and the general disturbance at Deerhurst lasted little more than a year, if that long, and this brevity may explain the otherwise inexplicable silence of the sources on the disputes that arose from Earl Richard's actions.

In any case, the timber was presumably necessary to repair buildings that locals scavenged and/or that the earl's crews had started to tear down before he and his resources began to be directed and indeed devoured elsewhere. Evidence for 1256 points in the same direction, that is to say, to the apparently successful reestablishment of relations as they were in place before the earl's purchase. In that year the prior presented Pagan de Mobray to the forest justices as the monks' woodward for its property at Taynton, where they had a manor originally given to Saint-Denis by Edward the Confessor. The justices swore him without incident.[23]

Yet, an important legal issue remained. Had the earl's purchase annulled the dependence on Saint-Denis of any future monastic community at Deerhurst? What did Earl Richard say to the Deerhurst monks? Did he represent his willingness to let them resettle as a new act of foundation with himself as founder? Or was the annulment conditional, which is to say, did reconstitution reestablish Deerhurst as an alien priory dependent on Saint-Denis? In the absence of the original sale documents, one cannot know for sure what had and had not been agreed to at the time of purchase or before then in the earl's negotiations with the pope. But the issue assumed importance in 1258. On 28 June Prior Robert de Tremblay was the beneficiary of a royal writ of protection, a routine issuance implying the crown's vigilance in looking after the welfare of the people and properties of bishops, heads of monastic houses and other prelates who were temporarily, but for a significant period, leaving the region or the kingdom. Robert was going to France. The writ of protection was due to expire about five months later at All Saints, 1 November 1258.[24]

My guess is that Robert de Tremblay, who had been prior of Deerhurst since 1251 and had endured the whole brunt of the crisis, including the expulsion of the monks early in the decade and the reconstruction of the community a year or so later, was sick. He would be returning to Saint-Denis to retire. Indeed, in October 1258 the English royal government issued an order, just as it had for Robert in 1251 and to the same cluster of officials, the sheriffs of Gloucestershire, Worcestershire, Northamptonshire, and Oxfordshire, to recognize Benoît, a monk of Saint-Denis, as Robert's successor as the new prior of Deerhurst and to commend to him the priory's temporalities in their counties.[25]

What Benoît discovered, undoubtedly to his horror, was that a bishop was claiming the right of jurisdiction over Deerhurst Priory. Since Saint-Denis was an exempt abbey, subject only to the pope within the church, and since it was well understood, though decried by bishops, that the exemption of a mother house extended to her daughters (saving the rights of the mother), the local bishop in question, Walter Cantilupe of Worcester, should have kept out of the priory's business, unless, of course, Saint-Denis could no longer properly be considered the mother house of the

[22] *CR 1251–53*, 370.
[23] *Oxfordshire Forests, 1246–1609*, ed. Beryl Schumer (Oxfordshire Record Society Series 64, 2004), 47 and 79 no. 76 and n. 28.
[24] *CPR 1247–58*, 639.
[25] *CPR 1247–58*, 653.

community now in place at Deerhurst.[26] Put another way and restating my earlier questions, was Deerhurst Priory in 1258 the same corporate entity as the Deerhurst Priory before the sale to Earl Richard or was it an entirely new community, a new corporation, and therefore no longer exempt or tied in any way to Saint-Denis?

A quite unmistakable answer came from Saint-Denis, and it was yes. I am persuaded that the new abbot of Saint-Denis, Mathieu de Vendôme, elected in 1258, thought the original sale invalid, and blamed it on his predecessors' incompetence. (There is abundant evidence that he had this attitude toward many of the *acta* of at least one of his predecessors, Henri Mallet.[27]) Or perhaps he believed there was an oral agreement, entered into at the time of purchase, that if the property ever resumed its status as a site of a monastic community, the original relationship with Saint-Denis would automatically revive. Unfortunately, from Abbot Mathieu's point of view, Henry III, who had so recently confirmed Benoît as prior, was swayed by Walter Cantilupe and seized Deerhurst into the crown's hand until such time as a final assessment of the situation could be made. This further riled the monks of the famous French abbey. What did the king really know about Deerhurst, this relatively unimportant priory? What did he know about points of law with regard to its status? Probably not much, but in his entourage now was the new abbot of Westminster, Richard de Ware, who knew a lot, simply because the great English monastery was a landholder in Deerhurst's vicinity.[28] Indeed, he was intimately involved in some of the properties in which Deerhurst had an interest. For example, the tenant, the Mucegros family, of the manor of Botinton held it in third parts from three lords, the earl of Gloucester, the abbot of Westminster, and the prior of Deerhurst (who received 28s 4d).[29]

Meanwhile the English king's trip to France to conclude the negotiations for the Treaty of Paris was approaching, and at some point he must have realized the anomaly of accepting the hospitality of Saint-Denis' abbot while the Deerhurst affair festered. By the way, I think Henry really wanted to stay at Saint-Denis and have nothing spoil it. The visit was bound to be something like a homecoming or a return to a favorite vacation spot, for it was at Saint-Denis that Henry stayed for a while when, on his trip to France in 1254, he first met his brother-in-law Louis IX.[30] Early on, the English king had not known whether their meeting would be cordial. The kingdoms were technically at war. Henry was even a little apprehensive about returning to England safe and sound. In a promise made on 14 October 1254 to indemnify the archbishop of Bordeaux for losses the latter had incurred wrongly at the hands of Henry's officials in Aquitaine, the king mentioned that he was soon going north to the French capital. He would authorize the archbishop's remuneration when he was there or at Saint-Denis, before returning to England – dead or alive, he added somewhat ominously, even melodramatically.[31] As it turned out he had a

---

[26] The details on the events chronicled in this paragraph have been reconstructed from entries in *CR 1259–61*, 21, 47–8, 226.

[27] Jordan, *Tale of Two Monasteries*, 27, 32–3.

[28] On Westminster's properties and rights at Deerhurst and relations with the village and priory in Abbot Richard de Ware's time, see WAM, Westminster Domesday, fols 31–2. See also Barbara Harvey, *The Obedientiaries of Westminster Abbey and their Financial Records, c. 1275 to 1540* (Woodbridge, 2002), 3; Emma Mason, *Westminster Abbey and its People, c. 1050–c. 1216* (Woodbridge, 1996), 84; Helen Cam, *The Hundred and the Hundred Rolls: An Outline of Local Government in Medieval England* (London, 1930), 267.

[29] *CIPM*, i. no. 311.

[30] *CPR 1247–58*, 385–6.

[31] *CPR 1247–58*, 344–5.

most delightful time, and the sojourn was the occasion for the opening soundings for making an end to the war. Now, four years later, he would be returning. Now he would be welcomed as a peacemaker. 'Blessed are the peacemakers for they shall be called children of God.'

The first task, though, was to make a lesser peace in the Deerhurst affair. Henry announced on 9 January 1259, perhaps on Richard de Ware's behest (the new abbot would become a ferocious defender of the rights of exempt monasteries),[32] he would lift the recently imposed royal guardianship and consign Deerhurst's temporalities to Benoît of Saint-Denis until Michaelmas. The sop Henry threw to Bishop Walter Cantilupe was the promise to further look into the status of the priory. Benoît, in other words, was not yet recognized formally as prior. Henry acted as a special favour ('de speciali gratia'), he said, and at the request of the abbot of Saint-Denis and the French king. In fact, he continued, he had only seized the priory's temporalities in the first place because the bishop of Worcester told him – insinuated to him – that it was vacant, the bishop not having recognized Benoît's accession as prior as licit.[33]

Walter Cantilupe did not give in readily and managed to delay the recognition of Benoît as prior for more than a year. But Henry was insistent in the end that the bishop of Worcester make peace with the abbot of Saint-Denis.[34] And as a result the English king's welcome and stay at the French monastery overflowed with warmth. Abbot Mathieu de Vendôme was the perfect host. He had his monks process for the English king's arrival arrayed in their ceremonial vestments. He put the royal entourage up in monastic apartments. He also, along with Louis IX, paid a significant part of the bills that the English ran up during their visit.[35] Henry in turn entered into the worship-life at the abbey with enthusiasm.[36]

Deerhurst did not immediately thereafter sink back into oblivion. On the presentation of Abbot Mathieu of Saint-Denis, it received another monk of the French house, Jean d'Estrennes, as its new prior in mid July 1260. The order went out to the usual suspects, the sheriffs of Gloucestershire, Worcestershire, Northamptonshire, and Oxfordshire, to deliver the priory's temporalities to Jean.[37] Routine enough, but clearly Abbot Mathieu de Vendôme had worries beyond a smooth succession at the priory. And fortunately for him he had Louis IX's ear and the ear of his wife Marguerite de Provence. Nine days after Henry mandated the delivery of the temporalities, he issued a second order (23 July 1260) in which he addressed other matters at Deerhurst. This order acknowledged that he had been lobbied by the French king and by his own wife, who was Marguerite's sister, on behalf of Deerhurst. Presumably Louis had written to Henry – and Marguerite had written to her sister Eleanor – about something troubling that they had heard, implicitly through Mathieu de Vendôme, about Deerhurst. During the vacancy preceding Jean d'Estrennes' appointment as prior, Henry (or, rather, his officials), strapped for money in the difficult struggle with the barons, appropriated more than was seemly of the priory's

[32] Jordan, *Tale of Two Monasteries*, 187–9, 192–200.
[33] *CCR 1259–61*, 21–2.
[34] *CCR 1259–61*, 226.
[35] A conclusion reached by David Carpenter, 'The Meetings of Kings Henry III and Louis IX', *TCE*, x (2005), 1–30 (at 9), by arguing back from Henry's household account rolls. In general on these accounts, see David Carpenter, 'Household Rolls of King Henry III of England (1216–72)', *HR* 80 (2007), 22–46.
[36] Carpenter, 'Meetings of Kings Henry III and Louis IX', 15, 19–20.
[37] *CPR 1258–66*, 81.

income. King Henry now promised to have his escheator on the hither side of the River Trent return to the priory's coffers £30 of the £40 that the officials had taken.[38]

Abbot Mathieu's watchfulness and his good connections through the French court to their English royal relatives had the potential for helping insulate Deerhurst Priory from transgressions of this sort in the future.[39] But the political situation in England in the early to mid 1260s was so unstable that nothing was immediately certain for the house. Proof of this is that there was another long vacancy at the priory in the late winter of 1265, which persisted through the spring.[40]

Could the prospect of a new prior appointed by the abbot of Saint-Denis even have been welcome in England at the time? On the one hand, the barons had seized power after the Battle of Lewes on 14 May 1264, and the visceral hostility of the French government, including counsellors like Mathieu de Vendôme, to this act was well known. On the other hand, the new rulers claimed to want to restore good government, and the right of the abbot of Saint-Denis to appoint a new prior had been reaffirmed in law and custom. Did the baronial partisan Bishop Walter Canti- lupe, who had blessed the rebel army at Lewes and said mass personally for Simon de Montfort, its commander, the next year on the morning of the Battle of Evesham (4 August 1265), try to prevent the admission of Saint-Denis' candidate as he had in 1259?[41] I do not know, but I strongly suspect that he did.

What is known is that by high summer, a new prior was finally in place. On 20 August this new prior and a number of other prelates received writs of protec- tion.[42] They would have been issued so as to facilitate their coming together to voice their collective support for the restoration of royal rule following the Battle of Evesham, where the rebellious barons were defeated and Simon de Montfort was killed. It was a time of celebration for the king's defenders, culminating in Henry III's crown-wearing at Westminster Abbey on 13 October, Edward the Confessor's feast day.[43] Something like normalcy was returning to England, to governance, and indeed to the alien priory of Deerhurst. Evidence is abundant from the late 1260s until the end of the thirteenth century, indeed until the Hundred Years' War and the end of the Middle Ages when the whole system of alien priories broke down, of the restitution at Deerhurst of the kind of equilibrium characteristic of the period before Earl Richard's purchase. This includes routine issuances of writs of protec- tion for its priors, arrangements for the reception of new priors from Saint-Denis, payments of aids, minor squabbles over fiscal and proprietary claims to feudal land, disputes with the mother house, and occasional petitions from Saint-Denis to the English crown to protect or show benevolence to the priory.[44] At long last *l'affaire Deerhurst* was history.

---

[38] *CCR 1259–61*, 82 (also pp. 47–8); London, TNA, Ancient Petitions, SC 1/3/133 and 144: on-line, http:www.nationalarchives.gov.uk/catalogue/
[39] See, for example, *The Parliament Rolls of Medieval England, 1275–1504*, I: *Edward I, 1275–1294*, ed. Paul Brand (Woodbridge and London, 2005), 150 (dated Michaelmas 1283), 'amercements [were] pardoned to the prior of Deerhurst at the request of the abbot of Saint-Denis'.
[40] *CPR 1258–66*, 405; *CLR*, v. *1260–67*, 173.
[41] The information on Walter's warm relationship with the baronial reformers and rebels is culled from C.H. Lawrence's entry on the bishop in the *ODNB* (on-line), 'Cantilupe, Walter de'.
[42] *CPR 1258–66*, 441–2.
[43] Björn Weiler, 'Symbolism and Politics in the Reign of Henry III', *TCE*, ix (2003), 15–41 (at 23).
[44] *CPR 1258–66*, 639; *CPR 1266–72*, 366–8, 397, 418, 605, 627, 669; *CPR 1272–81*, 49; *CPR 1281–92*, 66; *CIPM*, i. nos 123, 404, 407; *CCR 1279–88*, 181–2, 223; WAM, no. 8198; *Parliament Rolls of Medi- eval England* [PROME], I: *Edward I, 1275–1294*, ed. Brand, 150; PROME (on-line), C49 File 2 Text/ Trans, 1380 January Text/Trans, 1447 February Text/Trans, 1463 April Text/Trans; *Calendar of Chancery Warrants A.D. 1244–1326* (HMSO, 1927), 333; *CFR*, iv. 386, 419, 451.

The Treaty of Paris (1259) and
the Aristocracy of England and Normandy[1]

Daniel Power

King Henry of England came to France with the earl of Gloucester and
many knights and prelates from his kingdom and made peace with Saint
Louis, king of France. For he quitclaimed to the kings of France whatever right he was claiming in the duchy of Normandy and the counties
of Anjou, Maine, Touraine and Poitou and in their fiefs, by the express
wish of his brother Richard, king of the Romans, and the counsel of the
princes and prelates of England.

This passage, adapted from Primat's *Gesta Ludovici Regis* some time after the
canonisation of Saint Louis in 1297, was copied in the early fifteenth century into
one of the thirteenth-century cartularies of the Norman abbey of Saint-Évroult.[2] As
well as showing the interest that late medieval Norman monks had in their Anglo-
Norman past, the account reminds us that the peace of 1258–9 was concluded not
only between Louis IX and Henry III, but also between their barons; an exceptionally
large number of nobles are said to have accompanied the king of England to Paris.[3]
The active participation of the aristocracy in the Angevin-Capetian negotiations is
easy to explain. Like the kings of England, many landowners after 1204 aspired to
bring England and Normandy once more under a single ruler, and that hope shaped
Anglo-French relations throughout the period from 1204 to 1259. Furthermore, the

[1] I am grateful to the conference participants for their comments upon this article, which forms part of
a project to examine the fate of the estates and families affected by the collapse of the Anglo-Norman
realm. An AHRC-sponsored pilot study for this project, 'The "Lands of the Normans" in England 1204–
44', ran at the University of Sheffield in 2006–7 (http://www.hri-online.ac.uk/normans). The archival
research for this article was generously supported by the British Academy.
[2] BN, MS lat. 11056, fol. 195v, no. 1193: 'Henricus Rex Anglie cum comite Glocestrie et multis regni
sui militibus et prelatis veniens in Franciam, cum sancto Ludouico rege Francie pacificatur. Quitauit enim
regibus Francie de expressa voluntate fratris sui regis Romanorum Ricardi et consilio principum ac prela-
torum Anglie quicquid juris requirebat in ducatu Normannie et comitatibus Andegauie, Cenomannie,
Turonie et Pictauie ac in eorum feodis. Rex vero Francie sanctus Ludouicus dans eidem magnam pecunie
summam ac etiam assignauit sibi et suis successoribus magnam terram in Lemouicensi, Petragorensi,
Xantonensi, et Agensi episcopatibus tali condicione quod istam terram, Burdegalam, Bayonam cum tota
Gasconia de regibus Francorum in feodum ipse et successores reges Anglie retinerent. Et rex Anglie
ascriptus in numero baronum Francie par et dux Acquitanie de cetero vocaretur de quibus tunc rex Anglie
coram prelatis multis utriusque regni fecit homagium sancto regi Francie Ludouico.' It is not apparent
why this text was inserted into the cartulary at this date, amongst fourteenth-century acts, although
another late addition was a memorandum of the abbey's English revenues (fol. 179r). The relevant Latin
passage from Primat is preserved in Guillaume de Nangis' *Gesta Ludovici Regis* and Jean de Vignay's
French translation (*RHF*, xxiii. 410, 412, and 16–17); both contain details that the St-Évroult version
omits. For Primat, see G.M. Spiegel, *The Chronicle Tradition of Saint-Denis: A Survey* (Brookline, MA,
and Leyden, 1978), 83–92.
[3] *Flores*, ii. 437–8. The treaty was confirmed by many magnates and prelates (*Layettes*, iv. no. 4555).
In general, see M. Gavrilovitch, *Étude sur le traité de Paris de 1259* (Paris, 1899).

properties confiscated from landowners who had chosen to remain overseas in or after 1204 formed a distinct aspect of the context for the peace negotiations. These properties comprised the so-called *terre Normannorum* confiscated in England from landowners who opted to remain in France, and the less well-known French estates seized by the Capetian kings from landowners who remained in England. On both sides of the Channel, the seized possessions would play an important role in royal patronage; they also had an influence upon legal developments concerning the rights of 'aliens' and inheritance, and in the development of English and French national identity.

The present article considers the nature and extent of the *terre Normannorum* and their French equivalents, briefly tracing their history to 1259 and assessing their fiscal and political significance by the 1250s. In examining the material conse-quences of the 'loss of Normandy' for the Anglo-Norman aristocracy, it aims to depict the context for the peace agreement that the two monarchies and their leading subjects concluded in 1259.

The fate of aristocratic estates (1204–59)

The fate of cross-Channel aristocratic landholdings after 1204 has been a subject for historical inquiry ever since Thomas Stapleton published his introductions to the Norman exchequer rolls in the 1840s.[4] General surveys of aristocratic fortunes were compiled by Sir Maurice Powicke and Wendy Stevenson,[5] while case-studies of *terre Normannorum* have also proved important;[6] so, too, have studies of the prop-erty of French religious institutions north of the English Channel.[7] To date, however, there has been no comprehensive study of families and properties affected by the collapse of the Anglo-Norman 'realm', and the lands of the English in France have received very little attention indeed. Most previous studies have concentrated upon the top echelons of Anglo-Norman society. Yet the humbler landowner with a manor

---

[4] *Magni Rotuli Scaccarii Normanniæ*, ed. T. Stapleton, 2 vols (London, 1840–4).

[5] F.M. Powicke, *The Loss of Normandy 1189–1204: Studies in the History of the Angevin Empire*, 2nd edn (Manchester, 1961), 328–58; W.B. Stevenson, 'England and Normandy, 1204–59' (unpubl. Ph.D. diss., University of Leeds, 1974), 199–237, 360–485. Other overviews include L. Musset, 'Quelques problèmes de l'annexation de la Normandie au domaine royal français', in *La France de Philippe Auguste: le temps des mutations*, ed. R.-H. Bautier (Paris, 1982), 291–307; K. Thompson, 'L'aristocratie anglo-normande et 1204', in *La Normandie et l'Angleterre au Moyen Âge*, ed. P. Bouet and V. Gazeau (Caen, 2003), 179–87; D. Power, ' "Terra regis Anglie et terra Normannorum sibi invicem adversantur": les héritages anglo-normands entre 1204 et 1244', in ibid., 189–209; idem, 'L'établissement du régime capétien en Normandie', in *1204: La Normandie entre Plantagenêts et Capétiens*, ed. A. Flambard-Héricher and V. Gazeau (Caen, 2007), 319–43; M. Billoré, 'Pouvoir et noblesse en Normandie (fin XIIe – début XIIIe siècles)' (unpubl. Ph.D. thesis, University of Poitiers, 2005), 805–79.

[6] D.A. Carpenter, 'A Noble in Politics: Roger Mortimer in the Period of Baronial Reform and Rebel-lion, 1258–1265', in *Nobles and Nobility in Medieval Europe*, ed. A.J. Duggan (Woodbridge, 2000), 183–203; D. Crook, 'The "Lands of the Normans" in Thirteenth-Century Nottingham: Bingham and Wheatley', *Transactions of the Thoroton Society* 109 (2004), 1–7; K. Thompson, 'The Lords of Laigle: Ambition and Insecurity on the Borders of Normandy', *ANS XVIII*, ed. C. Harper-Bill (Woodbridge, 1996), 177–99; idem, *Power and Border Lordship in Medieval France: The County of the Perche, 1000–1226* (Woodbridge, 2002), 177–99 (at 192–6); D. Power, 'The French Interests of the Marshal Earls of Striguil and Pembroke, 1189–1234', *ANS XXV*, ed. J. Gillingham (Woodbridge, 2003), 199–224; N.C. Vincent, *Peter des Roches: An Alien in English Politics 1205–1238* (Cambridge, 1996); idem, 'Twyford under the Bretons 1066–1250', *Nottingham Medieval Studies* 41 (1997), 80–99; R.C. Stacey, *Politics, Policy and Finance under Henry III 1216–1245* (Oxford, 1987), e.g. 111–14, 160–9, 238–9.

[7] D.J.A. Matthew, *The Norman Monasteries and their English Possessions* (Oxford, 1962); J. Peltzer, 'The Slow Death of the Angevin Empire', *HR* 87 (2007), 553–84.

or two on each side of the Channel may be as significant for our understanding of Anglo-Norman landholding as the great noble who frequented the French or English courts with ease. Minor landowners typically had quite localised interests, often concentrated in one or two English counties or a single Norman *bailliage*. The determination of such people to continue to hold property on both sides of the sea, in defiance of great political and financial obstacles, testifies to the apparent viability of cross-Channel estates even decades after 1204. Their ability to keep track of the fate of relatives and estates overseas also demonstrates the continuing communications between the two countries, which are matched by economic and linguistic evidence.[8]

In 1204–5 King John's subjects were forced to choose between their Insular and continental possessions and allegiances. Most of their decisions were never reversed, but they were not necessarily irreversible. On both sides of the Channel many people initially assumed that the king of England would recover his lost territories, and that when he did so, the dispossessed landowners would regain what they had lost. A number of landowners changed their mind after 1204 and were allowed to swap lands and allegiance for what they had lost overseas, and a small but highly visible group managed to hold property in both countries for varying lengths of time.[9] The position of such landowners in England differed from their status in France in one very important respect. The kings of France treated King John's forfeiture of his continental estates as permanent, and so the lands of those who remained in England were likewise regarded as forfeited for good. By 1259 these lands had mostly been held by the kings of France or their subjects for over half a century and were not distinguished from other property. The king of England, by contrast, wished to reverse the losses of 1204, and so the confiscations in England were treated as reversible.

In the early years of Henry III's reign the English minority council devised several formulae that neatly expressed the uncertain legal status of the forfeited property. A piece of land, identified as 'the king's escheat as of the land of the Normans' (*escaeta sua de terris Normannorum*), would be granted 'until the land of England and the land of Normandy are one again' – often shortened in royal records to 'until the lands are one again' (*quousque terre communes sint*).[10] The recipient was to hold this property 'until the king restores it to the right heirs by his will or by a peace' – a phrase of particular resonance for the Treaty of Paris.[11] The language of royal charters and of pleading in royal courts therefore kept alive the memory of the collapse of the Anglo-Norman realm and sustained hopes that it might one day be restored. Such phrases were still a standard feature in royal charters when Henry III's envoys began the treaty negotiations in the late 1250s. They emphasised that the previous owner had the stronger legal right to the confiscated lands, just as the king of England was held to have the stronger right to Normandy than the king

---

[8] Power, '"Terra regis Anglie et terra Normannorum"', 194–6; L. Jean-Marie, 'Close Relations? Some Examples of Trade Links between England and the Towns and Ports of Lower Normandy in the Thirteenth and Early Fourteenth Centuries', *ANS XXXII*, ed. C.P. Lewis (Woodbridge, 2010), 96–113. For linguistic exchanges in the thirteenth century, see David Trotter's article in this volume.

[9] For some examples, see Thompson, 'L'aristocratie anglo-normande'; Power, '"Terra regis Anglie et terra Normannorum"'.

[10] E.g. *CRR*, ix. 300; cf. *Bracton on the Laws and Customs of England*, ed. G.E. Woodbine, rev. and trans. S.E. Thorne (4 vols, Cambridge, 1968–77), iii. 361.

[11] E.g. TNA, C 53/25, m. 9r (*CChR 1226–1257*, 132): 'donec nos vel heredes nostri predictam medietatem predicti manerii reddiderimus rectis heredibus per pacem vel voluntatem nostram'.

of France. The reversible nature of the confiscations shaped the patronage of the kings of England, who could grant out the *terre Normannorum* on conditional terms.

However, there were considerable shifts in royal treatment of the *terre Normannorum* between 1204 and 1259. Until the end of the minority of Henry III in 1227, the lands were normally granted in custody only (*de ballio regis*), and the custodians were frequently linked to the former 'Norman' owner by kinship or marriage.[12] Once he came of age in 1227, however, Henry III increasingly granted out *terre Normannorum* in hereditary fee, sometimes to the existing custodians, but often to his favourites or members of his household, regardless of whether they had any prior connection with the property or indeed with France. On 25–26 May 1231, for instance, Henry III converted the tenure in custody of five manors, which had been confiscated from different Normans and granted to five different English barons or courtiers and their heirs, into permanent grants on identical terms, adding the provisoes that the 'right heir' might still recover the lands through peace or by the king's will.[13] As Nicholas Vincent has observed, each of these permanent grants dealt a blow to the idea of the Anglo-Norman realm as well as to the practical possibility of its restoration.[14]

There were good reasons why the English crown became increasingly pessimistic about the possibility of reunion. Successive English royal expeditions to France between 1206 and 1242 made scant headway in recovering the lost territories, while the surviving Angevin possessions were eroded further, notably with the loss of Poitou in 1224 and further losses in Saintonge in 1242. By the late 1220s, English royal aspirations in Normandy were being reduced to the possibility of establishing a land corridor through the Cotentin and Avranchin to the provinces further south.[15] Moreover, the Normans were conspicuously indifferent to the kings of England who continued to sport the title of duke of Normandy, even when Henry III recovered the Norman fortress of Saint-James near Mont-Saint-Michel in 1230 and seemed poised to enter the duchy. It was in Poitou and Brittany, not Normandy, that the kings of England found substantial support for their abortive enterprises. It is true that the Paynel lords of Bréhal came out openly in arms for the kings of England in 1214 and 1230,[16] and a few other Normans were embroiled in plots in Henry's favour.[17] Ships from Dieppe and Richard Marshal's port of Leure transported Henry III's army to Brittany in 1230, and Louis IX is said to have feared the possibility of Norman desertion, not least when Henry III campaigned in Aquitaine in 1242.[18] Henry III's return to the continent in 1253 aroused new worries at the French court. Nevertheless, the king of England proved very unsuccessful in gaining either territory or affections in Normandy.

---

[12] A point emphasised by Vincent, 'Twyford and the Bretons', 92–4.

[13] *CChR 1226–1257*, 132: Oliver de Pontchardon received Faccombe (Hants), formerly of Richard de Soliers; Henry le Tyeis received Grendon Underwood (Bucks.), confiscated from Robert de Thibouville; Hugh Paynel the manor of his cousin Fulk Paynel at Drax (Yorks.); William de Canteloup the Tancarville manor of Aston Cantlow (Warks.); Richard de Gray was given Gertrude Paynel's manor of Barton-le-Street (Yorks.). Ibid., 133–4: on 9–10 June Herbert fitzMatthew was confirmed in Robert de Courcy's manor of Warblington (Hants), expressly on the same terms as Richard de Gray's grant, and the royal sergeant Henry de Helion received the land of Ernald *de Magne* at South Fawley (Bucks.).

[14] Vincent, *Peter des Roches*, 30–1.

[15] *DD*, no. 215; Stacey, *Politics*, 167–9.

[16] *RC*, 207 (1214); *CM*, iii. 197–8 (1230).

[17] *Jugements*, no. 623 (Thomas de Gorges, 1230); *QN*, nos 408, 439 (Enguerrand de St-Philibert, 1230); *Exc. e Rot. Fin.*, i. 370 (*CFR Henry III*, iii. no. 26/170–1) (Robert Malet, 1242). However, Malet was serving in the French army in Saintonge when he died later in 1242 (*CM*, iv. 225).

[18] Power, 'The French Interests of the Marshal Earls', 220–1; *CM*, iv. 204.

During the long periods of truce, many landowners did recover their overseas property, but each renewal of the conflict led to fresh seizures by royal officials. After each cessation of hostilities, many who were allowed to recover their property overseas attempted to dispose of it on favourable terms, whether through grants or sales to religious houses or sharp-eyed royal courtiers. The actions of Amaury, lord of Gacé, in southern Normandy, are typical. Soon after he came of age in the late 1220s, Amaury managed to acquire his share of the Derbyshire inheritance of his maternal grandfather William fitz Ralph, the distinguished seneschal of Normandy. In 1234, however, after another Anglo-French war, Amaury sold his English lands to the royal knight Ralph fitz Nicholas, converting his rights to cash while the possibility remained; he had already given part of his English estates to his sister as her dowry.[19]

With time, the uncertainties over the *terre Normannorum* grew in other ways. A well-known letter from a burgess of Caen to Henry III (c. 1227) advised the king of England to win over the Normans with the promise of restitution of their English lands; the author believed that Louis VIII would have conquered England if he had made a similar promise to the English barons during the Magna Carta civil war.[20] Yet, in practice, the tangled history of the *terre Normannorum* would have made any general restitution well-nigh impossible. The repeated granting of these properties in custody meant that they could accumulate a bewildering number of competing claims. Between 1204 and 1244 the manors of Willian and Lilley (Herts.), confiscated from the lord of Pavilly, were variously held by members of the Chaources (Chaworth), Argentan, Lacy and Peyvre families, as well as by junior members of the Pavilly dynasty.[21] Aspley Guise and Henlow (Beds.) had already had a complex history before 1204, and in the late twelfth century Simon de Beauchamp had used them to buy off claims to the barony of Bedford from Albereda Taillebois and her husband Guy de Saint-Valéry. Albereda and her son Renaud de Saint-Valéry attempted to maintain lordships in both England and near Bayeux until Renaud's death c. 1227, but Aspley came at various times to Falkes de Bréauté, Hubert de Burgh, and Robert Passelewe, three of the most ambitious courtiers of the age, as well as to Renaud's English half-brother Saher *de Wahull* (Odell) and the royal knight Henry *de Capella*.[22] When Passelewe and De Burgh drew up a final concord concerning Aspley in 1240, Thomas de Bréauté, Saher *de Wahull* and William de

---

[19] Matlock, Derbs. Record Office, D5236/3/1–2 (*Descriptive Catalogue of Derbyshire Charters*, ed. I.H. Jeayes (London, 1906), nos 1161–2; cf. no. 1160, now lost). *Cartulary of Darley Abbey*, ed. R.R. Darlington, 2 vols (Kendal, 1945), 535–6, and *The Cartulary of Dale Abbey*, ed. A. Saltman (London, 1967), 12–13 and nos 142 (dowry for his sister Agnes, wife of Robert of Muskham), 150, 508, show that Amaury's mother Avice (*alias* Amice) was William fitzRalph's daughter. For Amaury, see D. Power, *The Norman Frontier in the Twelfth and Early Thirteenth Centuries* (Cambridge, 2004), 452, 500–1. Cf. Jordan de Valliquerville's sale of Soberton (Hants) to Beaulieu Abbey (1234–5): Power, '"Terra regis Anglie et terra Normannorum"', 206–8.

[20] *DD*, no. 206; see J.C. Holt, 'The End of the Anglo-Norman Realm', *Proceedings of the British Academy* 61 (1975), 223–65 (at 264–5); D. Power, 'The End of Angevin Normandy: The Revolt at Alençon (1203)', *HR* 74 (2001), 444–64 (at 447).

[21] *Rotuli Normanniae in Turri Londinensi asservati*, ed. T.D. Hardy (London, 1835), 129; *CChR 1226–1257*, 57, 85, 140, 338; *CRR*, xvi. nos 1397, 1621, 1758; *VCH Herts.*, iii. 37–8, 177–8, 181.

[22] Stevenson, 'England and Normandy', 468–9; *HKF*, i. 64; *CIPM*, i. no. 461; *VCH Beds.*, ii. 281, 283; iii. 338–9, 342; G.H. Fowler, 'De St Walery', *The Genealogist* n.s. 30 (1914), 1–17 (at 14–17); *The Cartulary of Newnham Priory*, ed. J. Godber, 2 vols (Bedford, 1963–4), ii. no. 948; *PR 12 John*, p. 14; *CFR Henry III*, i. no. 8/422; ii. nos 9/336, 10/27. For Albereda's, Guy's and Renaud's Norman lands, see *RBE*, ii. 638 (*Registres*, p. 273); *RHF*, xxiii. 715; Caen, AD Calvados, G 822, liasse 19; J.W. Baldwin, 'Le Livre de Terres et de Revenus de Pierre du Thillay', *Cahiers Léopold Delisle* 51 (2002), 1–95 (at 79).

Beauchamp all put in claims.[23] Multiple claims to a single estate were not a new phenomenon in 1204, but such disputes over 'lands of the Normans' were a systemic consequence of their peculiarly uncertain title.

This uncertainty became particularly significant when Henry III's financial hardship in the 1250s set his officials upon an aggressive drive to test titles to property, foreshadowing the *quo warranto* proceedings of Edward I's reign. By then the bonanza of confiscations in 1244, when Henry ordered the seizure of all the possessions of French landowners in England, had been dissipated.[24] Even as Henry's proctors were negotiating the Angevin-Capetian treaty during the late 1250s, his officers were suing tenants of *terre Normannorum* in his courts. One plea roll, concerning proceedings *coram rege* in a short period in the Trinity term 1258, contains some thirteen entries relating to 'the lands of the Normans': these come from eleven cases that concerned fourteen properties in eight counties, ranging in size from a single messuage at Great Limber (Lincs.) to whole manors at Moulton and Cretingham (Suffolk) and one-and-a-half knights' fees at Northwold and Stibbard (Norfolk).[25] During the period covered by the roll, Henry III's régime underwent one of its greatest crises, including the parliament between 10 and 22 June that produced the Provisions of Oxford, and the flight of the Lusignans to Winchester a few days later;[26] yet the roll shows that the king's officers continued to prosecute royal claims to *terre Normannorum* before the king throughout the troubles.

There can be no doubt that the crown remained as aware in 1259 as in 1204 of the political, legal and fiscal significance of the *terre Normannorum*. It is harder to discern a precise role for the confiscated properties in the factional struggles that bedevilled Henry III's court. One exception is Henry's arbitary disseisin of Gilbert Basset of the Tancarville manor of Upavon Bassett (Wilts.) in 1233, undoing the king's own charter in Gilbert's favour, in order to restore it to Peter de Maulay who had previously held it in custody. This notorious case led directly to a major revolt led by Richard Marshal; and, as Nicholas Vincent has shown, it embodied broader issues concerning royal patronage during the ascendancy of Peter des Roches, bishop of Winchester.[27] It is harder to relate the Norman lands to later struggles for influence over royal patronage. Individual properties continued to trouble relations between the king and certain landowners: David Carpenter has shown the influence upon the early career of Roger de Mortimer of his uncertain tenure of two Gloucestershire manors to which he had a weaker title than his Norman cousin, the lord of Ferrières-Saint-Hilaire.[28] Yet during the treaty negotiations deep hostility developed between Richard de Clare and Simon de Montfort, two earls who might have been

---

[23] TNA, CP 25/1/2/18, no. 17; *A Calendar of Feet of Fines for Bedfordshire, Richard I – Henry III*, ed. G.H. Fowler, 2 vols (Bedfordshire Historical Record Soc. VI, 1919–28), no. 430 (cf. p. 206). Beauchamp's claim concerned services due to him as lord.

[24] H.W. Ridgeway, 'Foreign Favourites and Henry III's Problems of Patronage, 1247–1258', *EHR* 104 (1989), 590–610. In 1244 half of the *terre Normannorum* had been notionally awarded to the Lord Edward.

[25] TNA, KB 26/158: Moulton and Cretingham (m. 3r); Whatley (?) (Somerset, m.3r); Northwold and Stibbard (mm. 7d, 14r, and also probably 11r); Steventon (Hants, m. 10r); Seaford (Sussex, m. 12d); Great Limber (15r); (Slade?) Hooton and Laughton-en-le-Morthen (Yorks., 15r); Rode (Somerset, 16r); Sheldon and Derriads (Wilts., 16r); Denton (Lincs., 16r).

[26] *CM*, v. 697–8. The plea roll runs from 26 May to 3 July 1258.

[27] Vincent, *Peter des Roches*, 334–40, 396–7, 422: see also 377–9 for ensuing seizures of *terre Normannorum* from the enemies of Peter des Roches.

[28] Carpenter, 'A Noble in Politics', 183–203. The lords of Ferrières in 1247 and 1263 were Walkelin and Henry de Ferrières respectively (*QN*, no. 325; Rouen, AD Seine-Maritime, 16 H 14, fol. 265r), perhaps the nephew and great-nephew of Roger de Mortimer's mother Isabella de Ferrières.

expected to share similar attitudes towards the *terre Normannorum*.[29] By 1259 the confiscated Norman lands in England appear disconnected from Anglo-French relations and no longer the focus of factional conflicts, which now revolved around other aspects of royal patronage and taxation.

In sum, the lands confiscated in England from French landowners remained an important aspect of royal wealth and patronage throughout the period 1204–59, but with time they became increasingly divorced from the context in which they had come into royal hands, and most lost touch with the families that had the most venerable claims to them. Nevertheless, the expectation and hope that England and Normandy would be united once more under a single ruler outlived the extinction of the generation of Anglo-Norman barons who remembered the Anglo-Norman realm. By 1259, very few would have remembered a time when England and Normandy were under a single ruler, although one notable survivor was Loretta de Briouze, countess of Leicester, living as a recluse at Hackington (Kent) in 1265, who had held her dowry at Couvert near Bayeux and Tawstock (Devon) before 1204.[30] For most members of the ruling class, from the Lord Edward downwards, a functioning Anglo-Norman realm was something from their grandfathers' day; yet many still nurtured aspirations of reunion of the realms or recovery of their lost possessions.

Voluminous English royal records can help us to construct a narrative for the progressive alienation of the *terre Normannorum* from their original context. It is much harder to reconstruct a coherent account of the fate of lands confiscated in France. Since the Capetian kings had no wish to reverse the confiscations of 1204–5, no term or legal category comparable to '*terre Normannorum*' evolved.[31] Many confiscated lands passed out of royal hands quickly and permanently after 1204, and numerous families owed their fortunes to their acquisition of such estates, including Norman families such as Rouvray and Argences and incoming French families such as Branchard, Poucin, and Bourguignel.[32] However, a significant part of the distributed property eventually returned to the Capetian domain; indeed, Joseph Strayer argued that later kings of France regretted Philip Augustus's initial largesse, which the political exigencies of the conquest of Normandy had forced upon him, and sought to resume the alienated estates whenever the opportunity arose.[33] On the other hand, the Capetian kings appear to have used confiscated Anglo-Norman estates in exchange for property in more strategically sensitive areas, or as compensation for lost English lands. During the Breton campaign of 1230, Henry III

[29] *CM*, v. 744–5; see also *Thomas Wright's Political Songs of England from the Reign of John to that of Edward II*, ed. P. Coss (Cambridge, 1996), 65, 66–7; below, pp. 152–3.

[30] *Complete Peerage*, vii. 536 (d); F.M. Powicke, 'Loretta, Countess of Leicester', in *Historical Essays in Honour of James Tait*, ed. J.G. Edwards et al. (Manchester, 1939), 247–72 (at 267); J. Maddicott, *Simon de Montfort* (Oxford, 1994), 332–3. For her dowry, see ibid., 535–6; *Fees*, i. 265 (Tawstock); *Actes de Philippe Auguste*, iii. no. 1025, and Évreux, AD Eure, H 561 (Couvert, dépt. Calvados, cant. Bayeux, cne. Jouaye-Mondaye).

[31] *Layettes*, i. no. 733, contains an isolated reference to 'totam terram Anglicorum et Normannorum' in the castelry of Mortemer-sur-Eaulne (Dec. 1204); cf. *CN*, no. 437, for *Fovilla* (now Flottemanville, dépt. Manche, cant. Montebourg), in royal hands 'pro forefacto Anglorum' (Aug. 1238).

[32] Rouvray: D.J. Power, 'Between the Angevin and Capetian Courts: John de Rouvray and the Knights of the Pays de Bray, 1180–1225', in *Family Trees and the Roots of Politics: The Prosopography of Britain and France from the Tenth to the Twelfth Century*, ed. K.S.B. Keats-Rohan (Woodbridge, 1997), 361–84. Argences: idem, 'The End of Angevin Normandy', 454–5. Branchard: idem, *Norman Frontier*, 108, 168, 284. Poucin: J.W. Baldwin, *The Government of Philip Augustus: Foundations of French Royal Power in the Middle Ages* (Berkeley, CA, 1986), 109, 133, 166, 289, 432. Bourguignel: *Actes de Philippe Auguste*, iii. no. 1224; *CN*, no. 708; AN, S 4997^A (acts of Bourguignel lords of Claville, 1216–71).

[33] *RDBR*, 17–19.

had rewarded the Breton magnate Henry d'Avaugour with valuable 'lands of the Bretons' in England.[34] After d'Avaugour returned to Louis IX's side, he received the honour of Moyon in Normandy in exchange for his strategic town of Pontorson.[35] Philip Augustus and Louis IX gave Ralph de Meulan lands in the Bessin that had belonged to the Subligny, Gray, Glapion, and Chester families, rather than admit Ralph's strong claims to the vast Norman lands of the counts of Meulan.[36] In 1227 Count Robert III of Dreux and his wife Aanor de Saint-Valéry received lands in Caux as compensation for the loss of the English honour that Aanor and her father had usually managed to retain until 1226.[37] In general, though, the kings of France followed a policy of prudent conservation of confiscated estates, and if Louis IX had any doubts about his rights to them, he did not let his qualms diminish his royal domains.[38] The treaty negotiations of 1258–9 therefore took place against a much more secure land settlement in France.

The extent of confiscated property

Nicholas Vincent has called the *terre Normannorum* 'arguably the single greatest influx of land to the crown between 1066 and the dissolution of the monasteries', while David Carpenter has described them as the 'great bank on which the thirteenth-century kings [of England] drew for patronage'.[39] How great were the 'funds' in this 'bank'? This is very difficult to establish, for the *terre Normannorum* were in fact very fluid, both in definition and in extent over time. Royal letters, surveys and inquests, and court cases all specified lands that were 'the king's escheat as land of the Normans'; but many other properties, not identified by such phrases, had been taken from French landowners and were treated and used in similar fashion. Furthermore, the designation *terre Normannorum* – or at its most grandiose, the *terre Normannorum et Britonum et aliorum extraneorum*[40] – was used primarily by the crown, being rare in 'private' documents such as charters.[41] Deciding what to include as 'funds' from the Norman 'bank' poses methodological problems and involves a degree of arbitariness, owing to their shifting composition. A range of factors, ranging from genealogical accident to political opportunism or disgrace, could mean that at the death of an English landowner, the 'true heir' of a property was overseas, and so a property could become 'Norman land' for the first time long

---

[34] *CR 1227–1231*, 443–4, 452, 525.

[35] S. Painter, *The Scourge of the Clergy: Peter of Dreux, Duke of Brittany* (Baltimore, 1937), 71, 73; *Layettes*, ii. nos 2135, 2139, 2253, 2255 (*CN*, nos 400–1), promising either Trévières (a Chester property) or Seulles and Moyon; BN, MS lat. 10086, fol. 224v (Alan d'Avaugour, lord of Moyon, 1256).

[36] *Layettes*, iii. no. 4196; *CN*, nos 536–7; Caen, AD Calvados, H 176 (Bény); *Jugements*, no. 418; Powicke, *Loss of Normandy*, 345. Ralph was usually called lord of Courseulles, a former Subligny property: AN, L 970, nos 442, 444–6; Rouen, AD Seine-Maritime, 7 H 2131; *QN*, no. 286.

[37] *Layettes*, v. no. 330 (*CN*, no. 361, p. 311).

[38] For discussion of St Louis' alleged scruples, see Gavrilovitch, *Étude sur le traité*, 39–46; Powicke, *Loss of Normandy*, 270–1.

[39] Vincent, *Peter des Roches*, 30; Carpenter, 'A Noble in Politics', 188.

[40] E.g. *Fees*, i. 613.

[41] *Chartulary of the Priory of Boxgrove*, ed. L. Fleming (Sussex Rec. Soc. 59, 1960), nos 326, 333, refer to lands of William du Fresne, *Normannus*, at Groves (in Oving, Sussex), but they ultimately derived from acts of Henry III (ibid., nos 323, 325, 332; cf. nos 3, 324, 335; *CChR 1226–1257*, 238, 293; *Fees*, ii. 1153; *VCH Sussex*, iv. 167–8). In 1269 a charter of John and Alice of Luton (TNA, C 53/58, m. 9; *CChR 1257–1300*, 123) referred to the Norfolk lands of John *de Sanes*, *Normannus*, but this description had probably been taken from a charter of Henry III, now lost.

after 1204.[42] It is likely that some confiscated lands that were not held in chief went unrecorded.[43]

The extent of confiscations in France is even harder to gauge because of the much thinner French documentary record and the Capetian tendency not to make conditional grants of forfeited lands. Few traces of property seizures survive for Brittany, Maine, Ponthieu, or Flanders, although Philip Augustus sent a general order to his subjects to seize all fiefs whose tenants were in England.[44] Even for Normandy, our chief sources provide only snapshots of landholding, notably the feudal surveys of Philip Augustus, a roll from the *bailliage* of Lisieux (1205 x 1207), the survey of the *bailliage* of Rouen (c. 1265), and the *Querimoniæ Normannorum* submitted to the commissioners of Louis IX, of which about 120 out of 551 items relate to the duchy's connections with England and the Anglo-Norman aristocracy. Taken together, these sources document central Normandy in detail, but parts of north-eastern and south-western Normandy are almost wholly absent from them. As in England, the French sources pose grave methodological problems for identifying confiscated property. Without a legal categorisation comparable to the *terre Normannorum*, it is often difficult to establish whether a piece of property in the king's hand had been confiscated because its former owner was in England, or for some other cause such as a felony or default of heirs.[45]

Comparing English and French evidence also poses problems: many 'Normans' who lost lands in England have left no trace in Normandy and vice versa, even if we allow for the challenges posed by differing Norman and English orthography.[46] Admittedly, 'Norman' was a loose term in England: it embraced Manceaux such as Juhel de Mayenne, Bretons such as Gervaise de Dinan and Henry d'Avaugour, Flemings such as Hugh de Malannoy, and Picards such as Alan de Morville (from Ponthieu) and the count of Saint-Pol.[47] Nevertheless, the disjuncture between insular and continental sources in both genre and details is a further obstacle to any attempt to identify confiscated lands and dispossessed landowners.

---

[42] E.g. Overstone (Northants) and Preston Millers (now East Preston, Sussex), first treated as *terre Normannorum* after the death of Master Humphrey de Millières in 1241; his sister Felicia, a Norman, fined to recover them from the king, and although she soon made over Preston to the royal clerk John Mansel, her son Gilbert de Viarville, *alias* Millières, entered Henry III's service and retained Overstone until his death in 1271, when it became 'Norman land' once more. See *English Episcopal Acta*, 9, *Winchester 1205–38*, ed. N. Vincent (Oxford, 1994), 166–8 (app. IV (4)), and the sources there cited; also *CFR Henry III*, iii. nos 25/343–4, 470, 533, 570–2; 26/83–4, 128, 432; *Abstract of Feet of Fines relating to the County of Sussex*, ed. L.F. Salzmann, 3 vols (Lewes, 1903–16), ii. nos 522, 759; *VCH Northants*, iv. 96; *HKF*, iii. 31, 97–8. *Placita de Quo Warranto temporibus Edw. I. II. & III. in curia receptæ scacarij Westm. asservata*, ed. W. Illingworth and J. Caley (London, 1818), 84, refers to Humphrey as *Normannus*, but contemporary sources do not.

[43] For 'Norman' subtenancies, see N.C. Vincent, 'Simon de Montfort's First Quarrel with King Henry III', *TCE*, iv (Woodbridge, 1992), 167–77.

[44] See *Cartulaire de l'abbaye cistercienne de Fontaine-Daniel*, ed. A. Grosse-Duperon and E. Gouvrion (Mayenne, 1896), no. LXIV; Power, ' "Terra regis Anglie et terra Normannorum" ', 192.

[45] E.g. M. Nortier, 'Un rôle des biens tombés en la main du roi en la baillie de Lisieux après la conquête de la Normandie par Philippe Auguste', *Annales de Normandie* 45 (1995), 55–68, clarifies many of the entries in *RDBR* that would have otherwise been opaque, and shows that some were already in ducal hands before 1200.

[46] E.g. *Radulfus Huiguen* or *Huigan*, mentioned in Normandy as having died in England (*Jugements*, nos 172, 246), was presumably either Ralph fitz Wigan of Willoughby (Warks.) or Ralph fitz Wigan of Goldington (Beds.): see D. Power, 'Cross-Channel Communication and the End of the 'Anglo-Norman Realm': Robert FitzWalter and the Valognes Inheritance', *Tabularia* 11 (forthcoming).

[47] E.g. *Fees*, i. 387 (Morville), 612 (Mayenne), ii. 1395 (Malannoy); *CRR*, xvi. nos 1, 79, 86 (Ringwood, taken from Gervaise de Dinan), 1837 (St-Pol); *CChR 1256–1257*, 137 (Avaugour).

Allowing for the problems of identifying the seized properties, the following approximate figures give some sense of the amount of landed wealth tied up with the fate of the erstwhile Anglo-Norman realm in 1258–9. These figures relate mainly to lay landowners or to the lay fiefs of churchmen. In England, about 700 known estates fell into royal hands after 1204, ranging from demesne manors in great honours such as Brittany, Boulogne, Leicester and Perche, to a few virgates.[48] They were spread across most counties, although few have been identified in north-west England,[49] and they were heavily concentrated in the east and south Midlands and in Wessex. These lands had been taken from at least 200 continental families. These patterns were deeply rooted in the land settlement of England after the Norman Conquest as well as in the distribution of the royal domain both before and after 1066.

Assessing the value of these properties poses further challenges. It is unfortunate that the most complete survey of the *terre Normannorum*, from 1242–3, records almost no values.[50] The roll of confiscations from 1204 listed 102 lay properties in 18 counties. Tony Moore has calculated that the initial seizures were worth at least £1640 sterling per annum, but that income soon fell to a mere £526 per annum. However, he has also shown that the roll was an incomplete record of even the very early confiscations.[51] A more comprehensive record, the responses to an inquest of 1237, lists about 120 properties in 15 counties, valued at about £3000 per annum in total; most had been distributed to loyal courtiers and servants.[52] These values, though impressive, are not vast, and the property that remained in royal hands provided far less income than many other sources of revenue. Nor did the 'bank' of *terre Normannorum* hold these assets all at once. Admittedly these lands brought other financial benefits to the English crown, such as proffers to inherit or to have all the *terre Normannorum* in one's fief, farms at term and custodies, and feudal prerogatives over tenants such as reliefs, wardships, and control of marriages.[53] The real value of some estates must often have been much higher than admitted to royal assessors; in 1248 the Breton nobleman Henry d'Avaugour claimed that the English honour of l'Aigle, to which he was the next heir, was worth £3750 sterling per annum excluding the woods, whereas in 1236–7 inquests had assessed the l'Aigle lands in Sussex, Surrey, and Hampshire, the bulk of the English honour of l'Aigle, at only £294 sterling.[54] Yet their chief value surely lay in the conditional nature of so many grants: the revocable nature of the gifts gave the *terre Normannorum* an additional value that cannot be quantified in terms of cash income alone, although it diminished over time as sitting tenants tightened their grip upon the lands in their hands and as the number of forfeitures diminished after 1244.

Quantifying the lands seized by the French crown poses its own methodological challenges, and unlike in England it is almost exclusively those which remained in

[48] Figure derived from 'The "Lands of the Normans" in England 1204–44' (see n. 1) and subsequent research. It is almost certainly a significant underestimate, as we do not know how many lands confiscated from subtenants were recorded.

[49] For an exception, see *CIMisc*, no. 990 (*Trostormode*, i.e. Cross Dormont in Barton, Westmorland).

[50] *Fees*, ii. 637–1141: the *terre Normannorum* form one aspect of a much broader survey.

[51] T.K. Moore, 'The *Rotulus de Valore Terrarum Normannorum* and the Invention of the "Lands of the Normans"', *EHR* 125 (2010), 1071–1109 (values at p. 1093). I am grateful to Dr Moore for allowing me to consult this paper in advance of publication.

[52] *Fees*, i. 612–19.

[53] Moore, 'The *Rotulus de Valore Terrarum Normannorum*', 1095, calculates related proffers to King John in his sixth regnal year (2 June 1204 – 19 May 1205) of £1994 in cash and 18 horses.

[54] *RHF*, xxiv. I, p. 730; *Fees*, i. 617, 618; ii. 1366.

royal hands that can be valued. The roll from the *bailliage* of Lisieux (1205 x 1207) recorded 56 confiscated estates, which Michel Nortier valued at approximately 1300 *livres tournois* (£325 sterling) annually in total.[55] The 'Complaints of the Normans' of 1247 mentioned property confiscated because of connections with England that was allegedly worth over 4400 *li.t.* (£1100 st.) per annum, as well as very substantial renders in kind and numerous single payments of cash.[56] Amongst these properties the inheritance of Guérin de Glapion was said to be worth 1500 *li.t.* (£375 st.) per annum, Nicholas Malesmains' half of the Tillières inheritance was valued at 400 *li.t.*, and the dower of Margaret de Fougères, mother of Ralph de Meulan, at 500 *li.t.* (£125 st.).[57] In the 1260s, the survey of the royal domain in the *bailliage* of Rouen provided notional values of forfeited estates that totalled approximately 7750 *li.t.* (approximately £1940 sterling),[58] although the true figure was probably much larger; the survey itself shows that higher amounts could be realised from most of these estates in reality.[59]

Most of these lands represent actual wealth paid into the French king's coffers, whereas distributed *terre Normannorum* did not provide substantial income to the English crown; the value of lands given away by the king of France after 1204 does not show up in such surveys unless they had reverted to royal hands. Sources that identify redistributed lands, such as the surveys in the Registers of Philip Augustus, do not give many values, mainly assessing property by duties of knight-service. As in England, the distribution was very uneven: the confiscated lands in Normandy were more concentrated in northern and western regions such as the Cotentin and Pays d'Auge than in the southern and eastern frontier regions of the duchy. This pattern was often similarly determined by very venerable historical factors, such as the establishment of ducal power in western Normandy and the recruitment of supporters for the dukes' English ventures. At first sight, the confiscated lands in Normandy appear much more substantial than their English counterparts, since they included the honours of most English earls, the counts of Aumale and Meulan, and several other important Norman magnates such as the lords of Gournay and Tosny. However, this difference was more apparent than real, since the tenants of these honours mainly remained in Normandy after 1204.[60]

On both sides of the Channel, the seizure of lands was therefore a significant windfall for the monarchies, but between 1204 and 1259 they experienced very different fortunes. In both countries these estates remained an integral part of royal patronage. In England the possibility of restitution gave John and Henry III special leverage at first, but the pressure to make permanent grants to their loyal courtiers and members of their households had reduced this advantage over time, and by 1259 the crown had few *terre Normannorum* to give away. By contrast, the Capetians had no such pretext to make conditional grants, yet they were more successful in retaining their gains for themselves. It is possible that half of all lands confiscated from English landowners in Normandy remained in royal hands or reverted to the

---

[55] Nortier, 'Un rôle des biens', 61.

[56] *QN*, passim. The register does not permit a precise total value to be calculated.

[57] *QN*, nos 530, 54, 286.

[58] *RDBR*: figure based upon approximately 120 properties through comparison with other Capetian sources, and Strayer's excellent footnotes to his edition.

[59] E.g. *RDBR*, 185–8: the farm of land of Robert d'Angerville at St-Étienne-la-Thillaye was assessed at 140 *li.t.*, but realised income was 195 *li. 8s 2d*; it was leased to the prior of Beaumont-en-Auge for 190 *li.* p.a. (cf. *CN*, no. 641). For discussion, see Strayer, *RDBR*, 11–16, 20–3.

[60] This is most apparent for the Leicester honours of Breteuil and Grandmesnil: *RHF*, xxiii. 714–15 and 705–6 (*Registres*, 276–82), 643–4.

French kings within a few decades of the end of the Anglo-Norman realm. Neither monarchy can have wished for substantial restitutions to be made as part of any Anglo-French treaty in 1259: although not a fundamental part of royal wealth, they continued to be a valuable source of income and patronage for both monarchies.

The place of confiscated lands in the peace negotiations (1256–9)

By the mid-1250s, then, the French and English crowns had long since absorbed much confiscated property into their domains or given it away to their loyal followers. Nevertheless, the possible fate of these lands must have exercised many minds during the treaty negotiations, for most of the representatives of the two kings stood to be affected one way or another by a general restitution of property to dispossessed Anglo-French landowners. Of the four principal French negotiators, Simon de Clermont and the archbishop of Tarentaise had no potential English interests, but Count Alphonse of Eu still nurtured claims to the honours of Tickhill and Hastings, while Odo Rigaud, archbishop of Rouen, had his archbishopric's English property to protect.[61] Many of Henry III's representatives during the negotiations came from families that had lost substantial Norman lands in 1204, including the earls of Gloucester and Hereford, the count of Aumale, Richard de Gray, and Hugh Bigod the justiciar, although some had received lands of Normans as partial compensation. As for Simon de Montfort, he was overlord of numerous former Norman tenancies in the half-honour of Leicester, and husband of the king's sister, who proved very reluctant to renounce her claims in the erstwhile Plantagenet lands in France; moreover, during the negotiations Louis IX required Montfort to cede his residual claims to the Norman honours of Leicester and Évreux.[62]

Other English negotiators had no claims arising from the Capetian seizures of 1204, but stood to lose from any restoration of lands to their former holders. Peter of Savoy, Queen Eleanor's uncle, had been one of the chief beneficiaries of the redistribution of Normans' lands since his arrival in England in 1240, receiving the honours of l'Aigle, Hastings, and Richmond – a fact of particular relevance as Henry III aimed to use the treaty negotiations to arrange a marriage alliance with the duke of Brittany, who had a well-established claim to the honour of Richmond.[63] The king's half-brother Geoffrey de Lusignan had similarly received a scattered collection of *terre Normannorum* in eastern England.[64] Another negotiator, John Mansel, treasurer of York, had long had an eye for English lands of continental landowners, and royal gifts to him included the church of Haughley (Suffolk), on a demesne manor of the honour of Perche, and a manor at Poulders (Kent) taken from a Flemish landowner.[65]

---

[61]   The count of Eu requested Tickhill and Hastings in the wake of the treaty (*Rot. Parl.*, i. 23). Maddicott, *Simon de Montfort*, 296–7, notes that Simon de Clermont was married to Simon de Montfort's niece Alice.

[62]   Maddicott, *Simon de Montfort*, esp. 141, 155–6, 172–90, also demonstrating Simon's continuing ambitions in Bigorre. Évreux had formerly been held by the senior branch of the Montfort dynasty.

[63]   I.J. Sanders, *English Baronies: A Study of their Origin and Descent (1086–1327)* (Oxford, 1960), 120, 136–7; N. Vincent, 'Peter of Savoy, Count of Savoy and *de facto* Earl of Richmond (1203?–1268)', *ODNB*, xlix. 136–9; *DD*, nos 261, 307 (cf. no. 414). Peter no longer held the honour of Hastings by 1258–9.

[64]   See below, n. 88.

[65]   E.g. Preston Millers (above, n. 42), and the Courcy manor at Bilsington (Kent), acquired from the heirs of the last Aubigny earl of Arundel, although, curiously, an inquest in 1246 claimed that it was not Norman land. For Bilsington and Poulders (in Woodnesborough, described as 'de terris Flandrensium'), see *CPR 1232–1247*, 408, 426; *The Cartulary and Terrier of the Priory of Bilsington, Kent*, ed.

Consequently most of Henry III's representatives in the peace negotiations had Anglo-Norman connections and were either descendants of people who had lost lands in France in 1204, or had received gifts of 'Norman' land, or both. Of all the envoys, John de Balliol had most immediate cause to wish for Anglo-French harmony, on account of his privileged position as a landowner in both the Angevin and Capetian realms. Lord of substantial northern English lands and husband of one of the coheiresses of Galloway and the earldom of Huntingdon (through whom their son would become king of Scotland), John was also a leading baron of Ponthieu, where his grandfather and father had managed to retain their lordship since 1204.[66] Others faced severe conflicts of interest. As the king's brother, Richard of Cornwall had a direct interest in the recovery of the French dominions, but his English estates included very extensive *terre Normannorum*.[67] Peter de Montfort came from a family that had given up its Norman lands before 1204 and in a general restitution he stood to lose the former Harcourt manor of Ilmington (Warks.), which he held of Simon de Montfort. Yet his prominence in Simon de Montfort's affinity must have also made him eager to support his patron's claims in France.[68]

Such conflicts of interest help to explain why the final terms for peace said nothing about the claims of the aristocracy of England and northern France, despite the participation of numerous magnates and courtiers from both countries in the peace negotiations and ceremonies. Instead, it concentrated upon Henry III's rights in Aquitaine. The only Anglo-French magnate mentioned in the treaty was the duke of Brittany, with whom Henry III simultaneously arranged a marriage alliance, awarding the Agenais to the duke's son as a dowry for his daughter Beatrice. For everyone else affected by confiscations since 1204, any resolution of long-nourished claims would have to await the conclusion of peace.

The impact of the peace treaty upon the Anglo-French aristocracy

What were the consequences of the treaty for the aristocracy of England and northern France? The *Flores Historiarum* claimed that after Henry III did homage, he sent back to England, inviting his subjects to come to Paris to lay claim to their lost rights overseas. The author added ominously, 'But what was done about this is unclear to us.'[69]

The author of the *Flores* was right to be doubtful, for by and large English landowners failed to recover their lost rights in France. In November 1260, Lucy, wife

N. Neilson (London, 1928), 56–61 and nos 1–10, 26–8. Haughley: R.C. Stacey, 'John Mansel (d.1265)', *ODNB*, xxxvi. 530–3 (at 531).

[66] G. Stell, 'The Balliol Family and the Great Cause of 1291–2', in *Essays on the Nobility of Medieval Scotland*, ed. K.J. Stringer (Edinburgh, 1985), 150–66.

[67] N. Denholm-Young, *Richard of Cornwall* (Oxford, 1947), 165–70, lists the following estates (with dispossessed continental family in brackets): the honours of Eye (Brabant) and Beckley (St-Valéry), the latter including Isleworth (not recognised by Denholm-Young as a member of this honour), Exning (Boulogne), Haughley (Perche), Hailes (Tancarville), Benson (Harcourt), Princes Risborough (Semilly), and Oakham, Lechlade and Langborough (all Ferrières; see above, n. 28).

[68] Maddicott, *Simon de Montfort*, 65–6. Peter's grandfather, Henry de Montfort of Beaudesert (Warks.), had ceded Picauville (Manche, cant. Ste-Mère-Église) to his brother Hugh before 1204, but it had been seized in 1204 and given to the French baron Matthew de Marly: N. Vincent, *Norman Charters from English Sources: Antiquaries, Archives and the Rediscovery of the Anglo-Norman Past* (forthcoming, PRS), no. 30; *RHF*, xxiii. 611, and *CN*, no. 473.

[69] *Flores*, ii. 438: 'ut quicunque in Anglia jus aut clamium in partibus ultramarinis se credebant habere, ad eum quam tocius festinarent accedere, quod et factum est. Sed quid exinde sit actum, nobis est ambiguum.'

of Richard de Gray of Codnor (Derbs.), appeared before the Parlement de Paris and laid claim to the land that her father and uncle had held in Normandy. These brothers, from a junior branch of the constables of Normandy, had taken different paths after 1204. The elder, John du Hommet, had wavered between the two countries for more than a decade before eventually settling on his English estates, which included Humberstone (Leics.), Newbottle (Northants), and Sheringham (Norfolk), where he remained until his death in 1223, by which time he had forfeited his Norman lands near Caen.[70] His younger brother William du Hommet had inherited his mother's dowry near Lisieux and retained it until his death c. 1243.[71] Lucy's claim therefore posed a double problem to the Parlement. An inquest discovered that her father had forfeited his Norman land by crossing to England; this was taken to disbar Lucy from inheriting her uncle's land as well.[72] Hence the peace treaty did not enable Lucy to recover her lands. Gilbert de Clare, earl of Gloucester, similarly failed to recover his ancestors' lands in Normandy in the Paris Parlement in 1279: his claim was rebutted on the grounds that this land had not been in his family for four generations and been held peaceably by the king of France for sixty years and more (a standard period). The French court might reasonably have also thrown the claim out because Gilbert appeared ill-informed about his ancestors' Norman lands.[73] Meanwhile, the kings of France continued to make gifts from the lands of the English: much of the vast fortune that Philip IV conferred upon his chamberlain Enguerrand de Marigny consisted of former Anglo-Norman estates in north-east Normandy.[74]

Yet the peace possibly made it easier after 1259 for the small number of English landowners with relatives in Normandy to inherit any rights overseas that might pass to them. In the late 1260s the Oxfordshire baron John de Saint-Jean acquired a Norman manor, probably Héricourt-en-Caux, from his grandmother Emma, to whom the manor had come by descent. This branch of the Saint-Jean family therefore became cross-Channel landowners for the first time since the partition of the Saint-Jean inheritance in the reign of Henry I.[75]

---

[70] Stevenson, 'England and Normandy', 425–7; *Rotuli de liberate as de misis et præstitis*, ed. T.D. Hardy (London, 1844), 62; *Rot. Fin.*, 259, 503, 587; *CFR Henry III*, no. 8/156 (*Exc. e Rot. Fin.*, i. 127); *RLC*, i. 249; *CRR*, vi. 42, 93; *Fees*, i. 19; *RHF*, xxiii. 707, 709 (Cléville, Osmanville: *Registres*, 284, 289); *Jugements*, no. 145; *QN*, no. 287; *RDBR*, 161–2. John and William were sons of Jordan du Hommet (d. 1192), third son of the constable Richard du Hommet (d. 1179).

[71] *QN*, nos 1, 91; *RDBR*, 158–61; *CN*, nos 1018, 1044. William should not be confused with his uncle and cousin of the same name who were constables of Normandy.

[72] *Les Olim*, ed. le Comte de Beugnot (3 vols, Paris, 1839–48), i. 123, no. XIV.

[73] *Olim*, ii. 150–1, no. XXXVI. The earl claimed 'Montpinçon', but neither of the Norman places of this name formed part of the honour of Gloucester before 1204; he also claimed some of his great-grandmother Amice's inheritance as if it had been her dower.

[74] *Cartulaire et actes d'Enguerran de Marigny*, ed. J. Favier (Paris, 1965), nos 9–10, 32, 34–8, 41, 72–6, and no. A2: Longueville and Longueil (both Marshal lordships), Bellencombre (the chief former Warenne lordship), Sauqueville, Dénestanville (Dunstanville family), Neufmarché (Roumare family) and Gournay. See J. Favier, *Un conseiller de Philippe le Bel, Enguerran de Marigny* (Paris, 1963), 34–9.

[75] *CChR 1257–1300*, 156: confirmation (8 Nov. 1270) of the exchange of *Herecurt in Normannia* for three hamlets of the manor of Steeple Barton (Oxon.) (1265 x 1270), probably made at the royal court. John was descended from an earlier John de St-Jean (d. 1149 x 1153); the family's Norman lands, centred upon St-Jean-le-Thomas (Manche, cant. Sartilly), had passed to that John's younger brother Roger, lord of Halnaker (Sussex), whose successor William de St-Jean, *alias* Port, had abandoned the Norman lands in 1204. See *Complete Peerage*, xi. 316–25, 340–8; J.H. Round, 'The Families of St. John and of Port', *The Genealogist* n.s. 16 (1899–1900), 1–13; *Boxgrove Chartulary*, esp. nos 4–24; Sanders, *English Baronies*, 9; *HKF*, ii. 59–60; iii. 56–61; *VCH Oxon.*, xi. 62, 65, 71.

It was perhaps easier for Normans to consider recovering their property in England after 1259, given that the kings of England had never ceased holding out this possibility to them. David Crook has traced how William Paynel of Hambye revived his family's dormant interest in the manor of Bingham (Notts.) in the early 1260s. Indeed, Henry III acknowledged the undertakings that he had made to William's father during the Breton campaign more than thirty years earlier and promised to arrange an exchange with the current occupant of Bingham.[76] The king may have made similar promises to a Breton lord concerning an English pension that he had granted during the same campaign.[77] However, William Paynel proved no more successful at recovering his family's former lands in England than his kinswoman Lucy de Gray did in France. By then Bingham had been in the hands of the Ferrers earls of Derby for nearly three decades, and Henry III was understandably reluctant to unravel the arrangements that the earls had put in place – or it suited him to appear so.[78]

The Norman branch of the Harcourt family had more success in recovering its lands in England after the treaty. In 1260 Henry III's council even stated that the custom of England allowed John, lord of Harcourt, to plead in the king's court to recover the lands that he claimed. Would this open the floodgates to Norman claims to English lands? John duly acquired his father Richard's former manor of Ilmington, but only through a collusive action with Peter de Montfort, the man who had held it since Richard's death in 1236. This unusual agreement attracted the attention of the annalist of Pershore Abbey.[79] It was truly exceptional, for Harcourt recovered the manor in a very charged political situation: he had come from France with the archbishop of Rouen as Louis IX's envoy and to assist Simon de Montfort in his defence against a treason charge from Henry III. The immediate context of Harcourt's visit to England is a reminder that Anglo-Norman affairs were now subsumed into the local politics of each country, in essentially distinct contexts. The success of John de Harcourt's action for Ilmington also owed much to the fact that the king was not the warrant for the deforciant's possession: Henry III expressly stated that Harcourt could not implead anyone whom the king was bound to warrant.[80] Therein lay the difficulty for the Normans: despite repeated promises to make restitution to the 'right heirs', the king now alleged that his charters prevented him from doing so. In 1272, John de Harcourt ceded Ilmington to Peter de Montfort the younger, restoring it to the family that had held it as Norman land, and severing the link between the English and Norman lands of the Harcourts once more.[81]

Yet if the Normans struggled to recover their lands in England, their confiscated lands continued to have a very dubious status in English law. In 1268 an act of Henry III for John Mansel's sister admitted as much: 'If there is any flaw in fine or seisin and the manor escheats to the king as land of the Normans, Emma and her

---

[76] Crook, 'Lands of the Normans', 103–4. See especially *CPR 1258–1266*, 165–6, 211; *EYC*, vi. 29–30.
[77] *DD*, no. 317: *vidimus* by Richard, abbot of Mont-St-Michel (18 Sept. 1260), of Henry III's letters patent (Tréguier, 15 Oct. 1230) granting Roland de Dinan 100 marks p.a. from the exchequer. The *vidimus* survives in TNA, which suggests that the abbot or claimant sent it to England, presumably in the hope that this pension would be renewed. Its survival amongst Chancery, not Exchequer, records implies that the Dinans were unsuccessful.
[78] Crook, 'Lands of the Normans', 102–4.
[79] *CR 1259–1261*, 189; Powicke, *Loss of Normandy*, 343; Stevenson, 'England and Normandy', 423–4; F.M. Powicke, 'The Archbishop of Rouen, John de Harcourt and Simon de Montfort in 1260', *EHR* 37 (1922), 108–13.
[80] *CR 1259–1261*, 189–90.
[81] *CChR 1257–1300*, 182 (10 June 1272). See Maddicott, *Simon de Montfort*, 49, 65, 72, 198, 205.

heirs by the king's special grace shall retain the manor in the form under which the king has been accustomed to give the other lands of the Normans.'[82] Kings continued to grant out *terre Normannorum* by their special grace, with the assumption that the 'right heir' might still cross the Channel to claim them.[83] Royal acts after 1259 still referred to a future time when England and Normandy might be one again.[84] Meanwhile, the crown persisted in testing warrants to hold Norman escheats: in 1277, for instance, the king was suing Matilda of Lewknor for the manor of Langton Long Blandford (Dorset).[85] Inquests continued to seek out property that was rightfully the king's escheat as Norman land,[86] as did the inquiries that were recorded in the Hundred Rolls.[87] When John de Brienne, count of Eu, appeared before a parliament of Edward I in 1290 to claim the honour of Hastings and Tickhill, he received much the same response as had been given to a Norman noblewoman in 1220: French subjects would recover their former English lands only when the subjects of the king of England were allowed to recover their former possessions in France.[88] While two branches of the Étouteville family managed to hold onto English lands until the outbreak of the Hundred Years War,[89] they were exceptions to prove the rule that the treaty of 1259 had resolved nothing for the Anglo-Norman aristocracy. It is no coincidence that religious houses increasingly sought ways of commuting their overseas obligations, notably Bruton Priory and Troarn Abbey, which exchanged their estates in south-west England and the Cotentin in August 1260, just a few months after the treaty.[90]

The Treaty of Paris consequently marks not a final rupture between England and Normandy, but just one stage in the gradual uncoupling of aristocratic ties between England and northern France. We see a slow decline of family contacts, of double tenure, of knowledge and memory of the old holdings overseas. In 1259 the fate of overseas property still affected a small but significant number of families directly, and far more landowners stood to be affected by any process of restitution once peace was concluded. This explains why so many lords accompanied the king of England to France. Disappointment on both sides at the outcome of the negotiations is reflected in obscene satires about the king of England and his barons that

---

[82] *CChR 1257–1300*, 114.

[83] E.g. *CChR 1257–1300*, 42: grant to Peter de Savoy and his heirs of the honour, castle and rape of Hastings, with terms 'if the king wishes to restore them to the right heirs of his free will or by a peace or in any other way' (3 June 1262).

[84] E.g. *CChR 1257–1300*, 84: grant to William de Valence of the St-Amand lands in Wall (in Great Hallingbury, Essex), Exning (Suffolk), and Cleyndon (Kent) (6 Nov. 1267).

[85] TNA, KB 27/129, m. 9r.

[86] E.g. *CIMisc*, nos 344, 418, 460, 483, 990.

[87] *RH*, e.g. i. 50, 81, 90, 110, 185, 433.

[88] *Rot. Parl.*, i. 23; *Complete Peerage*, v. 170; cf. *CRR*, ix. 36–7 (response to Matilda de Courtenay, 1220). Edward I had already granted Tickhill to his kinswoman Constance de Béarn (*CPR 1281–1292*, 54). However, Ralph III of Eu (d. 1345) acquired lands in England and Ireland through marriage to Joanna de Mello, a descendant of Henry III's half-brother Geoffrey de Lusignan, including the former *terre Normannorum* of Wighton (Norfolk) with the hundred of North Greenhoe, Great Ponton (Lincs.), and Laughton-en-le-Morthern (Yorks.), which had belonged respectively to William de Cayeux, Luke de Crasmesnil, and the counts of Eu themselves: see *Complete Peerage*, v. 172; E. Lebailly, 'Raoul d'Eu, connétable de France et seigneur anglais et irlandais', in *La Normandie et l'Angleterre au Moyen Âge*, ed. Bouet and Gazeau, 239–48. For these manors as *terre Normannorum*, see *Fees*, i. 617, 619; *CChR 1226–1257*, 56–7; *CIMisc*, no. 414.

[89] *EYC*, ix. 55–65.

[90] *CN*, no. 673; Caen, AD Calvados, H 7780, H 7824; *Two Cartularies of the Augustinian Priory of Bruton and the Cluniac Priory of Montacute in the County of Somerset*, ed. M. Lyte et al. (London, 1894), nos 310–27; Matthew, *The Norman Monasteries*, 99–102.

were composed in the aftermath of the treaty, probably at the University of Paris.[91] In practice, however, the more stable and harmonious Angevin-Capetian relations that prevailed after 1259 appear to have made little difference to most of the heirs of the old Anglo-Norman families. Conversely, the Treaty of Paris did not mark a final rupture between the dominant classes of England and France, either magnates or 'gentry'; the communities of both countries would continue to have connections until the outbreak of the Hundred Years War in 1337 permanently altered relations between the two kingdoms.[92]

[91] *Thomas Wright's Political Songs*, 63–8 ('La Pais aus Englois'), which, *pace* Wright, concerns the treaty of 1259 rather than the Mise of Amiens (1264); E. Faral, *Mimes françaises au XIIIe siècle* (Paris, 1910), 48–50 ('La Chartre de la Pais aus Englois'). The manuscript for both texts (BN, MS fr. 837) has been linked to the University of Paris. I am grateful to Alison Williams, David Trotter, and Gaël Chenard for their help with these texts: I shall discuss their significance for the treaty of 1259 in a separate article.
[92] W.M. Ormrod, 'England, Normandy, and the Beginnings of the Hundred Years War, 1259–1360', in *England and Normandy in the Middle Ages*, ed. D. Bates and A. Curry (London, 1994), 197–213 (at 197–201), usefully discusses the 'lost' period of Anglo-Norman relations between 1259 and 1337.

Les traités de Paris des 22 et 23 octobre 1295 : la fin d'un système politique nordique ou de l'intérêt de l'alliance norvégienne

Florent Lenègre

Abstract

**The Treaties of Paris of 22 and 23 October 1295:
The End of a Nordic Political System or
of the Significance of the Norwegian Alliance**

The historiographical treatment of the Treaty of Paris, concluded on 22 and 23 October 1295 between the kingdoms of France, Scotland and Norway, has tended to relegate the Norwegian contribution to second place, privileging instead the Franco-Scottish agreement which established a durable alliance, the well-known 'Old Alliance'. Taking this as our point of departure, we here attempt to reassess the Norwegian participation in the Treaty and to consider its potential significance for the French crown at the moment of its conclusion. In order to undertake this analysis, we need to re-establish the Treaty within its immediate temporal context and also within an economic and political space focussed upon the North Sea, where, throughout the thirteenth century, English kings had affirmed their hegemony. After setting out the events which brought about the conclusion of this Treaty as well as analysing the negotiations along with the compositon of the Scottish and Norwegian embassies, we aim to show that the military aid of the Norwegians, irrespective of the promised numbers of ships and of men upon which the analysis to date has tended to focus, rested above all upon its far greater pyschological impact.

In fact, whatever the actual number of ships, the Norwegian navy was perceived at the time as a battle-hardened and redoutable force to the extent that its very presence represented a threat to the English crown and its German allies. In addition, through the Treaty, the French king had managed to ally with his Norwegian counterpart, until then a traditional ally of the English crown, and thereby had positioned himself as arbiter between Norway and Scotland, a role traditionally held by the English kings. By such an act, the king of France had broken the hegemony over the economy and polity of the North Sea region exercised by the English sovereigns and one which they had carefully constructed throughout the thirteenth century. By so doing, the French monarch was able to present himself as the one and only *rex pacificus*, natural heir to St Louis, with all that such implied in terms of leadership in the political theatre of western Christendom.

En conclusion de cette journée d'étude consacrée au traité de Paris, il nous a paru fécond d'opérer un léger saut temporel pour nous pencher sur ce qui peut apparaître comme un double maléfique de l'accord de 1259. L'inversion de ces deux derniers chiffres nous mène en 1295, les 22 et 23 octobre 1295. A ces dates furent conclus à Paris deux traités jumeaux par lesquels le royaume de France s'alliait aux royaumes de Norvège et d'Ecosse. En apparence, leur objectif pouvait se rapprocher de celui de 1259: il s'agissait en effet pour le roi de France de régler un différend financier d'origine territoriale entre deux souverains rivaux dans le but d'établir entre eux une paix durable. La différence majeure résidait dans le fait que cette paix devait permettre l'union des trois royaumes contre un ennemi commun: le roi d'Angleterre. Replaçons quelques éléments de contexte. Depuis l'attaque menée par des marins gascons sur La Rochelle au printemps 1293, les relations entre le roi de France et le roi d'Angleterre s'étaient nettement dégradées. Les demandes de compensation françaises assorties d'une convocation d'Edward devant le Parlement avaient abouti à la confiscation par le roi de France, le 19 mai 1294, du duché de Guyenne pour défaut de comparution.[1]

Les hostilités furent alors lancées et chacun chercha à renforcer son camp. Edward Ier activa ses réseaux et parvint à construire, dans un but certainement dissuasif, une alliance qui menaçait directement une partie du royaume de France. Cette série de traités d'alliance trouvait clairement son origine dans les limites mêmes du traité de 1259, et notamment dans son incapacité à résoudre les tensions qui ne pouvaient qu'exister entre le caractère souverain du roi d'Angleterre et sa position de vassal du roi de France pour le duché d'Aquitaine.

La riposte française ne tarda pas et prit des proportions similaires. Après s'être assuré quelques appuis sur sa frontière nord-est, Philippe le Bel tenta d'instaurer une menace directe sur le territoire anglais. Dans cette optique, l'alliance écossaise s'imposait naturellement. L'association des Norvégiens à cet accord peut aujourd'hui paraître plus intrigante mais elle répondait à une logique semblable et s'appuyait – nous allons le voir – sur une réelle capacité d'intervention. Malheureusement, cette alliance tripartite ne fut que de courte durée: quelques mois après sa ratification officielle le 23 mars 1296 en Ecosse,[2] l'accord fut dénoncé par les Ecossais sous la contrainte anglaise. Le traité norvégien, ratifié le 29 mars 1296,[3] n'a pas laissé de traces évidentes de fonctionnement, les négociations de paix reprenant rapidement entre France et Angleterre pour aboutir de trêve en trêve à un autre traité de Paris, celui de 1303.[4]

Malgré leur caractère éphémère, ces deux accords ont fait l'objet d'une étude complète. Publiée dans la *Scottish Historical Review* par Ranald Nicholson, cette étude souffle cette année ses cinquante bougies.[5] Arguant que ces traités n'avaient fait jusqu'alors l'objet que d'un traitement partiel, chaque commentateur se plaçant du seul point de vue du royaume qu'il étudiait, son ambition était de comprendre ce qui avait amené leur conclusion en les replaçant dans une perspective européenne. Analysant les contacts étroits tissés tout au long de la deuxième moitié du XIIIe siècle entre la Norvège, l'Angleterre et l'Ecosse, l'auteur parvenait à montrer

---

[1] Sur l'enchaînement des événements, voir, entre autres, F.M. Powicke, *The Thirteenth Century, 1216–1307*, 2ème éd. (Oxford History of England, 1962), 644–8.

[2] AN, Trésor des Chartes, reg. V, fols 132v–135v; K.M. Brown et al., éds, *The Records of the Parliaments of Scotland to 1707* (St Andrews, 2007–09), A1296/2/1; http://www.rps.ac.uk/mss/A1296/2/1

[3] C.C.A. Lange et C.R. Unger, éds, *Diplomatarium Norvegicum* (désormais *DN*) (Christiania, 1849–1972), xix. no. 406 (les volumes 1 à 21 sont consultables en ligne: http://www.dokpro.uio.no/dipl_norv/diplom_felt.html).

[4] Powicke, *Thirteenth Century*, 649–54.

[5] R. Nicholson, 'The Franco-Scottish and Franco-Norwegian Treaties of 1295', *Scottish Historical Review* 38 (1959), 114–32.

que ce rapprochement entre les trois royaumes était le fruit d'un long et tortueux cheminement dans cette relation triangulaire. Il concluait en soulignant le caractère éphémère de l'alliance franco-norvégienne, à la différence de l'alliance franco-écossaise, première quoique brève occurrence de la fameuse 'auld alliance' et cause directe de l'invasion de l'Ecosse par Edward Ier en 1296.

Le versant norvégien de l'accord se trouvait ainsi un peu relégué à l'arrière-plan. Le roi de Norvège aurait profité de ce traité pour obtenir uniquement des rentrées pécuniaires et se serait même engagé par la voix de son procureur à apporter une aide militaire qu'il n'était pas en mesure de fournir, rendant ainsi le traité inapplicable.

La plupart des manuels et des monographies, lorsqu'ils ont développé un peu le sujet, ont repris en partie ou en totalité ces analyses depuis la réédition du manuel de Sir Maurice Powicke[6] jusqu'à la récente étude de Narve Björgo sur la politique extérieure norvégienne au Moyen Age.[7] Plusieurs questions restent pourtant en suspens: pourquoi une réaction si violente d'Edward Ier lorsqu'il apprend la ratification du traité? Quel intérêt pour la France de recourir en plus de l'alliance écossaise à l'alliance norvégienne alors que ces deux royaumes sont à l'époque manifestement en conflit? La Norvège n'est-elle présente ici qu'à titre anecdotique? N'y a-t-il pas là de la part du roi de France un geste symbolique dont l'importance a pu être sous-estimée? Pour tenter d'apporter une réponse complète à ces questions, il convient de reprendre le dossier. Après avoir replacé ce traité dans son contexte immédiat, nous voulons pousser plus loin l'enquête commencée par Nicholson, en l'interprétant dans une perspective différente, celle d'un espace économique et politique centré sur la Mer du Nord, sur lequel les rois d'Angleterre tout au long du XIIIe siècle souhaitent affirmer leur hégémonie.

Le cheminement qui a mené à la conclusion de ce double traité a été, nous l'avons dit, bien mis en évidence par Ranald Nicholson. Il n'est pas inutile dans notre perspective d'en rappeler les grandes lignes, afin de fixer les grandes dates que nous serons amenés à évoquer au cours de notre propos. Au début de l'année 1295, l'Ecosse et la Norvège étaient en conflit depuis quelques années à cause d'un défaut de paiement, avec l'Ecosse dans le rôle du mauvais payeur.

La créance norvégienne avait pour source deux traités passés dans la deuxième moitié du XIIIe siècle: le premier conclu à Perth le 2 juillet 1266 prévoyait la cession par la Norvège des Hébrides et de l'Île de Man à l'Ecosse contre une rente annuelle de 100 marcs.[8] Le deuxième traité fut passé le 25 juillet 1281 à Roxburgh: il fixait les conditions du mariage de Margaret, la fille du roi d'Ecosse Alexander III, avec le jeune roi de Norvège Erik Magnusson. La dot de la jeune mariée s'élevait à 14000 marcs dont la moitié fut payée en espèce et l'autre moitié assignée sur les revenus de 4 terres écossaises à raison de 700 marcs par an.[9] La mort du roi Alexander III, le 19 mars 1286, sans autre héritier que la petite fille née de l'union entre Margaret et Erik, suivi du décès de cette dernière en septembre 1290, alors qu'elle venait d'arriver au large des côtes écossaises, plongèrent le royaume d'Ecosse dans l'instabilité.[10]

6 Powicke, *Thirteenth Century*, 612–13.
7 N. Bjørgo, Ø. Rian et A. Kaartvedt, *Selvstendighet og union fra middelalderen til 1905* (Norsk utenrikspolitikks historie I, 1995), 90.
8 *DN*, viii. no. 8.
9 *DN*, xix. no. 305.
10 Sur cet épisode, voir W.C. Dickinson, *Scotland from the Earliest Times to 1603* (Oxford, 1977), 27–38.

A la perspective d'une minorité, déjà peu réjouissante en termes de stabilité, succéda celle d'un processus de dévolution de la couronne d'Ecosse, au cours duquel il faudrait choisir entre plusieurs candidats. Pour trancher, les grands du royaume d'Ecosse firent appel à Edward Ier qui en profita pour se faire reconnaître seigneur supérieur du royaume. Commença alors ce que l'on nomme par la suite la 'Great Cause'. Douze candidats se déclarèrent, parmi lesquels le roi Erik de Norvège, Robert Bruce l'ancien, le grand-père du futur roi, vainqueur de Bannockburn, et John Bailliol qui finit par remporter la mise en novembre 1292.[11]

Les bouleversements que connut le royaume d'Ecosse entre 1286 et 1292 suffisent sans doute à expliquer l'arrêt des paiements liés aux traités de Perth et de Roxburgh, les uns en 1286, les autres après 1291.[12] Il est certain en tout cas que les Norvégiens ne goûtèrent pas vraiment la chose. Pour forcer une issue, le roi Erik de Norvège assigna en 1292 à deux marchands cahorsins, Guillaume d'Averson et Guillaume Servat, auxquels il avait emprunté 2800 marcs, quatre ans d'arrérages sur le paiement de la rente liée à la dot de son épouse, correspondant à la période 1286–1290. Edward Ier, en tant qu'arbitre du procès de dévolution, dominait la scène écossaise, Erik lui demanda logiquement d'intervenir en faveur des deux marchands qui se trouvaient, de plus, être originaires du duché de Guyenne. Edward intervint lors du Parlement de la Trinité 1292, tenu à Berwick et accorda à Erik la reprise du paiement de la rente et le rattrapage de trois années d'arrérage pour la période 1290–1292. Malheureusement, la somme versée, 802 livres, 16 sous et 10 deniers et demi, n'atteignit pas les 2100 marcs escomptés car les quatre terres attribuées ne produisaient visiblement pas assez de revenus. Erik revint rapidement à la charge par l'intermédiaire d'un Suédois, maître Peter Algotsson, auquel il avait prêté de l'argent et assigné remboursement sur le reste des revenus écossais en souffrance.

Celui-ci se présenta au Parlement de Berwick pour y demander une intervention royale. Edward tenta d'obtenir le paiement des revenus en s'adressant au nouveau roi John Balliol sans succès, certaines personnes s'opposant en interne à ce paiement. Lors du Parlement de Pâques 1293, Edward réaffirma le jugement rendu l'année précédente mais n'engagea pas d'autres actions. Une relance fut effectuée en novembre mais Balliol, étranglé par les difficultés financières, ne put répondre favorablement. La conjonction en 1294 des tensions naissantes avec le royaume de France et des révoltes galloises fit que cette réclamation resta sans réponse, malgré au moins une ambassade norvégienne envoyée auprès d'Edward à Aberconway entre juillet 1294 et juin 1295.[13] Lors de cette entrevue, le sujet des Hébrides et de la dot de Margaret fut abordé de façon certaine mais le roi Edward ne put apporter de réponse claire aux envoyés norvégiens: dans la lettre qu'il leur remit sans doute à destination du roi Erik, il conseilla à ce dernier de reprendre son droit le plus rapidement et le plus commodément possible.[14] Nicholson lui prête des intentions pacifiques, le contraire pourrait tout autant se soutenir. Quoiqu'il en soit, Erik prit le message au pied de la lettre: prenant acte de l'incapacité d'Edward à résoudre son problème, il se tourna vers le roi de France.

Côté Ecossais, les choses étaient plus simples: ce furent les vexations féodales imposées au roi d'Ecosse John Balliol par son seigneur Edward Ier qui poussèrent John et son aristocratie à se rapprocher de la France contre l'Angleterre dans un

---

[11] *DN*, xix. no. 372.
[12] Pour les deux paragraphes qui suivent, nous avons repris Nicholson, 'The Franco-Scottish and Franco-Norwegian Treaties of 1295', 122–9, en relisant les sources correspondantes.
[13] *DN*, xix. no. 394.
[14] Nicholson, 'The Franco-Scottish and Franco-Norwegian Treaties of 1295', 129; *DN*, xix. no. 412.

contexte d'hostilité ouverte entre les deux royaumes. Ce rapprochement se fit d'autant plus facilement que John était vassal du roi de France pour ses possessions françaises (Bailleul, Dampierre, Hélicourt et Hornoy).[15]

Le décor est planté, penchons-nous à présent sur la négociation des traités et sur leur contenu, en tentant particulièrement de montrer en quoi la Norvège peut être considérée comme un interlocuteur sérieux pour le roi de France. Les délégations norvégiennes et écossaises reçurent leur procuration dans le courant de l'été 1295, respectivement le 24 juin et le 5 juillet.[16] Leur composition était tout à fait différente et reflétait assez bien la situation politique des deux royaumes. La délégation écossaise était composée de quatre membres, deux ecclésiastiques, William Fraser, évêque de Saint Andrews et Matthew de Cranbeth, évêque de Dunkeld, et deux laïcs, John de Soules et Ingram de Umfraville. Elle fut envoyée au nom de John Balliol par un conseil de douze gardiens nommés en juillet 1295 pour contrôler les actes de John Balliol, afin qu'il ne compromette pas l'indépendance du royaume. Comme l'a bien montré Geoffrey Barrow dans son *Robert Bruce*, cette délégation, à l'image du conseil qui l'a envoyée, était chargée de représenter l'ensemble de la communauté du royaume d'Ecosse.[17] La figure dominante en était sans conteste William Fraser, évêque de Saint Andrews, déjà rompu aux missions diplomatiques, notamment auprès d'Edward Ier, gardien d'Ecosse entre 1286 et 1290, et probablement aussi membre du conseil de douze gardiens nommé de fraîche date.[18]

La délégation norvégienne était, quant à elle, beaucoup moins spectaculaire, si ce n'était par la liste des titres dont se parait son unique membre. Elle se résumait au seul Audun Hugleiksson, présenté dans sa lettre de procuration comme seigneur de Hegranes, dans le nord-ouest de la Norvège, parent et *secretarius* du roi Erik.[19] A ces titres, le texte du traité ajoutait ceux de baron et de conseiller du roi de Norvège.[20] Le personnage mérite qu'on s'y attarde quelques instants car il montre que le service du roi de Norvège évoluait à l'époque au même rythme que celui des rois plus occidentaux.[21]

Sans doute né vers 1245 d'un aristocrate de rang moyen, Audun pouvait se vanter d'être parent avec Inga de Varteig, mère du grand roi Håkon Håkonsson (1217–63), le grand père d'Erik. Après avoir certainement étudié le droit, il entra à la cour du roi Magnus Håkonsson dans les années 1270, aidé sans doute par ses relations familiales. Tout porte à croire que c'est par sa compétence qu'il s'y imposa. Chargé de superviser le tribunal de la cour, il participa dans les années 1270 à l'élaboration des réformes juridiques prises par le roi Magnus. Le titre de baron, qu'il reçut en 1277, le plaça parmi les proches du roi. Il devint trésorier du royaume sans doute dès 1280. Lorsque le jeune roi Erik fut couronné en 1280, il était une figure dominante du conseil de régence. A partir de 1290, il s'imposa comme le plus proche conseiller d'Erik, ce qui lui valut sans doute le titre de 'secretarius', qu'il faut entendre au sens de conseiller particulier, comme le fut John Mansell auprès de Henry III.

[15] Nicholson, 'The Franco-Scottish and Franco-Norwegian Treaties of 1295', 118.

[16] Ibid., 129.

[17] Sur ce sujet, voir G.W.S. Barrow, *Robert Bruce and the Community of the Realm* (Londres, 1965), 89.

[18] Sur ce personnage, voir *A Biographical Dictionary of Scottish Graduates to A. D. 1410*, dir. D.E.R. Watt (Oxford, 1977), 203–6.

[19] *DN*, xix. no. 398.

[20] *DN*, xix. no. 399.

[21] Sur ce personnage, voir *Norsk Biografisk Lexicon*, dir. K. Helle et J.G. Arntzen, nouvelle édition (Oslo, 1999–2005), i. 169 et K. Helle, *Konge og gode menn i norsk riksstyring ca. 1150–1319* (Oslo, Bergen, Tromsø, 1972), 579–81.

Le fait qu'il fût envoyé seul pour mener cette négociation délicate – il s'agit de rompre avec l'allié traditionnel anglais et de pactiser avec l'adversaire écossais – était inhabituel. Les ambassades norvégiennes envoyées dans les Îles Britanniques au cours du XIIIe siècle pour négocier des traités similaires ou pour participer à la 'Great Cause' comprenaient toujours au moins deux personnes, un aristocrate pour l'apparat et un expert en droit pour suivre les tractations juridiques.[22] Cette exception attestait la grande confiance du roi Erik envers Audun mais peut-être également le caractère hautement confidentiel, voire secret, de sa mission.

Cela peut également s'expliquer par le fait qu'Audun regroupait dans sa seule personne toutes les qualités attendues d'une délégation diplomatique. Son appartenance à la famille royale et à la cour du roi lui conférait une dignité qui lui permettait d'assumer pleinement son rôle de représentant de la personne royale et du royaume. Il était également doté d'une sérieuse expérience juridique et diplomatique.[23] Sa première mission documentée eut lieu en Danemark en 1276. Dans les années 1280–90, il mena quatre importantes missions diplomatiques dans les Îles Britanniques, dont la plupart étaient relatives aux paiements déjà évoqués. Si le but de ces missions est mis en relation avec sa charge de trésorier, apparaît alors une des caractéristiques saillantes de la diplomatie de la fin du XIIIe siècle: son caractère pragmatique. L'étude des missions diplomatiques échangées entre l'Angleterre, l'Ecosse et la Norvège au XIIIe siècle montre qu'outre la compétence et le statut social, l'intéressement direct du diplomate dans les résultats de la mission était un facteur important, sinon décisif, dans la composition d'une délégation.[24]

La figure d'Audun montre que la monarchie norvégienne évoluait à l'époque au même rythme que les grandes monarchies occidentales. Ses états de service étaient clairement ceux d'un légiste, du même type que ceux qu'on rencontrait à la cour de Philippe le Bel, mais son statut aristocratique, sa place de favori auprès du roi, la conjonction entre son poste de trésorier et ses missions diplomatiques forcent également la comparaison avec Enguerrand de Marigny, qui était toutefois d'une origine plus modeste.[25] Il incarnait un type de gouvernement, le gouvernement par favori, où le favori en question devenait tellement proche du roi et était réputé influer tellement sur ses décisions, qu'il s'attirait de féroces rancoeurs. De fait, lorsque le roi Erik mourut en 1299, Audun fut immédiatement arrêté et jugé sans doute pour haute trahison. Condamné à mort il fut, comme Matthieu de la Brosse et Enguerrand de Marigny, pendu en décembre 1302.

Poursuivons notre démonstration en nous concentrant maintenant sur les traités eux-mêmes. Le 22 octobre 1295, à l'issue d'une négociation préalable qui dura certainement pendant tous les mois de septembre et d'octobre, plusieurs documents furent établis. Le premier était un document détaillant les engagements militaires pris en faveur du roi de France par Audun Hugleiksson au nom du roi de Norvège,[26]

---

[22] Voir par exemple la composition des ambassades norvégiennes ayant participé à la conclusion des traités significatifs pour la période 1250–95 ou aux missions les plus importantes: *DN*, xix. nos 284, 305, 331, 377, 394.

[23] Les missions qui suivent sont présentées en détail dans notre thèse d'Ecole des Chartes, 'Les relations diplomatiques entre la Norvège et les Îles Britanniques 1249–1319: les ambassadeurs et le service diplomatique du roi', 2002, Annexe: dictionnaire biographique, II, no. 7.

[24] On peut citer comme exemple la mission diplomatique, citée plus haut, de maître Peter Algotsson auprès du roi d'Ecosse, en 1292, pour négocier le paiement de l'arriéré de la dot de Margaret d'Ecosse. Cet arriéré avait été concédé à Peter par le roi de Norvège en remboursement d'un prêt qu'il lui avait concédé.

[25] Sur le sujet, voir J. Favier, *Philippe le Bel* (Paris, 1978), 36–7 et 481–514.

[26] *DN*, xix. no. 399.

le second un engagement de non-agression envers la Norvège pris par les diplomates écossais,[27] les derniers, deux traités d'alliance en bonne et due forme, pris par Philippe IV à destination d'Erik de Norvège et John Bailliol, roi d'Ecosse.[28] Le traité franco-norvégien officialisait l'alliance initiée entre les deux royaumes et évoquait le subside militaire que devait fournir le roi de Norvège sans le détailler, renvoyant au document produit par Audun. De même, il précisait les relations que devaient entretenir le roi de Norvège avec le roi d'Ecosse et réciproquement. Conservés dans le trésor des chartes du roi de France, les deux premiers accords peuvent être considérés comme deux reconnaissances annexées à ce traité principal. Scellé du sceau de Philippe le Bel, il fut envoyé au roi Erik et conservé par la suite dans ses archives. Le lendemain, Philippe produisait un autre traité d'alliance similaire à destination du roi d'Ecosse.[29]

Penchons-nous sur le contenu de l'aide militaire promise par Audun dans son traité annexe. Conformément aux pouvoirs portés dans sa lettre de procuration, cette aide est tournée explicitement contre l'Angleterre et ses soutiens, le roi d'Allemagne étant cité particulièrement.[30] Cette aide était précisément chiffrée: 200 galées et 100 navires équipés ainsi que 50000 hommes devaient être mis à disposition pendant 4 mois tous les ans contre un paiement de 30000 livres.[31] Les historiens, de Knut Gjerset à Narve Björgo, en passant par Nicholson, n'ont pas manqué de souligner le caractère irréaliste de cette promesse, au moins en ce qui concerne le nombre d'hommes à fournir.[32]

Est-ce bien le cas? Le système du Leidangr qui avait cours en Norvège à l'époque permettait de lever des flottes importantes composées essentiellement de navires légers à rames.[33] Ce système autorisait tout à fait un rassemblement de 200 embarcations légères et 100 lourdes. En 1256, le roi de Norvège Håkon Håkonsson, grâce à une importante levée opérée dans la seule région du Vik (baie d'Oslo), parvint, selon la saga qui lui est consacrée – une source digne de foi – à lever 360 navires pour aller ravager les côtes danoises.[34] L'année suivante, il était à la tête d'une flotte de 375 bateaux pour retourner au Danemark.[35] 300 navires représentaient une mobilisation très importante à l'échelle du royaume de Norvège mais cela ne semblait pas être un chiffre rédhibitoire.

Les 50000 hommes paraissaient beaucoup plus difficiles à envisager mais il faut bien comprendre que l'équivalence 50000 hommes pour 30000 livres n'était sans doute ici qu'un ratio. Les clauses d'application de cette promesse précisaient bien quelques lignes plus bas que la somme versée était au prorata des hommes fournis, un tiers des hommes fournis déclenchant le paiement d'un tiers de la somme, sans

---

[27] *DN*, xix. no. 401.

[28] *DN*, xi. no. 5.

[29] On ne conserve de ce traité que la ratification écossaise du 23 mars 1296, voir note 2 ci-dessus.

[30] *DN*, xi. no. 399: '[...] in presenti querra quam contra dictum Regem Anglie, fautores et confederatos, tam regem Allemannie quam alios quoscumque valitores ejus habere dignoscitur, assistet ope et consilii et auxilii efficacis [...]'.

[31] *DN*, xi. no. 399

[32] K. Gjerset, *History of the Norwegian People* (New York, 1915), 482; Bjørgo et al., *Selvstendighet og union fra middelalderen til 1905*, 90; Nicholson, 'The Franco-Scottish and Franco-Norwegian Treaties of 1295', 130.

[33] *Medieval Scandinavia: An Encyclopedia*, dir. P. Pulsiano et K. Wolf (New York, Londres, 1993), 388.

[34] G. Vigfusson, éd, *Hákonar Saga* (désormais *HS*), *Rerum Britannicarum medii aevi scriptores* 88/2 (Londres, 1887), § 285.

[35] Ibid., § 293.

que le nombre de bateaux pût varier pour autant.[36] De la sorte, le roi de Norvège comme le roi de France gagnaient une certaine souplesse dans la gestion l'un de ses troupes, l'autre de ses deniers. Les modalités de mobilisation de cette aide militaire, détaillées un peu plus loin dans le texte apportaient des éléments qui allaient dans ce sens. Le roi de France devait, avant la mi-mars de chaque année, transmettre au roi de Norvège la taille du subside qu'il souhaitait obtenir,[37] ce qui plaide pour une flexibilité de la demande et sans doute aussi de l'offre sur la base du ratio porté dans le traité. Si les chiffres maximums promis pouvaient paraître au-dessus des capacités du royaume de Norvège, la teneur du traité prévoyait une certaine souplesse dans la fourniture du subside militaire. En l'état, il n'était pas totalement inapplicable.

Et il était important que ce fût le cas, car le fait d'avoir la flotte norvégienne à ses côtés était, en cette fin de XIIIème siècle, moins anodin qu'il ne paraît de prime abord. Qu'elle intervînt en masse ou non, la flotte norvégienne faisait peur. Elle était en effet, à l'époque, particulièrement aguerrie et avait prouvé à quelques reprises qu'elle pouvait frapper hors de ses bases, et particulièrement dans les Îles Britanniques.

A partir de 1253, le roi Håkon effectua plusieurs raids sur le Danemark à la tête d'une flotte importante, forçant en 1257 la négociation d'un traité.[38] Après une pause sous le règne de Magnus Håkonsson, les expéditions de grande ampleur reprirent à partir de 1289. Le harcèlement norvégien sur les côtes danoises aboutit à la conclusion du traité de Hindsgavl en septembre 1295, qui permit à la Norvège de poser son empreinte sur la politique danoise et de renforcer son contrôle sur le détroit commandant l'accès à la mer baltique.[39] Quelques mois avant la conclusion du traité, la Norvège apparaissait comme une puissance maritime qui avait le vent en poupe. Dans des circonstances similaires, Alphonse X de Castille avait recherché en 1258 à s'allier la flotte norvégienne pour l'aider dans sa lutte contre les Maures.[40]

Les Norvégiens pouvaient-ils intervenir loin de leurs côtes? Ils l'avaient prouvé en 1263 en envoyant une flotte d'une centaine de bateaux au large de l'Ecosse afin d'affirmer leur contrôle sur les Hébrides et l'Île de Man.[41] Cette expédition fut considérée comme un échec car elle fut contrainte de se replier à l'arrivée des tempêtes automnales mais sa suprématie navale pendant la campagne active ne fut pas contestée, le roi d'Ecosse se contentant d'attendre que le mauvais temps la chasse de ses côtes. La présence de territoires norvégiens pouvant servir de bases d'opérations au large de l'Ecosse et sur la route maritime qui y mène,[42] la nouvelle amitié écossaise, tous ces éléments permettaient aux Norvégiens de frapper aisément les côtes anglaises.

---

[36] *DN*, xix. no. 399: '[…] Si vero minorem personarum numerum habere volueret, quot infra predictum numerum sibi habere placuerit, idem Dominus noster Norwegie rex sibi tenebitur ministrare: quo casu pro rata sive numero personarum quas habere voluerit idem rex Francie, de quantitate predicte summe pecunie detrahet; ut si tertiam partem personarum habere voluerit, tertia pars pecunie totalis summe predicte detrahetur […]'.

[37] *DN*, xix. no. 399: '[…] quod idem Francie rex annis singulis infra medium mensem Martii predicto domino nostro Norwegie regi significare debebit qui subsidium ipse Francie rex tempore vernali sequenti juxta prescriptam formam habere voluerit ab eodem […]'.

[38] Bjørgo et al., *Selvstendighet og union fra middelalderen til 1905*, 66–7.

[39] Ibid., 87.

[40] Ibid., 64–5; *HS*, §§ 290 et surtout 294.

[41] Bjørgo et al., *Selvstendighet og union fra middelalderen til 1905*, 71–7; *HS*, §§ 318–29.

[42] On pense ici notamment aux Shetlands et surtout aux Orcades, territoires sous domination norvégienne, qui peuvent servir de base arrière pour lancer un assaut contre les Îles Britanniques.

L'alliance norvégienne faisait peser une menace réelle sur le territoire anglais doublé e d'un manque à gagner sur le plan commercial. Une fréquentation march-ande réciproque importante est en effet attestée dès le XIIème siècle qui se développa tout au long du XIIIe siècle et obtint une reconnaissance officielle par la passa-tion de traités de libre commerce entre les deux royaumes en 1223 et en 1269 à Winchester,[43] accord qui est renouvelé en 1284.[44] Un conflit avec l'Angleterre dérè-glerait cet ensemble et pourrait se traduire par des saisies de navires commerciaux et leur réutilisation à des fins guerrières, comme cela avait été précisément le cas avant l'expédition de 1263 contre l'Ecosse.[45]

A la lumière de ces éléments, on peut penser que l'alliance norvégienne était considérée en octobre 1295 plus dissuasive que ce qu'on avait pu imaginer de prime abord. Dissuasive non seulement pour le roi d'Angleterre, mais aussi pour ses prin-cipaux alliés, et notamment les princes allemands, qui devaient s'accommoder de la récente mainmise norvégienne sur le détroit commandant l'accès à la Baltique.

Mais bien plus significatif que tout cela fut le coup immense que ce double traité porta au prestige d'Edward Ier et à sa position au sein d'un ensemble économique, politique et culturel centré sur une Mer du Nord qui faisait figure à l'époque de véri-table Méditerranée septentrionale. Cet ensemble, qui reposait sur le lien traditionnel qui unissait tous les royaumes qui bordent la Mer du Nord depuis les invasions anglo-saxonnes et viking, avait été entretenu tout au long du XIIIe siècle par les rois d'Angleterre qui cherchaient à y imposer une forme de *pax anglica*, recherchant l'alliance, notamment familiale, des souverains voisins et se plaçant vis-à-vis d'eux dans la position de l'arbitre impartial, du *rex pacificus*.

On connaît les liens dynastiques et d'entraide tissés entre les rois d'Angleterre et les rois d'Ecosse.[46] Ils justifièrent l'intervention de Henry III pendant la minorité d'Alexander III en 1249 qui permit de stabiliser la situation. Le roi d'Ecosse et son aristocratie le lui rendirent bien lorsqu'en 1265, ils lui fournirent une aide décisive lors de la bataille d'Evesham qui assura sa victoire sur Simon de Montfort et ses amis. Les relations triangulaires entre l'Ecosse, la Norvège et l'Angleterre obéissent pendant l'essentiel du XIIIe siècle à cette logique.

Le roi Henry III entretint tout au long de son règne d'excellentes relations avec le roi Håkon Håkonsson, basées sur des échanges commerciaux fructueux. De Norvège arrivait le poisson nécessaire aux périodes de Carême, du bois de construction, des peaux et quelques marchandises de luxe fort prisées, en prov-enance d'Islande et de Groënland: les fourrures, les faucons, notamment le précieux faucon blanc, et l'ivoire de morse dont on fabriquait entre autres des pièces d'échec. En échange, l'Angleterre fournissait essentiellement du blé et du tissu. Entre 1222 et 1253, le dépouillement des 'rolls' anglais ('close' et 'liberate') ainsi que de la correspondance royale laissent apparaître des échanges annuels entre les deux rois, les données basculent ensuite sans doute dans les 'household accounts' qui n'ont pas été dépouillés. En 1230, il est fait mention de présents de bonne année.[47] Les faucons étaient échangés contre du blé, des tissus précieux ou encore des bijoux. Parmi ces nombreux présents offerts par Håkon et ses successeurs, se trouvaient

---

[43] *DN*, xix. no. 284.

[44] *Regesta Norvegica 1264–1300*, éd. S. Bagge et N. Bjørgo (Oslo, 1978), ii. no. 355.

[45] Une lettre de Henry III adressée à Håkon atteste d'une telle saisie lors de la préparation de l'expédition norvégienne de 1263: *DN*, xix. no. 276.

[46] Powicke, *Thirteenth Century*, 580–95.

[47] *DN*, xix. no. 198.

quelques cadeaux pour le moins originaux: un élan en 1222,[48] de l'ivoire de morse et des peaux d'ours blanc en 1225,[49] une ourse blanche avec ses petits en 1252 gardée à la tour de Londres,[50] une tête de baleine entière en 1276.[51]

Ces relations très cordiales aboutirent à plusieurs tentatives de rapprochements concrets: en 1223, le jarl Skuli formula une demande de renouvellement du traité de libre commerce qui liait les deux royaumes,[52] en 1224, Håkon demanda à obtenir un fief en Angleterre, apparemment sans succès.[53] En 1259, après avoir marié sa fille Kristin avec un frère d'Alphonse X, Håkon s'enhardit et demanda la main de Beatrice, fille de Henry III pour son fils Magnus. La demande fut poliment rejetée par Henry qui expliqua qu'un mariage était prévu pour Beatrice précisément dans le cadre du traité de Paris.[54]

Henry III entretenait de très bonnes relations avec les rois de Norvège et d'Ecosse qui de leur côté voyaient un contentieux territorial se développer entre eux autour de la souveraineté sur les Hébrides. Cet ensemble d'îles sous domination norvégienne depuis la fin du XIe siècle contrariait le 'winning of the west' écossais, mouvement d'assimilation par le royaume d'Ecosse de ses franges occidentales. Plusieurs tentatives de négociation avec la Norvège sur la base d'un rachat de ces îles avaient échoué sous Alexander II, déclenchant une invasion écossaise des Hébrides en 1249 au cours de laquelle le roi d'Ecosse trouva la mort, plongeant le royaume dans l'épreuve d'une minorité.[55] Alexander III parvenu à la majorité, les tractations reprirent. Une ambassade écossaise fut envoyée en Norvège fin 1261 qui, non seulement, se vit signifier une fin de non-recevoir mais qui fut, en outre, retenue de force en Norvège.[56]

C'est à ce moment qu'intervint le roi d'Angleterre, sur plainte de son gendre, Alexander III. Plutôt que de favoriser son parent, Henry chercha à apaiser le conflit en prenant la position d'arbitre. Plusieurs raisons expliquaient cette position: la pression que l'opposition baronniale exerçait sur son pouvoir amenait Henry à redouter un conflit entre la Norvège et l'Ecosse, qui l'aurait privé du soutien militaire de l'aristocratie écossaise. D'autre part, Henry s'accommodait fort bien de la lointaine souveraineté norvégienne sur l'Île de Man, qui lui permettait de développer librement sa politique irlandaise. Une Île de Man écossaise aurait été une épine dans le pied du roi d'Angleterre.[57]

Henry III écrivit au roi de Norvège pour obtenir la libération des envoyés au printemps 1262.[58] Puis il lui écrivit à nouveau le 15 novembre 1262 pour s'assurer qu'il n'attaquerait pas l'Ecosse, promettant d'inciter le roi d'Ecosse à régler les contentieux commerciaux qui opposaient les deux royaumes si, de son côté, il

---

[48] *DN*, xix. no. 137b.

[49] *DN*, xix. no. 167.

[50] *CLR 1251–60*, 70.

[51] *DN*, xix. no. 293.

[52] *DN*, xix. no. 152.

[53] *DN*, xix. no. 153.

[54] *DN*, xix. no. 269.

[55] Sur ce point, voir G.W.S Barrow, *Kingship and Unity: Scotland 1000–1306*, 2e édition, (The New History of Scotland, 2003), 139–40.

[56] *HS*, §§ 307 et 310. Voir à ce sujet notre article 'Redorer le blason: écriture de l'histoire et intégration à l'Occident dans la *Saga d'Håkon*', dans *Le passé à l'épreuve du présent*, éd. P. Chastang (Paris, 2008), 251–63.

[57] Bjørgo et al., *Selvstendighet og union fra middelalderen til 1905*, 73.

[58] Cette lettre ne nous est pas parvenue mais elle est citée dans une autre lettre adressée le 23 mars 1262 par le roi d'Angleterre au roi d'Ecosse: *DN*, xix. no. 271.

s'engageait à faire de même.[59] Cette tentative de médiation se révéla vaine et Håkon leva sa flotte pendant l'hiver 1262.[60] Devant la menace d'une intervention norvégienne le long des côtes écossaises, Alexander III leva de son côté une armée pour envahir les Hébrides et les annexer à son royaume. Juste avant l'été 1263, Henry III tenta de dissuader Alexander de se lancer dans une telle expédition en rappelant que ce type d'opération n'avait pas porté chance à ses prédécesseurs,[61] mais le mécanisme était déjà enclenché.

Une fois le conflit terminé, les tentatives d'arbitrage reprirent malgré la situation précaire dans laquelle se trouvait le roi d'Angleterre. La dernière lettre que Henry III envoya avant d'être mis sous tutelle, le 28 juin 1264, fut à destination du roi Magnus, le successeur d'Håkon, mort dans les Orcades au retour de son expédition en décembre 1263. Il y proposait un marché simple: le traité commercial de 1223 pouvait être renouvelé et les marchands norvégiens qui avaient subi des dommages en Angleterre trouveraient compensation, à la condition que la paix se fît avec l'Ecosse.[62] Ces efforts aboutirent cette fois à la conclusion du traité de Perth en 1266 qui, en plus de régler le problème des Hébrides et de Man, institua le libre commerce entre les deux anciens adversaires. Le roi d'Angleterre tint ensuite sa promesse, le traité commercial anglo-norvégien de 1223 fut renouvelé à Winchester en août 1269.

Par cette médiation, le roi d'Angleterre atteignait un double objectif: il renforçait sa position vis-à-vis de ses barons en cultivant des alliances utiles et construisait en même temps un espace économique et politique où la paix était garantie en dernier ressort par son arbitrage. Il se plaçait, en concurrence avec saint Louis, dans la position du *rex pacificus*, à même de fédérer les autres princes chrétiens dans le but ultime de les mener en Terre Sainte. Cette tradition fut reprise en 1272 par son fils Edward, dont on connaît l'attachement à l'idée de Croisade.

Cette communauté nordique fut dans un premier temps cultivée et développée. Lorsqu'en 1280 le roi Magnus sentit la mort venir, significativement, il écrivit à Edward pour le remercier d'un don de reliques et lui recommander ses deux fils Erik et Håkon.[63] Comme pour l'Ecosse en 1249, le roi d'Angleterre apparaissait comme une garantie de stabilité alors que le royaume se préparait à affronter une minorité royale, et où l'existence de deux héritiers pouvait faire renaître le spectre de la guerre civile. Edward ne prit pas cette recommandation à la légère et ce fut sans doute lui qui incita son gendre Alexander III à marier sa fille Margaret au jeune roi Erik à l'été 1281. Par ce geste, il faisait entrer le roi de Norvège dans sa propre famille et se garantissait ainsi une possibilité accrue d'intervention dans les affaires du royaume.

En 1286, lorsque mourut Alexander III en laissant comme seule héritière Margaret, la jeune fille d'Erik de Norvège, les négociations pour la reconnaissance de cette dernière comme reine d'Ecosse et son arrivée dans son royaume, qui aboutirent au traité de Salisbury de 1289, furent pilotées par Edward Ier et son conseil, à la demande des grands d'Ecosse et du roi de Norvège. L'année d'après, fidèle à ses

---

[59] *DN*, xix. no. 272.

[60] *HS*, § 314.

[61] Il fait référence évidemment à la mort d'Alexander II en 1249 dans des circonstances similaires: *DN*, xix. no. 273.

[62] Henry III, dans la guerre qu'il menait contre ses barons, avait besoin du soutien des aristocrates écossais et devait donc éviter que le conflit avec la Norvège ne les empêche de le soutenir, Bjørgo et al., *Selvstendighet og union fra middelalderen til 1905*, 78–9; *DN*, xix. no. 276.

[63] *DN*, xix. no. 302.

habitudes, Edward obtint, par les traités de Brigham et Northampton, le mariage de Margaret avec son fils dans le but de renforcer son emprise sur le royaume d'Ecosse.[64] Après la mort de Margaret, c'est naturellement Edward qui s'imposa comme arbitre de la 'Great Cause', le procès de dévolution du trône d'Ecosse. A ce moment précis, le long travail mené par les rois d'Angleterre de consolidation à leur profit de cet ensemble nordique porta tous ses fruits: dans la continuité des arbitrages passés, Edward fut naturellement chargé de départager plusieurs princes en provenance de l'ensemble du pourtour de la Mer du Nord (Norvège, Hollande, Ecosse). Il apparaissait clairement à cette occasion comme le prince dominant d'un ensemble nordique élargi, en termes de puissance mais aussi de prestige moral, faisant de la Mer du Nord une sorte de '*mare nostrum*' anglaise.

L'étude des lettres de sauf-conduit accordées par le roi d'Angleterre pendant la période 1270–90 atteste du prestige acquis par le roi d'Angleterre outre-mer. A la fin du XIIIème siècle, celles-ci sont adressées à tous ses baillis et amis ou à tous ses amis et fidèles, une adresse fort large et riche en sous-entendus. La protection qu'elles accordaient valait sur son territoire mais également pendant le séjour à l'étranger et pour le retour.[65] Les ambassades anglaises se rendant en Norvège étaient ainsi dotées d'une protection valant pour tout le trajet, un document qui revendiquait une valeur internationale. Par comparaison, les ambassades norvégiennes qui se rendaient en Angleterre se voyaient systématiquement dotées d'une telle lettre de sauf-conduit signée du roi d'Angleterre, la protection du roi de Norvège ne suffisant manifestement pas pour traverser paisiblement les terres du roi d'Angleterre.[66]

Mais ce fut également à cette occasion qu'Edward précisément sortit de son rôle d'arbitre bienveillant pour tenter de s'imposer directement sur un des membres de la communauté. Au lieu de rendre un avis consultatif, comme le fit saint Louis lors de la mise d'Amiens, il préféra rendre une décision de justice, ce qui impliquait qu'il devînt seigneur d'Ecosse. Cet acte politique sema les graines de discorde qui allaient mener '*in fine*' au délitement de cet ensemble, dont les traités de 1295 furent le premier acte. La radicalisation des Ecossais face aux prétentions seigneuriales anglaises annihila le rôle d'arbitre efficace que le roi d'Angleterre avait eu jusqu'à présent auprès notamment des Norvégiens. Ces derniers se tournèrent donc vers une autre puissance pour obtenir justice.

Au terme de ce cheminement, l'intérêt pour le roi de France de recourir à l'alliance norvégienne, parallèlement à l'alliance écossaise apparaît plus nettement. Potentiellement dissuasive, cette alliance revêtait surtout un caractère profondément vexatoire pour le roi d'Angleterre. Incapable de régler un différend au sein de son propre jardin, il se fit supplanter par le roi de France qui affirmait par là non seulement l'échec d'Edward en tant que seigneur féodal, mais également son statut de seul et unique '*rex pacificus*', dans la droite lignée de saint Louis, avec tout ce que cela impliquait en termes de 'leadership' à l'échelle de l'Occident Chrétien. Dans le contexte d'une guerre franco-anglaise où le roi de France mettait en avant sa supériorité féodale sur le duc d'Aquitaine, le trait fit mouche et de façon d'autant plus insupportable pour Edward que John Bailliol se trouvait être également vassal du roi de France et pouvait à ce titre le soutenir contre Edward, affirmant par là que la fidélité due au roi de France était supérieure à celle due au roi d'Angleterre.

---

64   Sur la chronologie de ces événements, voir note 10.
65   'Ibidem morando et redeundo'. Voir par exemple, la lettre de sauf-conduit accordée à Robert Bruce pour aller marier sa fille Isabella en Norvège avec le roi Erik: *DN*, xix. no. 379.
66   C'est le cas, par exemple, pour la délégation norvégienne qui vient négocier en Angleterre, en 1294, un renouvellement du traité de Winchester: *DN*, xix. no. 394.

La réaction d'Edward, épidermique, ne se fit pas attendre et il ne fut plus question de médiation. Au printemps 1296, il envahit l'Ecosse et fit déposer John Bailliol, ce qui rendit vaine la médiation initiée par la France entre l'Ecosse et la Norvège. Maître à présent de l'Ecosse, il obligeait la Norvège à s'adresser à lui pour obtenir ses paiements, ce qu'elle fit à partir de 1297.[67] Mais l'interventionnisme anglais avait durablement déréglé le fonctionnement habituel de l'ensemble politique nordique. Les Norvégiens n'obtinrent jamais gain de cause: le traité de 1269 ne fut pas renouvelé à l'avènement du roi Håkon V en 1299.[68] La communauté nordique dont la stabilité avait été garantie pendant presque un siècle par la médiation anglaise explosa et finalement ce fut l'Angleterre qui s'en trouva exclue. La tradition rapporte que lorsque William Wallace fut arrêté en 1305, on trouva sur lui un sauf-conduit du roi de Norvège – dont le contenu exact est inconnu – qui lui aurait permis certainement de trouver refuge en Norvège ou, plus probablement, dans les Orcades.[69] Cet épisode, qu'il se soit véritablement produit ou non, est révélateur du réchauffement des relations entre l'Ecosse et la Norvège. Le remariage d'Erik Magnusson avec Isabella Bruce conclu en 1293 fit que les ennemis d'autrefois finirent par se rapprocher. Le divorce avec l'Angleterre fut consommé en 1312 lorsque le renouvellement du traité de Perth fut conclu à Inverness entre le nouveau roi d'Ecosse Robert Bruce et Håkon V.[70] Par cet accord officiel, Håkon fut, en effet, un des premiers rois occidentaux à reconnaître officiellement Robert Bruce comme roi légitime d'Ecosse, à la grande fureur des Anglais qui cherchaient à l'enfermer dans un rôle d'usurpateur.

---

[67] Une importante délégation norvégienne reçoit, le 23 juin 1297, une lettre de sauf-conduit pour se rendre en Angleterre, sans que soit précisé son but. On peut supposer qu'il s'agit de récupérer les fameux paiements et de renouveler le traité de Winchester: *DN*, xix. no. 409.

[68] Les instructions données par le roi Håkon à Snare Aslaksson, dans le cadre d'une mission effectuée en Angleterre aux alentours de 1299 mentionnent en effet les difficultés que les marchands norvégiens rencontrent pour exercer leur activité en Angleterre, signe que le traité de 1269 n'est plus pleinement appliqué: *DN*, xix. no. 412.

[69] Cette lettre de sauvegarde est mentionnée dans: *Antient Kalendars and Inventories of the Treasury of His Majesty's Exchequer*, éd. Sir F. Palgrave (Londres, 1836), i. 134.

[70] *DN*, xix. nos 481–2.